DATE DUE			
JAN 8			
MAR 10 '70			

Lament for the Molly Maguires

Other books by Arthur H. Lewis

The Aaronsburg Story
The Worlds of Chippy Patterson
The Day They Shook the Plum Tree

Arthur H. Lewis

Lament for the Molly Maguires

Harcourt, Brace & World, Inc., New York

For Gezo

From the Beginning

Vengeance has never ceased to play its cruel role in the affairs of men. Consorting with violence, it has laid its bloody stains across the pages of history. In those remote times that we now comfortably call ancient, an act of savage vengeance scarcely raised a question of morality or reason. We have come to accept as "classical justice" the utter destruction of Troy by the victorious Greeks; conversely, we consider Hannibal's failure to obliterate Rome, defenseless before his massed army, as something of an historical puzzle.

The concept of vengeance as an instrument of justice in the hands of man goes back at least as far as the Old Testament. Genesis admonishes, "Whoso sheddeth man's blood, by man shall his blood be shed"; Leviticus elaborates, "Breach for breach, eye for eye, tooth for tooth."

As western man moved unsteadily into the Christian era, a profoundly different spiritual guide was advanced. The New Testament declares vengeance the province of God, not of man; and, in the Sermon on the Mount, explicitly brands as evil the code of "eye for eye and tooth for tooth."

The gentle echo of the Sermon on the Mount has mingled with other voices across the vast chasm of years. In the 14th century, Geoffrey Chaucer philosophized that "Vengeance is not cured by another vengeance, nor a wrong by another wrong; but each increaseth and aggregeth the other." Some two hundred years later Francis Bacon advised that "Revenge is a kind of wild justice; which the more man's nature runs to, the more ought law to weed it out."

Neither law, nor philosophy, nor reason, nor spiritual counsel has prevailed against this primitive element in man's nature. The upward path of civilization, and it has been upward, is twisted by it, leaving grim milestones in appalling quantity.

The story of the Molly Maguires in Pennsylvania is one such milestone. It would be worth recording for its dramatic values alone; it is compelling and exciting, and within it are such varied elements of conflict and adventure that most fiction pales beside them. Far more important, it is a story for our time. Here are men faced with a choice of avenging wrongs or of righting them. Men were faced with that choice two thousand years ago. They face it today.

In gathering material for this book I had the help and cooperation of many people and wish to express my gratitude to them. I am particularly indebted to Thomas Barrett, Joseph H. Davies, and James F. Haas for searching deeply into their memories as well as for permitting me to use factual material gathered by them over many years; to Florence Collis, Renee Marke, and Arthur L. Redstone for their editorial help; to the publishers and staff members of the *Anthracite Tri-District News, Catholic Standard and Times,* Jim Thorpe *Times-News,* Mahanoy City *Record-American, New York Times,* Philadelphia *Evening Bulletin,* Philadelphia *Inquirer,* Pottsville *Republican,* Shamokin *Citizen,* Shamokin *News-Dispatch,* Shenandoah *Evening Herald,* Tamaqua *Evening Courier*; to David W. Davis, curator of the Historical Society of Schuylkill County; to Miss Ellen Shaffer, Herbert Davis and members of the staff of the Free Library of Philadelphia, Miss Mary E. Harvey, former librarian of the Pottsville Public Library and members of her staff, Zelma K. Snyder and members of the staff of the Mahanoy City Public Library, Louis Rauco of the Library of the Commonwealth of Pennsylvania, and John McMahon, librarian of the Boston *Herald*; to staff members of the Jim Thorpe Dimmick Memorial Library, Shamokin and Coal Township Public Library, Hazelton Public Library, and Tamaqua Public Library; Mrs. Patrick William Callahan, James Corrigan, George J. Curilla, Jr., Charles H. Engle, Edward E. Henrie, Herrwood E. Hobbs, Father Francis Hoey, Herman and Isadore Janowitch, Mrs. Mary Kane Kerns, Mrs. Goldie

Kerstetter, Mrs. Ruth Krause Lewis, Theodore T. MacFarland, Mrs. Mary A. McDonald, Dr. Edwin Mendelssohn, David L. Miller, Mrs. Charles D. Neast, Roland Newhard, Father Francis M. Philben, Louis Poliniak, Miss Frances Rowe, John U. Shroyer, William B. Weist, Mrs. Isabel Wilford, and Elwood M. Young.

I owe special thanks to two friends of my boyhood, the late Joseph Xavier Kaier and the late Harold Aloysius Xavier Kelly. Lastly, I must acknowledge my debt to Thomas C. O'Connor, editor of the Mahanoy City *Record*; W. P. Ramsey, Esq., member of the Schuylkill County Bar, and Dr. John Reilly, our family physician. These three men, all deceased, were friends of my father; their gatherings at our house in Mahanoy City and their talk of the Molly Maguires was an exciting experience from which, obviously, I have never recovered.

Reported conversations included herein have been examined, wherever possible, by the actual participants and are as accurate as individual memory and the passage of time allow.

ARTHUR H. LEWIS

Philadelphia, Pennsylvania

Lament for the Molly Maguires

Chapter One

On a warm and pleasant morning, the first day of the summer of 1877, two young Irishmen, immaculately dressed in quiet clothing, their hair neat, their expressions serene, spoke softly to each other as they walked slowly down an old brick path inside a walled garden. In each man's hand was a full blown red rose which, from time to time, he pressed to his nose, inhaling deeply. Each glanced upward at the hills less than half a mile away. Twenty minutes later both men were dead, hanged from a gallows in the prison yard at Pottsville, Pennsylvania, about one hundred miles from Philadelphia.

Within two hours, four more Irishmen would walk the same path, kiss their priest's hand, touch their lips to the crucifix, bless their friends, grant forgiveness to their enemies, mount the same gibbet, and die.

Coevally, a similar event would take place at Mauch Chunk, some forty miles to the east. In that mountain village, four more Irishmen would be hanged, one by one, in the corridor of Carbon County's new jail.

This was Irish-America's "Black Thursday," when the first ten of twenty convicted and condemned members of the Molly Maguires were executed. So ended a reign of terror begun nearly three decades earlier and without parallel in American history. During that fearful time, less than six hundred men, banded together under the aegis of a secret society, grew so powerful that they could commit any crime they wished, secure in the knowledge that alibis would be furnished them, that few witnesses had the courage to testify against them, and that jurymen must acquit them or risk death by murder. And finally, if a courageous jury voted a conviction, there was always the assurance that the "old man" up in Harrisburg could be "prevailed upon" to grant an immediate pardon.

From 1850 until 1877 three entire Pennsylvania counties and large portions of two more, with a total population of more than a quarter of a million, were without effective law and order in the face of an increasingly savage onslaught against on-the-spot representatives of absentee London, Boston, New York, and Philadelphia mine owners.

During the thirteen years between 1862 and 1875, there were 142 unsolved homicides and 212 felonious assaults in Schuylkill County. Many of the victims were mine superintendents, foremen, or colliery supervisors, who had incurred the wrath of a Molly or a friend of a Molly. Before the crime was committed, each victim might have received a crude, anonymously served warning, a "coffin notice," signed by a "Son of Molly Maguire."

The name "Molly Maguire" has many supposed origins, all apocryphal, based on a legendary Irish heroine who led poverty-stricken farmers of the "ould sod" in revolt against the brutal bailiffs whose task was to collect house and cattle rents for absentee English landlords.

There never was any doubt that the operators of coal mines drove the hardest possible bargain: miners worked long hours, lived in squalor, died hungry, and their children lived without hope. Since the owners lived a hundred or more miles from their mines, they regarded the Molly Maguires with loathing rather than fear. What terrified these absentee owners was the emergence of labor unions; these they tried to crush using any means they could, including use of their own private armies, which operated without regard for the Fourth Amendment.

Hostilities between the Molly Maguires and the operators were not battles between capital and labor, although on one side there surely was capital and on the other the working man. In vain have Molly apologists tried to intertwine their protagonists and the labor movement: The facts do not bear this out. While a long, continuing conflict between employer and employee raged, the Mollies remained outside it; the aid these tough men

4

might have contributed to labor's cause was dissipated in senseless crimes of revenge—murder, arson, mayhem. A foreman was beaten, his home burned, the colliery that employed him dynamited—not because of basic injustices, but simply because he had fired a Molly. Whether or not the dismissal was based upon good reason never seemed a factor meriting consideration or even concern by the Mollies.

Perhaps, in the beginning, when individual gangs of Mollies were no more than "regulars" of some saloon, these embittered, disillusioned men might have sought, if not abstract justice, recognition that they, too, were human beings worthy of at least as much consideration as the mine mules their twelve-year-old sons drove.

There is a strong likelihood that at the inception of Molly Maguirism thousands of law-abiding Irish immigrants must have taken quiet pride in the fact that at least some sons of Erin were fighting back when "No Irish Need Apply" signs were posted with increasing frequency at the doors of nearly every colliery hiring office.

Generations of subjection by, if not subservience to, English landlords had not stilled the Irishman's desire for respect. The open contempt with which "Paddy" and his Church was regarded by many of his aristocratic Episcopalian employers and their Welsh Nonconformist representatives was alleviated partially when the much-bedeviled Irishman began to stand up for his rights even if it meant he'd be fired from his job.

Later, when the Mollies degenerated into gangs of murderous thugs, they were opposed by most decent Irishmen. However, except for a very few courageous citizens, mainly Roman Catholic priests, opposition to the Mollies was rarely overt. Reprisals against those who spoke ill of the secret society were swift. Even "offending" clergy were not immune to physical attacks. A man never knew which of his neighbors was a Molly or a friend of a Molly. A word whispered in the wrong place to the wrong person could bring about a brutal beating with unbelievable speed.

One thing was certain, as this dreaded secret society grew more and more powerful: members of the Mollies or friends whom they took under protective wings no longer had to swallow pride, anger, or fear in silence when they were berated by a foreman or fired by the "super." Within hours the foreman might have his ears cut off and the super be shot to death on a lonely road. It might even happen in sight of a hundred witnesses who had been taught, by bitter experience, to see nothing, hear nothing, and say nothing, and not attempt a rescue. Vengeance for those who interfered arrived swiftly and unfailingly.

While no one in his right mind would deny that the crimes the Mollies committed for which they finally paid the extreme penalty were unspeakable, it is also a fact that charges of inhuman cruelty justly could be laid against the operators. One ruthless method mine owners used to force workers into near slavery was regulation of the flow of labor into the country. By manipulating immigration laws to their own advantage mine owners would flood the coal region labor market with eager "greenhorns" willing to work at any wage. This happened whenever it was thought "agitators" were having even small success with union organization.

The great Irish migration to the United States began shortly after the potato famine of the dreadful winter of 1847-1848. Into the promised land, seeking escape from the poverty and persecution which had dogged them for generations, poured thousands and thousands of the desperately poor. Their clothes were in rags and their bellies were empty.

What sustained them was hope. In the hard coal regions of America they would find work for which they would be adequately paid; they would find decent homes in which to raise their families; their children would have both time and opportunity to learn to read and write; they would have religious freedom; and best of all, they would be 3000 miles away from their English landlords. So went the propaganda spread by American mine owners just beginning to feel the need for cheap unskilled labor to dig and prepare the hard coal which was becoming the nation's most desired fuel.

For most of the first eight or ten years after his arrival, the Irish immigrant found work, even though it was dangerous and backbreaking. He was paid about seven dollars for a sixty-hour week, with which sum he might have been barely able to keep

6

his family from starvation had he been permitted to buy his groceries and other supplies wherever he wanted to.

But most mine operators compelled employees to deal at a "pluck me," the miners' name for company-owned stores. There, prices were at least twenty per cent higher than in nearby towns. Buying was done on "tick," and the "book" which recorded purchases was never revealed to the purchaser. (It wouldn't have mattered, anyway, because in all likelihood the Irish immigrant was illiterate.) Should a worker refuse to deal with the local pluck me, the store manager would report this disloyalty to a foreman and the miner would be out of work. In addition, his name would be blacklisted throughout the region. Such an ingrate would find it impossible to get a job anywhere in the anthracite fields.

To remove even the slight possibility that the Irishman might rebel and secretly buy elsewhere, wages were paid monthly, making it practically impossible for workers to deal in stores where cash was required. All this discussion of money is, for the main, purely academic. Most of the time what the miner received at the end of the month was a "bobtail" check, good for absolutely nothing, which merely showed his current debt at the company store.

"If a miner with a family of eight or ten . . . once gets into debt with the 'pluck me,' he remains in debt until his sons have grown up, and then their earnings, perhaps, will help to decrease the burden . . . There are families who for ten years have never received a dollar in cash from their labor," said the Philadelphia *North American* on May 25, 1881.

When times got hard, a miner's pay dropped to fifty cents a day, and there were desperate men with starving families who were willing to work fourteen hours to get that.

Except for the Civil War period, when demand for coal far exceeded supply, the unskilled mine laborer averaged only thirty-six weeks of work per year in the decades between 1857 and 1877.

After his twelve or fourteen hour stint of dangerous, back-breaking labor, the Irishman went to what could only euphemistically be called a home. This was a shack in a "patch." A patch was a cluster of a few dozen company houses along a crooked, unpaved street, built within the shadow of a towering colliery.

7

The frames of these two-room houses were of one-inch planks, the walls of clapboard that had never been painted. Each room had one narrow window without glass. Only in summer were these slits open. Otherwise they were sealed off with cardboard in a vain effort to keep out the cold. The roof leaked and there were holes in the side walls. The floor was Mother Earth, tramped hard by generations of bare feet. Heating was little better than primitive. There was usually a small coal stove for both cooking and warmth, fed with fuel the Irishman's wife and daughters garnered from spillage (accidental or deliberate, depending upon the humor of the train crew) as loaded coal cars passed by on their way from the colliery to the railroad's main line.

In each of these two miserable rooms lived a separate family, consisting of the man of the house, his wife, their six, eight or ten children, and even an occasional boarder. Cowsheds or chicken coops resembled human habitations more than did these shacks.

Added bitterness came to the Irishman at his daily sight of the "super's" house. This was an attractive three-story white dwelling, built in the center of a half acre of ground at the edge of the patch and away from the railroad tracks. It was surrounded by a freshly painted picket fence. On the front gate, which opened on a tree-lined path to the home itself, was a mailbox which usually bore the name of Llewelyn, Jenkins, Jones, James, or Davies—never O'Brien, O'Toole, Kehoe, Murphy, or Kelly.

At least the Irishman was spared a view of the great mine owner's house. With the exception of a few like that of Asa Packer, who built his feudal castle on a Mauch Chunk hillside, these were on Rittenhouse Square, Fifth Avenue, or in Back Bay. As a matter of fact, many of these houses were in Leicester Square. The same absentee owner still managed to control the immigrant's destiny even though the latter traveled 3000 miles to escape English tyranny. It was the Englishmen's money and that of their Anglo-Saxon cousins which ran the mines and the company stores and built the hovels in which the Irishman lived.

So much for dreams of his own decent home in which to raise a family in America. Quickly banished, also, were aspirations to educate his sons. When the boys were old enough—and this could be soon after their seventh birthday—they went to work. Sometimes, if his home was at the far end of the patch and the youngest of his brood was too small to walk a half mile to the colliery, "Pop" carried him there on his own broad back, the older boys walking ahead, single file, in early morning darkness, while the rattle of lunch pails, half empty even before the day began, broke the silence.

Yet from these careworn, browbeaten lads with so little time for fun in their dreary existences, came heroes, who for the moment made Welsh supers and straw bosses and even absentee English mine owners forgive the Irish their ancestry and forget their fears of the Molly Maguires. One such hero was Martin Graham, a breaker boy risen to the stature of mule driver. He was twelve years old and one of the eleven sons and daughters of Peter and Margaret Graham, formerly of County Donegal, now residents of Buck Mountain patch in Carbon County.

There had been an explosion in the mine where Martin worked. A "fire boss" had given the warning and the mule driver was about to enter the cage which would lift him to safety, 800 feet above. But Martin remembered a crew of men working in a corridor which he had left ten minutes before. He turned to warn them.

By the time the boy came back to the cage it had already been raised to the surface. Frantically Martin retraced his steps through the black tunnel to the miners whom he had apprised of danger. But they, meanwhile, had thrown up a barricade which gave them temporary protection against the smoke and gas. This was their only chance of life until the fire was extinguished.

"Martin stood at the barrier and begged piteously to be admitted," said the Mauch Chunk *Gazette*, on Friday, April 20, 1876. "The few survivors who heard him say the little fellow cried. But to have made a passageway for him would have been death to all, so they were obliged to refuse him.

"After a little he went quietly away to the stable. He had been promoted to the position of a mule driver only the day before; and now he went to his mule and there wrote with chalk upon a piece of board the names of those who were dear to him, and then lay down beside his mule to die. His body was found close to that of the poor animal, which, in its death agony, had rolled upon him and wounded his breast with a portion of the harness. "So died this little hero in the dark."

But the tolerance verging on respect with which the Irishman was treated after an occasional demonstration of the latent courage he and his progeny possessed soon faded, and again the sons of Erin were objects of ridicule. For example, in Mahanoy City, a Schuylkill County coal town, there was a line, invisible but just as effective as if it were a ten foot barbed wire fence, beyond which no Irishman was permitted to pass. Should a "Pape," before the emergence of the Molly Maguires, venture east of Catawissa Street, where the spire of St. Canicus Roman Catholic Church cast its shadow, he was in for a beating by the Modocs, a group of Welsh and English toughs. Finally, of course, the Irish, shillelaghs in hand, thumbed their noses at the Welsh and everyone else and marched in a body up Center Street to the east end of the town and back without casualties.

In an era and in an area where Catholics were a barely tolerated minority, it took immense courage for a prelate to acknowledge not only the existence of the Molly Maguires but to admit that its members were Catholics. The Church of Rome made this dreaded secret society an anathema to practicing Catholics of the day, and its re-emergence an impossibility.

"The Molly Maguires," said Bishop Wood of the Philadelphia Diocese in an editorial which appeared October 17, 1874, in the *Catholic Standard,* official diocesan spokesman, "is a society rendered infamous by its treachery and deeds of blood—the terror of every neighborhood in which it existed . . . the disgrace of Irishman . . . the scandal of the Catholic Church. . . ."

Many of Bishop Wood's priests, in the face of threatened (and frequently executed) physical abuse, had the courage to castigate the Molly Maguires. Scowling leaders of this dreaded society often sat in pews not a dozen feet from the pulpit and heard their organization and themselves denounced in no uncertain terms.

Among these clerics who dared speak openly in the presence of murderers with little regard for the supposedly "sacred body of a priest," several of Bishop Wood's hardy emissaries are worthy of special mention. One such is Father Daniel Ignatius

McDermott. This tall, frail, Irish ascetic began his coal region career with a denunciation of all secret orders. He was promptly warned that a repetition of this sort of loose talk would result in violence to himself.

With alacrity, the twenty-five-year-old Father McDermott mounted his pulpit at St. Ignatius Church in Centralia the following Sunday and preached even more strongly on the sins of Molly Maguirism. Three masked men seized the priest that evening and dragged him to the church cemetery where they slapped him about lightly. "It'll be worse next time, Father," one assailant warned him. "So will my sermon," retorted the cleric.

Unless you have lived in the hard coal regions of Pennsylvania, it is difficult to conceive of the power enjoyed by the Molly Maguires. As early as 1862, this society was so strong that it was able to defy the President of the United States, who retreated rather than subject two regiments of Army Regulars to the bloodshed their appearance in Cass Township, fountainhead of the Mollies, would have caused.

Even now, discussion of the Molly Maguires is taboo among a fair portion of the population of Schuylkill, Carbon, Northumberland, Columbia, and Luzerne counties. It is hardly to be wondered at that books have disappeared from the stacks of public libraries throughout the hard coal regions, that newspapers of the day have been lifted from their files, that public documents of the famous trials have vanished mysteriously from courthouses. Mention the names of those men who were hanged from the scaffolds to a resident of Pottsville, Mahanoy City, Girardville, Sunbury, or Shamokin, and you might very well be talking about his grandfather.

To those who lived in the Keystone State's hard coal counties during that bitter period, the "war" seemed endless. For nearly thirty years the fight went on; in tiny patches, on the well-lighted streets of Shenandoah, Tamaqua, and Gilberton, a thousand feet beneath the earth's surface in dark and gloomy passageways, on country roads, and on speeding express trains.

For the hated informer there were no boundaries over which to escape from vengeance. The savage arm of the Molly Maguires stretched everywhere—to a lonely Iowa farmhouse, to an abandoned Nevada mining camp, to a ship sailing off the coast of Capetown, South Africa.

The war's climax came that summer morning soon after the sun rose over the laurel-covered mountains of Pennsylvania.

"At last the long wished for, greatly dreaded and never to be forgotten day has arrived," wrote Tom Fielders in the Shenandoah *Herald,* June 21, 1877. "In this region of memorable occurrences all will pale before the tragic events of June 21. A hundred years from now, when this generation will have passed away and be laid beneath the sod, the descendants of the men today will relate, with bated breath, to their offspring, the terrible legal tragedy that was enacted so long ago and, at the same time, thank God that times have changed."

Chapter Two

According to many students of anthracite's stormy history, it was in Cass Township, Schuylkill County, Pennsylvania, that the American "branch" of the Molly Maguires started. The late Thomas P. O'Connor, editor of the Mahanoy City *Daily Record* a little more than a decade after the last Molly was hanged, shared this belief.

It is O'Connor's theory that roots of the Molly Maguires sprang from a Cass Township saloon owned by one Jeremiah Reilly.

"Saloons, or shebeens, as we used to call them," said the editor, "were the poor man's club. It wasn't unusual for a miner to stop off at his favorite barroom for a fast snort or two after work if only to wash down the coal dust. We Irish, as you may have heard, are a thirsty lot.

"Reilly possessed the quality of leadership and it was through his efforts that a priest came over from Pottsville twice a week to hear confessions and to hold Mass. That was ten years before St. Keiran's was built at Heckscherville and there was no church in Cass Township.

"This saloonkeeper had a rig and his fourteen-year-old daughter used to drive the Father back and forth to the Cathedral. It was quite a chore, what with the rough roads plus the danger from thugs who roamed the countryside."

According to O'Connor there had been a series of anti-Irish riots in the villages surrounding Pottsville due to the influx of immigrants whom the Welsh and English miners were sure would displace them at greatly reduced wages. That this was perhaps true, the editor admitted readily.

"In any event," O'Connor continued, "one of the times Reilly's little girl was driving the Father back, the pair was set upon by a bunch of toughs in front of a tavern outside of Yorkville, just beyond the Pottsville borough limits. They insulted the priest, then overturned the rig. Both of them were tossed out. I don't think they laid a hand on either but they were hurt when they fell. Somebody whacked the horse on his rump and off he ran. So the Father and Reilly's daughter entered Pottsville on foot.

"Reilly went wild. In Ireland he'd been a Ribbonman, White-boy, Molly Maguire, or whatever you want to call them, but he thought that was all over when he came to America. The saloonkeeper knew exactly where the tavern was at Yorkville and was aware it was a hangout for the English and Welsh.

"One night, shortly afterward, Reilly led a few dozen boys from his bar and they marched on to Yorkville. They beat the hell out of the customers there and may have smashed a few innocent skulls but Reilly was confident they got most of the guilty ones, too. It isn't unlikely that during the course of the brief encounter one Irishman shouted, after banging his homemade shillelagh on an Englishman's head, 'Take this from a son of Molly Maguire!' "

Another newspaperman and student of coal region history, Tom Barrett, shares O'Connor's theory about the Molly Maguires' origin.

"While I think this was the beginning of the Molly Maguires in Pennsylvania," said Barrett, current city editor of the Shenandoah *Herald,* "I don't believe for one moment that immediately after the Yorkville fracas lodges of Mollies suddenly sprang into existence all over the coal regions. What I do think, though, is that word of what happened in Yorkville spread quickly and that Irishmen in other patches took similar action when they felt badly put upon.

"Within a few years I'm sure there was some kind of informal link between the boys at Mickey Clarke's in Gilberton, Paddy Murphy's at Branchdale, or 'The Armagh' on top of Broad Mountain. It could be the tie-up was as loose as a patron of one saloon dropping into another a few miles away and bragging about what *his* boys did to an abusive Welsh foreman or an English straw boss. And getting, in return, gossip about deeds of glory or revenge the boys performed in *that* neck of the woods.

"I doubt if in those early days of Molly Maguirism they went as far as murder. Just administered some pretty solid beatings, with a few cracked noggins, spattered teeth and bloody noses. And maybe the victims deserved what they got!"

But by the end of the 1850s the only organized body of men willing to fight the operators was the Molly Maguires.

Their spread was rapid and their crimes, or those with which they were charged, became far more serious. No longer were insults, unfair treatment, unjust dismissals, and cuts in pay or working time avenged by simple assault. Mayhem, arson, dynamiting, savage beatings, and even murder followed too swiftly on the heels of some superintendent's "injustice" to be purely coincidental.

The rare witnesses (and the even rarer ones willing to testify) to a considerable number of these acts of violence, frequently reported that right before the crime, or immediately afterward, he saw "four Irishmen" assembled or fleeing. Why the number "four" was selected is a mystery. The press of the day is filled with such stories. "Four Irishmen" were suspected of having done this; "Four Irishmen" were thought to have done that; while "an Irish quartette" was believed to have done something else.

How were the suspects so clearly identified as to their ethnic origin? "Well, they *looked* like Irishmen; they *acted* like Irishmen; they *smelled* like Irishmen." Perhaps, in at least a few of these positive identifications, it was a matter of giving the dog a bad name.

Not that any arrest or subsequent conviction was likely to follow. When an Irishman occasionally was taken into custody, indicted and brought to trial, twenty other Irishmen were happy to testify, under solemn oath, that the gentleman in question never for one minute left Murphy's saloon where he and they were having a quiet glass of beer or two, a dozen hours before and a dozen hours after the crime was committed.

The anger and frustration felt by these Irish coal miners were basic causes for the birth of the Molly Maguires and for the fact that they were able to operate as long as they did, But, as the Shamokin *Citizen* pointed out, "Not every man who's hungry goes out and kills somebody whom he blames for making him hungry. Some hungry men kill themselves. The Mollies sought revenge and the objects of their revenge were the 'mine bosses,' and the owners, the men who hired, fired and set wages."

Chapter Three

By the end of 1860 the rate of pay had fallen to $6.48 for a sixty-hour week. However, no miner was certain of more than four days' work out of seven.

"As the year progressed," said Eveland and Harris in their *History of the Molly Maguires,* published at Tamaqua in 1877, "it was apparent that a mysterious society was growing in strength throughout the county. People who for years had never spoken to a soul on the subject, came out openly and advocated it.

"The Molly Maguire songs were sung and at their drinking bouts, . . . some of the members would tell of their prowess . . . The young and inexperienced soon became conversant with the objects of the society and many thoughtless young men joined them. . . .

"At the time, the ranks of the organization were being swelled in the different coal towns throughout the county, business men and politicians eagerly joining, the former for the money it would bring them, the latter for the popularity and chances for positions it would open up to them. In this way the society waxed strong . . . Thus did Irishmen who had previously borne characters which were above reproach join them from every city and mining village . . . The Civil War meant little to these renegades. . . ."

As the Mollies grew in strength, an elite group rose from their ranks. This inner circle took over control of the organization and welded it into a tight chain of "divisions," each headed by a carefully selected "bodymaster." They planned strategy, chose victims, punished the disobedient, and appointed executioners.

They provided alibis, furnished counsel, rigged juries, and bought elections. And they issued "coffin notices," and rewarded the worthy for "good, clane jobs" of murder, mayhem, or arson. An informer's "crime," the most heinous of all, called for no body-master decision. The penalty was death.

At the very pinnacle of this select company of twenty-eight bodymasters was one man. The whisper of his name struck terror into the hearts of many a straw boss, superintendent, or any other who, in a rash moment, had spoken against him or dared cross him in some way. He was Jack Kehoe, a virile, ruthless, clever leader who feared no one, not even Franklin Benjamin Gowen, president of the Reading Coal and Iron Company, who had sworn not only to destroy the secret society Kehoe headed, but to assist personally in the hanging of the "King of the Mollies."

At twenty-two, the future leader of the Mollies had already spent a third of his life at work, which had begun weeks after he, his mother, his father and at least ten brothers and sisters arrived at Pottsville from County Donegal in 1849.

"The Kehoes were good, hardworking people," said the Philadelphia *Times,* December 18, 1893, quoting someone who obviously knew not only "Black Jack," but his parents as well.

"They were poor like all of us in those days; never going to bed with a full belly. Waking up at five o'clock on a freezing morning, the outhouse ten yards down a snow-covered path and your shoes, the only thing you took off at night, nothing more than eight-inch strips of thin leather pockmarked with holes. No soap for washing, even if you had the ambition to dip your hands and face into the oily, icy water you drew from the pump.

"Breakfast? Miserable, lukewarm gruel and no milk to wash it down with and no sugar either. That was it and sometimes not even that. But if your parents were good Catholics, and the Kehoes were, they said Grace before they swallowed it and thanked God for His bountiful gifts.

"In summer, the never-ending heat baked the patch shanties into one big oven. A dozen sweaty bodies bumping, trying to keep out of each other's way. This was how we lived. This was how the Kehoes lived. Children dying like flies of consumption, two of Jack's sisters and one brother. Now can you understand why Jack got bitter?"

Another picture of Kehoe comes from Tom Barrett, editor of the Shenandoah *Herald*.

"I wrote a piece about him a long time ago," said Barrett, "and talked to some of his contemporaries. Now in all honesty I have to add that these were Irishmen and so their opinions might have been somewhat flavored. But this is what they said—that Kehoe was a *man* from the time he was a boy and took no gaff from anybody. If he had anything to say for himself or his buddies he said it openly.

"He had strong loves and strong hates. Included in the former were his family and, of course, Ireland! In the latter were the English, the Welsh, informers, Franklin Benjamin Gowen, and above everybody else, James McParlan, the detective."

When he reached manhood, "Kehoe was tall and rather handsome in person, intelligent, daring, selfish and unscrupulous," said the *New York Times* on December 18, 1878.

"Even as a youth," said the Mauch Chunk *Coal Gazette,* on July 16, 1876, "Jack Kehoe . . . was a leader and might well have used his great influence for good instead of bad . . . He stands six feet, two inches in his stocking feet. His jaw is firm and his teeth are white and even. He has jet black, curly hair, bushy eyebrows and bright blue, piercing eyes."

When Kehoe was about twenty he and his family had moved from a patch near Pottsville to another company town called Honeybrook. Kehoe's father, a victim of "miner's asthma," was unable to work; several sons and daughters had moved away, married or died, and Jack became the sole support of his parents. His skill, experience, and dependability landed him a good job at the Number Two Breaker of the J. B. McCreary and Company Colliery, near Audenried.

Kehoe, like other "contract" miners, was paid for actual coal tonnage rather than the total weight of the cars he filled below the earth's surface. Refuse, silt, and other waste was deducted from the gross weight and a "ticket" given for the net. There was no accurate method of determining the amount of waste and the ticket boss's estimate had to be accepted. Unfair supervisors easily could cheat the miner to favor the company and there is little doubt that many did. Frank Langdon, Kehoe's ticket boss, had a reputation for being tough but fair.

Kehoe, however, claimed that Langdon was constantly stealing from the Irish; but the foreman would not be drawn into an open argument. Some three weeks before Langdon's death, Kehoe, after a bitter altercation with his boss, turned away muttering, "I'll get you for this, you son-of-a-bitch!" If Langdon heard he gave no sign.

A community leader, Langdon, with his friend John Myers, was in charge of a celebration held on the evening of Saturday, June 14, 1862, at Audenried. The purpose of the gathering was to bolster President Lincoln's plea for more Pennsylvania volunteers. A German band was the center of attraction and hundreds of men, women and children gathered around to listen.

For a short time the crowd of English, Welsh, Germans, and Irish mixed good-humoredly. After a while most of the audience drifted away either to begin drinking or to renew that which they had started hours before.

Audenried had two saloons: Williams', which catered to the English and Welsh, and Boch's, where the Irish congregated. Not all the Irish stayed away from Williams' nor did all the English and Welsh boycott Boch's.

By seven o'clock that Saturday evening the crowd was getting unruly and women and children were sent home. A gang of a dozen men piled out of Boch's and began to heckle speakers and toss pebbles into the tuba's tempting opening. Included in the hard-drinking crew that staggered from Boch's were Kehoe and three of his intimates, Charlie Gallagher, Dennis O'Toole and Columbus McGee.

Foreseeing possible trouble, Myers cut the program short. Langdon was the last speaker. Just before he finished someone from the audience shouted, "Come down here, you bastard, and we'll kill you." The voice was never identified positively, although some spectators thought it was Kehoe's. William Canvin, an outside foreman at McCreary's, who was on the dais, seized the

American flag, placed it in front of himself, and walked down from the platform to the porch of Williams' hotel.

"I stood there for a minute holding the flag when Jack Kehoe came up and spat on it," Canvin said. "I asked him what the hell he was doing and while we were arguing, Jack's father came up and said, 'Jack, you shouldn't have done that.'

"Kehoe answered, 'Let me alone, Pop. I'll do worse than that before this night's over.'

"I had a feeling Kehoe was talking about Langdon and I went down to warn him. Then me and some buttys went into Williams' for a drink."

From this point on, exactly what happened during the balance of the evening is partly obscured by the passage of time. The first report of trouble that evening was from William R. Davis, whose evidence was succinct even if his actions were more discretionary than valorous.

"I was sitting near the door of Williams' with Jerry Sweeney. Suddenly, I heard a man cry out, 'Oh, don't! Oh, don't!'

"And what did you and the other fellows do then?" Mr. Davis was asked.

"We got up and ran down into the cellar."

Others who heard those same desperate pleas for help from somewhere in the starless night took cover wherever they could. One patron of Boch's, only a few yards away from where a man was being stoned to death, paused momentarily to handle a routine chore before turning on his heels.

"I seen Mr. Langdon in a white shirt running as fast as he could," he said. "He was about three feet away from me and there was five or six men following him, throwing rocks. Langdon hopped over the fence in front of Hamburger's livery stable with the crowd jumping after him."

"What did you do?" he was asked.

"I took another snootful of whiskey from the bottle I was carrying, tossed it away, turned around and went home."

"Was that all?" was the final question.

"No, sir," was this gentleman's answer. "First, I made sure the bottle was empty."

A similar display of courage was shown by two of Langdon's neighbors. A few moments had passed from the time the ticket boss leaped over the fence. Langdon had crawled along the ground outside the gate where he was clearly visible to two passers-by.

"Me and Sam Hoover were walking along the railroad track near the stable yard," said one of the men. "Sam stopped all of a sudden. 'Watch out!' he told me, 'or you'll step on a man.'

"I looked down, held a match and seen it was Mr. Langdon. He was moaning. Me and Jim ran over to talk to a couple other men who was standing around."

Whatever good intentions this pair may have had were dispelled almost at once. By the time they reached other gentlemen who had been observing the passing scene, the gang that had attacked the ticket boss returned.

"Then we heard Langdon cry out again and some stones smashed against his body and the gate."

The witness was asked what he did next.

"I went home," was his reply.

A local justice of the peace had a grandstand seat at the murder.

"I was in my house, which was near the stable fence. I heard a row and looked out the window. A man yelled, 'My God! Men, don't kill me.' It was Langdon. I heard stones rattle against the fence. Then I shut the window." (And presumably went to bed.)

Still another witness was asked why he neither went to Langdon's aid not offered to identify the killers.

"I was afraid to," he said, "because then I knew there'd be a double murder. I had my wife and family to think about."

When rumors of a brawl reached Williams', several of Langdon's friends became alarmed about the ticket boss's safety. Canvin, the foreman, recalling Kehoe's threats, looked around, and when he couldn't see Langdon, ran back to organize a search party. On his way back to the saloon, he passed Boch's. As the doors opened, he saw Kehoe and several of Jack's gang sweep onto the porch and into the bar. There were red stains on Kehoe's shirt. Kehoe, the last to enter the saloon, paused for a second and stared at Canvin. Their eyes met and held: then each went his way.

When Canvin pushed through the doors of Williams' he told his companions that Langdon was missing. Canvin and a dozen others dashed out of the saloon and into the dark and now empty street.

"We found Langdon in Hamburger's yard," recalled one of the men. "As we went to pick him up he said, 'Don't, boys, I've had enough,' thinking we were the party that beat him. We carried him back to the hotel. He never said who did it."

Langdon was badly hurt, his lips cut through, nearly all his teeth knocked out, his nose broken, and one ear completely severed. He was bleeding through his mouth and had difficulty breathing.

"Clean me up as good as you can," he whispered to Canvin, "and take me home. I'm afraid it's all up with me. I don't want the missus to see me the way I look now."

Langdon died in his wife's arms two days later. "I said to him, just before he passed on," Mrs. Langdon told Canvin, "I'm afraid this is the last of you. He made no reply but looked at me, oh so sorrowfully."

The verdict of the coroner's jury was "Death at the hands of persons unknown."

Little or no effort was made to arrest anybody and a troubled peace settled on Audenried. Men talked in subdued voices and discussed the murder only in the privacy of their homes. A noisy drunk at Boch's bar who began to boast of what he'd seen and heard the night of June 14 was choked from behind and hurled into the street before he knew what was happening. Canvin's home was stoned; John Tyrell, who told authorities he thought that Kehoe was one of the men who attacked Langdon, narrowly escaped a premature dynamite blast; Pat Brady claimed somebody fired a pistol at him.

A few weeks later Jack Kehoe quit his job at McCreary's and left Honeybrook to live in Girardville, forty miles away, near the west end of Schuylkill County.

Chapter Four

At about the time that Kehoe moved to Honeybrook, Franklin
Benjamin Gowen was being sworn in as District Attorney of
Schuylkill County.

No more cynical, tenacious, and shrewd antagonist could have
been chosen to lead the opposition, to plan the destruction of the
Molly Maguires, and to preside at their ruin than this handsome
aristocrat. Without any self-delusions of righteousness, Gowen
felt only amusement and contempt for the heavenly rewards
promised to all Philadelphia gentlemen by Episcopalian priests
and for the hypocrisy of so many of his colleagues.

Gowen was an Irishman but not a Roman Catholic. His fore-
bears, members of the Church of England, emigrated from the
north of Ireland early in the eighteenth century and settled in
Philadelphia. Gowen's father was a wealthy merchant; his mother
was a descendant of one of the Quaker City's oldest families.

Franklin Benjamin Gowen was born February 9, 1836, on his
family's estate in Mount Airy, a section of Philadelphia just a
bit south of Chestnut Hill geographically and socially. After
attending private schools (one of which was Mount St. Mary's
Academy, a strict Roman Catholic institution at Emmitsburg,
Maryland), Gowen matriculated at Moravian Institute in the
heart of the Pennsylvania Dutch country. He was graduated with
honors in 1854.

He was a handsome youth, with fine features, a high forehead,
and wavy dark brown hair. He was six feet tall, slightly built,
but wiry and strong. He possessed almost hypnotic charm for

both his contemporaries and his elders. He was a superb debater, sharp-witted and cool, and had almost total recall. He made friends easily. However, as William Weist, former editor of the Shamokin *Citizen* and one of Gowen's biographers, pointed out, "Later on in Gowen's life, it seemed that he wanted to be fighting all the time. Only then was he in his element."

The elder Gowen had made money in coal land speculation and owned stock in a mine near Centralia, Northumberland County. Franklin Benjamin was sent there to learn the business. At the age of twenty he became manager of his father's Shamokin Furnace Colliery, where he remained for little more than a year. (It was here he first heard rumors of the Molly Maguires.) Young Gowen then moved to Schuylkill County, where he and a partner, William Turner, bought a small mine of their own at Mt. Laffee, a few miles from Cass Township. The firm went into bankruptcy after less than two years, but Gowen eventually paid off all company obligations in full.

Publicly, Gowen attributed this failure to his own lack of judgment. But he told intimates that the pressure of rising unionism was forcing independent mine operators to the wall, and that unless incipient labor organizations were crushed they would soon rule the coal trade. He predicted that unionism could be defeated only by close co-operation of all mine owners, who would have to abandon destructive competition to survive.

Gowen now turned to the study of law, and was admitted to practice before the Schuylkill County bar in May, 1860. One year later, he was the Republican candidate for district attorney. He was elected that November and sworn into office on January 15, 1862. He was not quite twenty-six years old.

This was a period of increasing uneasiness throughout the hard coal regions. A sudden spurt in the demand for coal coupled with a loss in manpower due to army enlistments, brought an influx of many more thousands of Irish into the patches and towns of the anthracite counties. These immigrants, most of whom were hungry, were understandably disinterested in the Union's cause.

The District Attorney, with a limited budget and a small staff,

25

did a creditable job. Content for the time to increase his trial experience, Gowen made no effort to join the armed forces, and, by reason of his position, was not drafted.

Gowen gradually became concerned with the development of a secret body of men he felt was being organized all over the anthracite area. During his first six months in office there were eleven unsolved murders in Schuylkill County. Most of these homicides, the District Attorney claimed, fitted into a peculiar pattern. The victims were Welsh, English, or German, held positions of authority in the mines, and the ubiquitous "four Irishmen" were usually observed leaving the scene of the crime.

Another of Gowen's fears was that in the coming election, the Democrats, the bulk of whose strength lay in the solid Irish Catholic vote, would take over row offices, including the office of county commissioner, who spun the jury wheel. Then jury regulation, a polite term for "rigging," would pass from friendly hands. Schuylkill County Republicans, who had excluded Irish Catholics from jury lists for some time, felt no qualms of conscience as long as it was *they* who violated the Sixth Amendment. Gowen, who never deceived himself, must have viewed this example of smug Anglo-Saxon hypocrisy with amusement.

There was reason for Republican alarm. In neighboring Carbon County, two Irishmen, one of them an alleged Molly Maguire, had been elected majority county commissioners, while another son of Erin was sent to Harrisburg to represent his district in the lower house.

On May 5, 1862, miners whose working hours had been cut twice within six months to give jobs to newly recruited immigrants, struck at the Heilner Breaker in Cass Township. Violence flared within minutes of the walkout—foremen were beaten, the engineer was gagged and tied to a pipe, and the hoisting equipment was smashed.

Gowen acted promptly, sending the sheriff and a posse of armed citizens to the colliery in a coach provided by the Reading Railroad. When this force of law was routed Gowen telegraphed to Governor Curtin for help, and within hours, two hundred members of the state militia arrived from Philadelphia to restore order.

Bitterness over the Heilner Breaker incident increased the tension between employer and employee, Protestant and Catholic, and Union and anti-Union sympathizers everywhere in the hard coal regions, but particularly in Schuylkill and Carbon counties. One direct result of this smoldering passion had been the murder of Frank Langdon.

Chapter Five

By the autumn of 1862, Union troops were seriously depleted, and although Lincoln hesitated before requesting state conscription because he feared public reaction, he finally called upon the states to draft additional manpower. Except for a few isolated rural areas and some large eastern cities, the national response was better than Lincoln expected. The most bitter pocket of resistance was Cass Township.

From the swift spread of this "rebellion," it was evident to observers of the day and to current historians that those who defied Pennsylvania's Governor Curtin were skillfully organized. This opinion is shared by James E. Haas, former newspaperman, a Civil War enthusiast, and author of many scholarly monographs on the Molly Maguires.

"It couldn't have happened any other way," said Haas. "A spontaneous uprising wouldn't have taken the definite structure of this one. Within days after Colonel McClure, in charge of the state draft, put the Governor's orders into effect, armed bodies of Irish from this little township marched off to designated positions all over the county. They assembled promptly; they knew where they were going, and they got there on time.

"An accurate manpower census had been completed late that September. On October 16, a list of conscripts was drawn and Schuylkill County men were ordered to report to Pottsville. But when they checked the arrivals, there were a hell of a lot of Irishmen missing, and practically none present from Cass Township.

"This was damned strange, because only six months before that the Irish, who made up most of the Glen Carbon Guards, couldn't wait until they got into battle. Many a Civil War hero came from these Cass Township Irishmen.

"The Cass Township draft rebels had to have been told what to do by somebody who knew the score. The tavern owners were smart, natural leaders, and each one had his 'constituents.' Most were Democrats, not too sympathetic to the Union cause. They were plenty sore, too, because it looked like the rich were buying their way out of the draft. There was a lot of truth here. A disproportionate number of Irishmen were being called. Employers, too, were using conscription to get rid of Irish 'trouble-makers' by taking them out of the mines and putting them in the army.

"The Mollies were the only group which possessed all the necessary qualifications for this insurrection. They had leadership, mobility, homogeneity, dislike for superimposed authority, a tradition of rebellion, courage, and above all, hunger."

Shortly after the Pennsylvania draft law went into effect, a small body of Irish rebels stamped out of the patches of Cass Township. They were met by others all along their way. Soon, hundreds of shouting men, their numbers swelling hourly, picketed scores of Schuylkill County collieries, screamed protests against the draft, and damned Colonel McClure.

"A gang of five hundred armed men stopped a train of conscripts at Tremont and promised protection for any unwilling draftee who left the cars. The rebels prevented many of them going to Harrisburg," reported the *Miners' Journal*, October 20, 1862.

As the President was debating what steps to take, Bishop Wood hurried to Schuylkill County, where he conferred with political and spiritual leaders. The following Sunday, said the Pottsville *Journal*, "All priests throughout the region preached strong sermons on the duties of good citizens under law."

Secretary of War Stanton took sterner measures: he ordered two regiments of regulars to Pottsville. While this armed force was on its way, Colonel McClure, who feared added bloodshed in Cass Township, went over Stanton's head and sent a cipher to Lincoln explaining his desire to avoid a conflict between the military and civilians. The President understood and dispatched the following message to an aide in Harrisburg:

"Say to McClure that I am very desirous to have the laws fully executed but it might be well, in an extreme emergency, to be content with the appearance of executing the laws. I think McClure will understand."

McClure understood.

"The Colonel summoned Benjamin Bannan, publisher of the Pottsville *Miners' Journal,* and asked him to run a story stating that the quota in Cass Township had been filled," Haas continued. "The clash was averted and the two regiments were turned back. But nobody was fooled. You can imagine the delight among the Mollies over the fact that they had forced the Federal government to back down.

"Molly exploits grew more reckless and you couldn't get a witness to testify against them. People reasoned, and who can blame them, that if the Government of the United States wasn't big enough to take on the Mollies, certainly no individual was."

All through the Civil War open defiance of the law continued, with the core of resistance remaining in Cass Township. The first of many attacks on collieries where it was claimed hiring bosses would not employ "Irish draft dodgers" came on December 18, 1862, near Heckscherville, Cass Township. A mob of two hundred men, brandishing clubs, forced their way inside a colliery at eleven o'clock in the morning. After knocking down a dozen employees, rioters looted the company store and left the shelves bare. There were at least fifty witnesses to this brief but open assault, but not one was willing to testify.

"It . . . (the riot) seems to have been a movement originating in Cass Township where a secret association termed the Molly Maguires exists," claimed the *Miners' Journal* of December 20, 1862.

No mention was made of the fact that the rioters had been jobless for weeks, that they were blacklisted at every coal mine in the area, and that their families were starving in freezing patch hovels.

Audenried, resting uneasily since Langdon's murder, erupted violently again on November 5, 1863, with a murder as savage as Langdon's. This one was attributed directly to the Molly

Maguires. The cause of the murder, according to the *New York Times,* was the widespread belief that the victim, George K. Smith, had turned over names of draft dodgers and deserters to government authorities.

"Smith was a coal operator," said the *Times.* "He was accused of giving information to the Government, at that time hunting deserters. For this it was determined to 'put him away.'

"His murder was one of the most wanton and deliberate assassinations ever committed by the Molly Maguires. It was a committee of Mollies at Audenried, on the night of November 5, 1862, . . . which made the decision. . . .

"The thing [murder] was not done in a corner. A doctor making professional calls . . . saw a number of men loading firearms. A boy looking for cows came upon fifteen men holding a meeting in the woods; but boy and doctor had lived long enough in that wild society not to take notice of what they saw. They passed on, made no remarks, and so kept out of trouble.

"Mr. Smith, who had been to Philadelphia to report deserters, it was believed, came home that day on an evening train, sick, and went to bed at once. His wife had received some intimation of coming trouble and asked George W. Ulrich, a clerk in the colliery store, to spend the night in their house."

Ulrich armed himself with an ancient horse pistol and arrived at the Smith home before dusk. He went upstairs, spoke to his employer for a few moments, then went down again. He and Mrs. Smith had a cup of tea in the kitchen where the lady remained while the clerk walked through the rooms, locking windows and bolting front, rear, side and cellar doors.

As the night deepened, candles were snuffed. The house was dark except for the glow of coals in the kitchen stove and a kerosene lamp, its wick turned so low that only dim shadows flickered across the parlor from the huge square piano to the rocker where Ulrich had seated himself, cocked pistol on his lap. The stillness was broken by an occasional cough from the sick man upstairs, a troubled sigh from Mrs. Smith in the kitchen, or the howling of a dog far off. Ulrich waited.

"About eight o'clock," the *Times* continued, "two men knocked

31

at the door saying they had a letter for Mr. Smith, . . . which must be delivered into his own hands. They refused to place it under the door."

Mrs. Smith came in from the kitchen, turned up the wick, and looked at Ulrich for advice. He nodded his head and Mrs. Smith unbolted the door. The clerk, pistol in readiness, stood behind curtains which separated the parlor and dining room. Two men pushed their way inside.

"Smith, hearing the commotion and some of the conversation," said the *Times*, "called downstairs and said he was too sick to receive the letter and that the men should leave it and call again in the morning. On receiving this message one of the men fired his pistol . . . and at the report, a crowd of men entered the room.

"At the same time Ulrich came into the parlor and Mr. Smith, in alarm, sprang out of bed and hurried downstairs. He was immediately shot down and died in a few hours. Ulrich also was shot and beaten. He, in the meantime, was using his revolver with good effect . . . 'Long John Donohue,' whom the clerk recognized, was wounded, and another Molly was killed but carried off by his friends."

The usual pattern followed. The widow and the clerk told their stories; the authorities promised immediate action; the English and Welsh threatened retaliation; the decent Irish were horrified, and the boys at Boch's provided alibis.

It should have been easy to establish the identity of at least one more of the murderers—the widow and clerk were in accord on his description. He had, they said, a long, dirty, white, straggly, uncombed beard which stretched from his greasy, hatless head to a rope that dangled about his waist to hold up a pair of tattered pants, and the hand which fired one of the pistols was covered with thick, matted, grey hair.

The only gentleman in Carbon or Schuylkill counties fitting that description exactly was James McDonell, known widely as "The Hairy Man of Tuscarora." But Mr. McDonell apparently never left McBride's saloon in Tamaqua for twenty-four hours before and twenty-four hours after November 5, 1863. A dozen honest citizens were willing to swear to this on a stack of Bibles.

Chapter Six

As the Civil War drew to a close and the market for coal fell, wages dropped again and unemployment increased.

Except for weak, unaffiliated "locals," the miners had no union to speak for them. These ineffectual groups, led by the Welsh, refused to allow impetuous sons of Erin to join them. So the Irishman found a spokesman in the only place open to him besides the church—his saloon.

Democratic party leaders in the western end of Schuylkill County saw in young Jack Kehoe a man who might go far politically. He had already made a name for himself, and his reasons for leaving Honeybrook were accepted. He was strong, loyal, and honest, feared by his enemies and respected, if not liked, by his friends. Since the Langdon murder, he had learned to control his tongue and temper.

Sometime late in 1864 party chiefs helped Jack Kehoe open a tavern, the Hibernian House, on Third Street in Girardville. Just outside was a wooden bridge, which crossed a yellow sulphurous branch of the Schuylkill River to join Girardville, with a population of two thousand, to a half-dozen patches scattered on the other side of the stream.

Within sight of Kehoe's were dirty banks of silt growing higher each year. On a windy day dust from these piles was blown into thirsty throats. Within sound of Kehoe's were the whistles of four collieries whose workers passed the Hibernian House on their way to and from their jobs. Many of these Irish coal miners got into the habit of stopping into Black Jack's. Kehoe's power, and that of other saloonkeepers throughout the hard coal regions, grew enormously.

"The new Irish elite," said Tom Barrett, "was the saloon-keeper. The 'bhoys' were his loyal supporters. They did what he told them to do. He was smart. He could read and write and often he held a political job. Maybe he was despised by Protestant political leaders but he controlled a solid bloc of votes.

"Sure the men on top played along with him. He even was courted by the Republicans. Maybe they knew what went on in those backrooms. And maybe they didn't want to know."

In Barrett's opinion, one shared by many students of Pennsylvania's history, the period from the Civil War's end to the late 1870's marked the true ascent of Molly Maguirism. It was then that the links lightly binding loose, voluntary associations of men were forged into one strong chain stretching from Pine Grove to Mauch Chunk and surrounding a hundred patches, villages, and towns. The secret ritual was devised, passwords were created and changed to avoid recognition, and formal meetings were held where murder for profit, revenge, or pleasure was arranged.

"You must keep in mind," Barrett cautioned, "something which a hell of a lot of coal region chroniclers and spinners of anthracite fairy tales forget—that a very small percentage of Irishmen were involved and the rest of them, my grandfather included, were heartily ashamed of what was going on. They were particularly disturbed when Irishmen, and there were thousands of them fighting with the Federal troops, felt the lash of scorn from anti-Union Irishmen."

On one occasion the bitterness felt for Irish patriots by Irish Copperheads erupted with murderous results. Late in October, in 1864, James Shields, a private in Pennsylvania's 48th Volunteer Regiment, on leave after his third enlistment, walked into a saloon at Silver Creek, a patch in Cass Township. With Shields was a companion, James O'Hanlon, another enlistee from the same regiment. Although the saloon was owned by the widow of Shields' brother, it was, according to Gowen, a Molly Maguire hangout.

No sooner had the pair walked into the bar when Hugh Curran, a "regular," deliberately spilled whiskey on Shields' uniform. The soldier wiped it off and ignored the drunken Curran. A second or two later, John Stinson, another bar habitué, tossed his glass into O'Hanlon's face and called him a "bloody English bastard."

O'Hanlon, as Irish as anybody, swung at Stinson and knocked him down. Then O'Hanlon and Shields, seeing they were badly outnumbered, tried to edge their way to the door but were surrounded by a dozen jeering men. One of the attackers, whom O'Hanlon identified as Curran, drew a knife and plunged it seven times into Shields' body. The soldier fell, mortally wounded, and the mob scattered out front and rear doors.

District Attorney Gowen, acting on information furnished by the surviving soldier, ordered the arrest of Curran and Stinson. The former was taken into custody the following day, in the same saloon, surrounded by the same drinking companions. But Stinson was dead, "killed accidentally," reported the Tamaqua *Courier,* October 25, 1864, "by one of Stinson's friends in the back of the saloon because he thought it was O'Hanlon and was afraid O'Hanlon would not keep his mouth shut."

Curran was brought to trial in a courtroom crowded with toughs who vociferously showed their sympathy for the prisoner. O'Hanlon, now labeled "informer," was the sole prosecution witness, while a dozen of Curran's friends swore that the pair of soldiers were the aggressors and that Curran acted in self-defense.

The prisoner was found guilty of "involuntary manslaughter" and sentenced to one to three years at Eastern State Penitentiary. He was paroled after less than four months. Gowen was angry with the verdict and attributed its lightness to the panel's fear of reprisals. He felt the time was not yet ripe for the destruction of Molly Maguirism and when the Philadelphia and Reading Railroad offered the twenty-nine-year-old District Attorney the position of chief counsel, Gowen accepted.

During Gowen's last year in office no fewer than seventeen men were murdered in Schuylkill County; of these, eleven held supervisory jobs in the mines. All eleven, shortly before their deaths, either discharged an employee, had altercations with others, or were accused of being unfair to still others. In every single instance, fellow supervisors were able to recall an incident in which an Irishman had a part in some unpleasant episode involving the deceased.

In addition to homicide, that year six collieries were dynamited, scores of tool sheds, storage rooms, and engine houses were burned, hundreds of coal cars were overturned, and countless citizens were beaten or had their ears cut off.

Local police were ineffectual and the courts were unable to enforce the law. Gowen was fully cognizant of these facts and of the impossibility of mining and shipping coal without constant harassment. The Reading, which Gowen represented, was the largest operator in the anthracite region and a major victim of sabotage. Under pressure by this corporation, the state legislature passed an act permitting the formation of a private police force. That Gowen had a hand in drawing this piece of legislation is unquestioned.

The Act of February 27, 1865, set up an organization responsible not to the public but to the railroad and mining corporations that did the hiring. In theory, at least, the powers of this new arm of the law were limited to protection of mine and rail property; but in actual practice there was no limit to the privileges usurped.

The right of *habeas corpus* was suspended and search and seizure warrants bypassed. When a man was suspected of a crime the Coal and Iron Police entered his home, by force if necessary, and removed the suspect to the county jail. They guarded him, extracted his "confession," and assisted in his prosecution.

This new police force was outfitted with impressive uniforms and carried riot sticks and revolvers which they knew how to use. Compared to the members of local police forces, whom they supplanted *de facto* if not *de jure*, they were well paid. Certainly not all and probably not even many Coal and Iron policemen were the anti-Catholic sadists they were accused of being, although considering the circumstances of their hiring, it is likely that the majority were Protestants.

While they may have been given a smattering of proper law enforcement duties, they were told their first duty was to the company; and as far as the Irish coal miner was concerned, here was an extra enemy to be fought. The "Bloody English" had provided another foe, first cousin to the Constabulary which sons of Erin thought they had left behind them.

As the Coal and Iron Police grew in numbers and experience the underground opposing them expanded and developed cunning. No longer were the usual "four Irishmen" of local origin. Now, if a brave but foolhardy witness identified the quartet at all except ethnically, the criminals were strangers.

On July 10, 1865, two men walked into a hotel at New Philadelphia, a small town eight miles east of Pottsville. The bartender-owner was William Williams, whose brother, a foreman at the Tamaqua Steam Mill, had fired three drunken employees, Dennis Murphy, Dennis Magee and William Kehoe (no relation to Jack).

Just as William Williams looked up from the beer spigot where he had drawn lager for a half-dozen patrons, one of the strangers pulled a revolver from his pocket and fired at the tavernkeeper's head. Williams fell to the floor, mortally wounded. The murderer, gun leveled at the frightened customers, walked out with his companion and vanished into the hills. The two Dennises and William Kehoe were picked up on suspicion. All three provided alibis. No arrest was ever made.

On August 16 of that same year, a Cass Township colliery fire boss disappeared on his way home from work. He was never seen again. Two days previously he had discharged three frequenters of Reilly's saloon. The trio was questioned; each had an alibi and no one was held.

On August 22, the superintendent of another Schuylkill County colliery laid off two men for quarreling and two others for drinking on the job. All four were Irishmen, hated and feared by the decent Irish who populated the patch in which the quartet lived. Three days later in the presence of at least two hundred employees, the mine official was shot to death on a public highway in broad daylight, fifty yards from his office. Not one person was willing to describe the murderers.

There was no let-up in atrocities. Some colliery superintendents and small independent mine owners (most major operators lived outside the coal regions) who had been threatened were escorted to and from work by Coal and Iron Police. But they could not be guarded constantly and when vigilance was relaxed, they and sometimes their families were beaten. Many independent owners, unable to stand the strain, sold out to large producers.

Until the murder of Henry H. Dunne, one of Pottsville's most distinguished residents, there was no great cry for law, order, and justice in the press. But Dunne's murder aroused public opinion, temporarily at least, everywhere in the anthracite regions. Dunne was forty-eight years old, a vestryman at Trinity Protestant Episcopal Church, and a civic leader. He was in charge of all operations for one of the largest coal producers in the Schuylkill County.

On January 10, 1866, Dunne was shot to death by five armed men while driving his rig on a well-traveled road less than two miles from Pottsville. Although there was a score of witnesses, the murderers escaped unmolested and the only fact gleaned was that the five men were strangers.

Before moving to Pottsville, Dunne had made many enemies in Cass Township by publicly urging that draft laws be enforced and that all able male citizens be compelled to serve in the armed forces.

On the day of Dunne's funeral, the Pottsville *Journal* called for help from the state legislature.

"The time has arrived when protection, in Schuylkill County for life and property must be demanded imperatively . . .

"The curse of Schuylkill County is miserable, inefficient officials, who are either afraid to or do not know how to discharge their duties. The fact is that we must turn . . . to the State for protection from the bands of secret assassins that infest the County. If we do not, it will be a question soon whether a man's life will be safe on his own threshold . . . Murderers, in consequence of the secret, oath bound organization that exists in this County, remain to this day undetected."

But the corrupt political machine that took over Pennsylvania in 1867 ignored petitions from Schuylkill County citizens, and murder, assault, and mayhem continued unabatedly.

Soon afterwards, Cass Township was the scene of another homicide, when an official of the Glen Carbon Coal Company was shot to death a mile from his home. He had had an altercation with a trio of Irish miners and discharged all of them. After the murder the men were questioned but each provided an alibi. The widow was convinced her husband's murderers took an additional precaution to destroy possible identification.

"My grandmother told me the superstitious Irish used to believe the last thing a dying man saw was made into a permanent picture on his retina," said the victim's granddaughter. "So when the Mollies killed my grandfather, they shot out both his eyes."

The list of atrocities was endless. On March 23, Henry Johnson was bludgeoned to death by "four Irishmen" when he attempted to help an aged neighbor who was being robbed. On March 25, a fire boss at an Ashland colliery disappeared with his dog, which used to accompany him on his rounds. Neither was seen again until ten years later when the bones of a man and animal were found together in an abandoned mine entrance at Turkey Run, a patch outside of Shenandoah. A Masonic ring, which had rolled underneath the victim's body, was identified as the fire boss's.

The Tamaqua *Courier,* on September 5, 1867, published a list of serious unsolved crimes that had occurred in Schuylkill County during the preceding eight months. Included were twelve murders, sixty-four atrocious assaults, twenty-seven armed robberies, and thirty-five colliery and mine fires of suspicious origin.

"It was an unbelievable situation," James Haas commented. "Nobody seemed able to do a damned thing about it. My grandfather, who moved from Schuylkill County to Wyoming Territory in the '70s, said there never was anything like it even in the wildest days of the Wild West.

"It was obvious that most of the coal region crimes were planned down to the escape routes, and that some one person or an oligarchy of criminals was heading a secret society and would have to be smashed from the inside, not from without."

Chapter Seven

On September 1, 1869, Franklin Benjamin Gowen had been elevated from chief counsel to president of "The Road." He was then only thirty-two years old. The following year Gowen took the first of a series of steps by which he hoped to gain control of the entire hard coal industry.

Gowen believed that unless a strong and ruthless hand ruled the steadily weakening independent collieries, through merger or absorption, it was only a matter of time before "anarchists" would make "unreasonable" demands upon management. Gowen's initial move was to persuade the state legislature to pass a bill permitting railroads to own mines.

After a few minor difficulties, a measure satisfactory to the President of the Road passed both state houses by wide margins.

"Immediately thereafter," said the Shamokin *Citizen*, "the name of the company was changed to the Philadelphia and Reading Coal and Iron Company. Floating a loan of $25,000,000, Gowen set about to purchase lands in Schuylkill and Northumberland counties. Aided by strikes and financial difficulties, Gowen convinced individual operators to sell. He soon acquired a total of more than 100,000 acres, more than any other corporation. It could be said that he controlled almost one-third of the total anthracite region."

Gowen's next step was to divide and so destroy unions by creating dissension within the ranks of the miners themselves. He stirred up trouble wherever he could, by innuendo, by calumny, and by job discrimination, sometimes favoring newly arrived Irishmen over long established, experienced Welsh or Englishmen, sometimes reversing the process. He had his informers everywhere, in the pits, in the breakers, in stables, in engine houses, and at outside workings. Each whisper of incipient unionism was promptly reported.

He would often throw his miners off balance by promoting a "troublemaker" instead of firing him, and so Gowen would gain a "company man." The next time, another organizer would find himself out of work and blacklisted everywhere in the hard coal regions while his family starved. Even the operators themselves were never sure where Gowen stood. With company stores furnishing added profits to corporate coffers, Gowen refused to allow a single "pluck me" in any of his company's patches and permitted his employees to buy where they wished. In addition, he openly scolded his colleagues for permitting what he called "petty thievery."

Because they were tougher, less willing to be "bought," had abler leaders, and perhaps possessed greater physical courage than any other ethnic group among the miners, Gowen feared the Irish above all. And yet the President of the Road felt no personal animosity toward these embittered, disillusioned sons of Erin who lost at least as much as they gained by giving up the "ould sod" for the new. It is likely that he had more respect for the Irish than for those who gave in without a fight. He proved this often by refusing to allow the hated "No Irish Need Apply" signs to be posted at his hiring offices. Regardless of religion or ethnic origin, anybody could work for Gowen, provided he was willing to accept Gowen's terms.

All this is not to say that Gowen did not lend a helping hand to anti-Catholicism whenever he could, if he thought that in so doing he would create suspicion within diverse assemblies of men who had risen above prejudice to fight a common foe— Gowen and the operators he already dominated.

The Avondale disaster of September 6, 1869, which took 111 coal workers' lives including those of nineteen children under fourteen, united, if only briefly, all factions of labor and joined

Irishmen, Welshmen, Orangemen and Englishmen into a sodality which, properly exploited, could have advanced the workers' cause by several decades.

The mine at Avondale was owned by the Delaware, Lackawanna, and Western Railroad. Populated almost entirely by Welshmen, Avondale was a large patch in one of the dreariest sections of the mountainous terrain between Wilkes-Barre and Scranton. It was dominated by the breaker, a tall, black structure towering two hundred feet above the ground. Any physically fit males past the age of twelve worked either in the breaker or in the mines below.

Adjacent to the colliery was an engine house furnishing power for a hoist which lowered and raised men and coal and for a huge fan which pumped fresh air into the intricate passageways of a labyrinth stretching for miles as much as a thousand feet beneath the earth's surface.

The only entrance to the coal chamber 298 feet below the ground where the luckless 111 worked was through a shaft in the colliery itself. The fire began about 10 A.M. in a pocket 150 feet below the breaker. In seconds, an updraft swept it into the colliery, and minutes later the dry wood of the building was a mass of flames. Through a ghastly error, the fan in the fireproof engine house kept on pumping.

"For ten hours the fan, intended to purify the mine, had been driving into its depths the full volume of poisons and stifling gases thrown off," said the Philadelphia *Public Ledger* on September 8, 1869. "Men who somehow might have escaped were trapped horribly."

Rescue attempts were started at midnight while the smoldering embers of the ruined breaker lit up the sky. But even before the first body was brought to the surface and identified by a relative who stood at the open end of the shaft, hope was abandoned. There were no survivors.

"The hardest heart must be moved to offer substantial pity to all those unfortunates. Come forward quickly. A good work is yet before us," pleaded the Philadelphia *Evening Bulletin.*

Response to the newspaper's appeal for help was immediate. Miners who could barely sustain their own families walked to Avondale from as far as Pottsville, ninety miles away, bearing gifts of clothing and even cash. For a short while all miners were united and religious differences forgotten. At a protest meeting held in Wilkes-Barre, the speakers were Gwyllam Evens, Edward Merriman, James Boyd O'Connor, and Thomas Mulligan. "All the speakers," said the Wilkes-Barre *Sentinel,* "were greeted alike by thunderous applause."

From Lackawanna County to Schuylkill County, Irishmen previously banned from union "locals" now paraded spontaneously with the Welsh and English up and down the streets of Scranton, Hazelton, Mauch Chunk, Bloomsburg, Sunbury and Pottsville. They carried placards reading SUPPORT THE AVONDALE VICTIMS, DEMAND PROTECTION IN OUR MINES, GIVE US A LIVING WAGE.

Gowen and other operators viewed with justifiable alarm the obvious peril in this quick spread of unity. While the ruins of the breaker were still smoldering, a vicious anti-Catholic rumor spread from Scranton to Pottsville with almost the same speed as the news of the fire had traveled a few days before: Irishmen, led by the Molly Maguires, had started the blaze.

The lie was spread by word of mouth. Newspapermen on the scene of the disaster were quick to spot its source. Declared a correspondent for the conservative, reliable *Evening Bulletin* on September 11, 1869, under a Scranton dateline, "I can only give it [the rumor] for what it is worth, surmising that it was probably set afloat in the interest of the mine owners."

Irishmen were spat upon in the streets of Plymouth, Moosic, Wilkes-Barre, Mahoopany, Scranton, and in the patches of Luzerne and Lackawanna counties, where they were outnumbered and disorganized. On September 13, the newly formed Wilkes-Barre Miners' Union, which rose from the ashes of Avondale, dropped plans to include the Irish on its all-Welsh executive board.

While it would be impossible to pinpoint the source of the destructive rumor, chroniclers of the time were of the opinion that the touch was that of Gowen, spokesman and strategist for most miner owners, including the Delaware, Lackawanna, and Western.

A drop in wages and working hours in the winter of 1871-1872 brought on a new wave of terror. After a series of dynamitings, overturned coal cars, and derailed engines, a half-dozen men whom Coal and Iron Police swore were led by the Molly Maguires ignited the Franklin Benjamin Gowen Colliery at Shamokin, on February 13, 1872. The structure burned to the ground.

At this personal affront, Gowen, who rarely displayed temper, went into a cold rage. He sent his investigators into the area; they worked for months, but could prove nothing which would hold up in court. No arrest was ever made for this crime, committed during daylight hours in the presence of at least 150 witnesses.

On April 24, Henry Yiengst, a boss carpenter in Mahanoy City, told a few of the cronies with whom he spent nearly every evening that he'd never hire an Irishman because "they're all a bunch of goddamned Mollies." On April 26, Yiengst was found wandering about in a daze along the bed of Mahanoy Creek, which flows through the town. His skull was fractured, both arms were broken, and his tongue had been pulled out by the roots.

On May 1, Charles Green, a Centralia school teacher, made a disparaging remark about the Mollies at a teachers' meeting. On May 5, Green was discovered on the steps of his house. Both ears were cut off.

On June 16, after a Fair Association meeting, William Fenstermacher, a farmer, displayed a horse pistol which he said he'd use on any Molly who dared steal from his barn. On June 22, Fenstermacher's hired girl found him stripped, gagged, and tied to the base of a watering trough. He was bleeding profusely from wounds in each buttock inflicted by his own horse pistol, which was left dangling at the pump.

On June 28, employees at "The Road's" New Boston colliery were notified that their work week would be reduced from four to three days. To protest this, John Siney, the St. Clair labor leader, called a meeting of colliery workers in nearby Frackville on June 30 and for the first time in a year he was able to attract a large number of men. Included in the audience were many Irishmen, none of whom were alleged to be Mollies. Undoubtedly Gowen was furnished a detailed report of this angry gathering.

On July 1, fifty-five gondolas filled with coal prepared for market at the New Boston colliery were sent tumbling down a ravine. Coal and Iron Police, who investigated the wreck, said the train had been sabotaged.

Whether it was the cumulative effect of previous outrages, the danger of rising unionism, or the recent train wreck, Gowen finally concluded that if he wanted to smash the Molly Maguires and simultaneously tar all "rebels" with the same pitch, he would have to bore from within. As Schuylkill County's district attorney, Gowen had learned that even his best planned cases were lost by juries too timorous to convict. As counsel for "The Road," and finally as its president, he was aware that the conspiracy of silence which surrounded the Mollies had become impenetrable. All the Coal and Iron Police could do was protect the company's own employees and keep down property losses.

What Gowen needed, he realized, was a private detective who would join the Mollies, learn their secrets, and gather enough evidence to hang their leaders. This would require someone with unusual talents, but Gowen was prepared to pay any price for the right man.

During the late summer of 1867, one more Irishman was ready to exchange the Old World for the New. He was the twenty-three-year-old James McParlan, born in Ulster, County Armagh, Parish of Mullabrack, Ireland, on July 7, 1844. Not much is known about his early life except that he left home for England at the age of sixteen to work in a boiler factory at Gateshead on the River Tyne.

By then he had grown to his full height of something under five feet seven inches, and weighed nearly the 145 pounds he was to carry the rest of his life. Since only a few years later he was able to demonstrate his talents as an excellent boxer and an even more deadly rough-and-tumble fighter, a nimble dancer of Irish jigs, a sweet-voiced tenor, a ladies' man of considerable sophistication, and a man who could drink unbelievably large quantities of whiskey and still retain his faculties, it must be assumed that McParlan put his spare time to good use.

When he arrived in America, he spoke English well, although with a brogue, and wrote intelligibly. It might be deduced from

this that McParlan spent at least a few hours each week further-
ing his childhood education in whatever schools Gateshead had
to offer.

McParlan spent about three years in the boiler factory, quitting
his job, he afterward hinted, "because of woman trouble." He
joined a small traveling circus which toured the Continent. "I
was a roustabout, gambling shill, and barker," he told Jim Haas's
grandfather, whom he knew in later life. "Besides, I took on all
comers for two bits, if I didn't throw them with both shoulders
on the mat in less than two minutes. I can tell you we didn't pay
out many quarters!"

Chapter Eight

There were some two hundred passengers on board the *S. S. Valencia,* which sailed from Queenstown for New York on August 24, 1867. Among the steerage passengers was James McParlan. The voyage was stormy almost from the first day out but McParlan was a good sailor although the only open water he'd been on before was the Irish Sea.

"If you can believe the stuff he told me, and I'm inclined to, though some of it was pretty wild," said Jake Haas, Jim Haas's grandfather, "it was one hell of a crossing. Damned near everybody from first to steerage including plenty of the crew was seasick. But not Jimmy. He said he never missed a meal the whole trip.

"Told me he was all over the place during the day preparing meals for mothers too ill to cook for themselves or their broods, diapering infants, consoling youngsters homesick for parents they'd left behind. And in the evenings he'd gather a group of kids around him and croon lullabies until they'd fall asleep. Jim had a sweet tenor voice, even when I knew him, and he used to accompany himself on a lute.

"Then, after a few drinks (a few *he* said) in a makeshift bar the men set up in a corner of the eating section of his deck, he'd dance jigs, do soft-shoe and tap, and maybe sing some more songs for those well enough to sit up and listen.

"I guess all the steerage passengers were 'papes' and they had a priest along to say Mass. Probably the lads who would have been pressed into service as altar boys were seasick, so McParlan helped the priest serve.

"I'll bet before that ship was two days out everybody was calling him 'Jim' or 'Jimmy.' He was that kind of guy. Sort of soft and easy with a good sense of humor. His eyes were bright blue and they had a twinkle. When I knew him his hair was nearly all white but you could see a few traces of reddish brown hair. And he certainly loved the ladies! You can bet your life he got the prettiest colleen aboard and played up to her the whole trip. But he wasn't the marrying kind."

Those who thought this slightly built Irishman was meek and mild were not disabused of that idea until the last night out. During the voyage McParlan avoided trouble and walked away from the many sudden brawls which sprang up. It was difficult to pick a fight with a man who refused to get angry, brushed aside offers to "put up your mitts," and smiled at drunken insults.

"On the night before the *Valencia* docked," Haas continued, "Jimmy got into one he could hardly avoid. There was a lot of drinking that evening and McParlan did his share. For hours he and a pair of fellow Irishmen had been passing the bottle between them. I guess McParlan *looked* like or *was* reasonably sober, maybe because he didn't drink as much or maybe because he could hold his liquor better.

"Well, the other two guys went through all the stages of a drunk, happiness, sorrow, and then they wanted to lick anybody in the house starting with McParlan. When they got to this point Jim tried to get away. He said 'good night' and turned to leave when one of the guys who'd been calling him 'Jimmy boy' a moment before, hauled off with a fist like a ham, caught McParlan on the jaw, and knocked him on his ass.

"Jim got up, shook his head to clear it, and stood there for a second or two. Then he ducked a long swing he could see coming and sent two short savage punches, the first to the man's kidneys and the other to his gut. The big guy toppled over and was out like a light. I'll bet the whole thing was over in less than a minute. Jimmy wiped off his hands and walked off."

On the morning of September 8, 1867, the *Valencia* docked in New York. Within hours McParlan was on his way to Chicago. Once in the Middle West, he had no trouble getting a variety of jobs. He was a deckhand on a Great Lakes freighter, from which he drifted to lumbering in the rugged country of upper Michigan. Back to Chicago again, he was a well digger, fireman, stevedore, entertainer in a German beer garden, bartender, horsecar driver, coachman in a public livery stable, boxing instructor in a gymnasium, bodyguard for a wealthy liquor dealer, and a member of the Chicago police force.

It was only a short hop from this last job to the possessive scrutiny of "the eye that never sleeps," one of a sharp pair owned by Major Allan Pinkerton, operator and owner of the largest and oldest private detective agency in America. Details of the missions young McParlan undertook are lost to posterity.

For a time Gowen had considered asking the Philadelphia Police Department to release one of its best detectives and put him on the railroad payroll. But he decided against it because the man he chose might be recognized almost before he began his dangerous mission. In the end, the President of the Road called in Major Allan Pinkerton, head of the National Detective Agency, "The Eye That Never Sleeps."

Pinkerton was a native of Scotland who came to Chicago in 1842. He was able, honest, discreet, intensely loyal to those who paid for his services, and could never be justly accused of entrapment. After capturing a gang of counterfeiters in rural Illinois he was appointed a deputy sheriff of Cook County. This led to the establishment of his detective agency in 1852. His subsequent triumphs, and there were many, included the detection of Confederate spies and the development of the United States Secret Service.

The session between the President of the Road and the president of the National Detective Agency was recorded by the latter in his autobiography. In the weighty words of Major Pinkerton the meeting took place "in Gowen's private, elegant apartment in the company's building on Fourth Street."

While the essentials are probably accurate, it is apparent that the detective placed more than a few fanciful phrases into the mouth of Mr. Gowen, who normally used plain but expressive language, saving his rhetoric for the courtroom.

The Major continued, " 'I have sent for you, Mr. Pinkerton,' said the President of the great Pennsylvania corporation after we exchanged greetings, 'upon business of importance.'

"I made known my willingness to hear what it was, then the President declared, 'The coal regions are infested by a most desperate class of men, banded together for the worst purposes—called, . . . the Molly Maguires, and they are making havoc with the country.

" 'It is a secret organization, has its meetings in hidden and out of the way places, and its members are guilty of a majority of all the murders and other deeds of outrage. We want to get within this . . . impenetrable ring; turn to the light the hidden side of this dark and cruel body to probe to its core this festering sore upon the body politic which is rapidly gnawing into the vitals and sapping the life out of the community.' "

It is extremely likely that the pragmatic Gowen dwelt upon his fear of a miners' union, particularly one which might be led by the Irish, and expressed his desire to crush such a movement before it made headway. But the Major made no mention of this subject in his lengthy autobiography. He did, however, pay homage to Mr. Gowen's humanitarian instincts. Still professing to quote the president and without a trace of irony, but with obvious difficulties in matching pronoun and antecedent, Major Pinkerton continued:

" 'We want a laboring man protected in their right to work, to secure substance for their wives and little ones, to go forth cheerfully to the slope, the shaft or wherever it may seem to him for the best, void of the fear in their hearts when he parts from his wife at the cottage.' " (To Gowen, the patch hovel had become a cottage, but at least the president hadn't covered it with ivy.)

After accepting the assignment (just what the Major's fee was is not to be found in his book), Pinkerton outlined qualifications of the operative, still to be chosen, and set up a number of reasonable working conditions.

"It is no ordinary man, Sir, that we seek in this manner," the chief of the National Detective Agency went on in the same oratorical manner (and with additional problems in grammar). "He must be an Irishman as only these class of persons can find admission to the Molly Maguires . . . He must be hardy, tough and capable of laboring and I shall have to extract from you a pledge that whoever I may dispatch upon this errand, he shall not become known to any person as a detective.

"Take the precaution, Sir, that my name and those of my employee does not appear upon any of your books. Keep my reports in your own custody away from all prying eyes. I would also ask that if my agents are engaged for one week, one month, or for years, that these requests will still be complied with; and further, whatever may be the result of this, no person in my employ, unless circumstances are greatly changed and I demand it—shall be required to give testimony upon the witness stand."

Major Pinkerton's final candidate for the job was McParlan, who had done little to distinguish himself in the service of "The Eye That Never Sleeps" yet met all requirements. When the dangerous assignment was offered to the little Irishman he accepted for any number of reasons, none of which was altruism. He was bored with routine activities and here was a chance for action. The salary of twelve dollars per week was no particular inducement, but the unlimited expense account that went along with it was. Besides, as McParlan once told Jake Haas, "A girl I'd been courting was getting too close for comfort. All she could hear was wedding bells."

So, on a crisp afternoon late in October, 1873, James McParlan set out on his mission. No longer dressed in the dapper clothing he sported in Chicago, the detective was disguised, according to Major Pinkerton, "with his head covered by an old dilapidated slouch hat, plenty of space for his cutty pipe in its narrow, faded band; a greyish coat of coarse material, ragged shirt, frayed cuffs, frayed vest, and brown, woolen pantaloons, too large for his body; strapped tight at the waist with a leather belt, yellow and broken.

"In his waistcoat was seen a heavy grey shirt with no collar and a red cravat. The undergarment had a pocket at the left inner side for tobacco. His boots were hobnailed and high topped. His face was unshaven for ten days and his hair dry and straggly. He carried no razor or strop."

After a three-hour ride from Philadelphia in a dimly lit Reading Railroad coach, McParlan, alias James McKenna, stepped off the train into the village of Port Clinton, at the very edge of the hard coal country. Here he was to begin a deception which would last for almost five years, surrounded with potential danger from the moment he walked into McGillicuddy's noisy saloon on a back street opposite the dirty Schuylkill Canal and ordered his first whiskey "with a beer chaser and make it fast, butty!"

Chapter Nine

While McParlan had no firm plans, he had a general method of operation, based partly on a two-day briefing session with Superintendent Franklin, in charge of Pinkerton's Pennsylvania offices, and partly on several weeks' study of voluminous reports gathered throughout the years by private and public investigators and turned over to Gowen.

Franklin was thoroughly aware of the problems facing McParlan. He knew the fearful chances the detective would have to take and the swift and bloody retribution that would follow discovery of his identity. A means of communication between Franklin and McParlan had to be established and an operative selected to act as liaison. For the former, it was decided that the detective should try to mail a daily report to the Philadelphia office. This alone would take skill and daring on McParlan's part and extreme caution on Franklin's. The detective would have no legitimate reason to carry postage stamps and certainly none to buy them in the quantities he would need. To conceal sufficient paper was a job requiring considerable ingenuity. McParlan solved this by oiling the paper so it would not crackle and then sewing it inside the lining of his jacket.

There were no corner mail boxes in those days and McParlan was afraid to use coal region post offices except as a drop for notes he wanted to be read. It was decided that whenever possible McParlan would send his reports via train mail where it would not be sorted by local clerks.

No correspondence could be left about where it might be seen even by trusted Pinkerton office employees. Only two people would see McParlan's reports, Superintendent Franklin and Gowen.

For a liaison, Franklin wisely chose Captain Robert J. Linden, of Philadelphia. The Captain was a huge man, six feet four inches tall, and weighed well over two hundred pounds. He was dour, a teetotaler, devoted to his wife and four children. He was not only an Episcopalian of Scotch ancestry but also an active Mason, a member of the Philadelphia Commandery, Number Two, Knights Templar.

"He was the biggest, most powerful looking son-of-a-bitch I ever saw," McParlan told Jake Haas. "He had hands like hams and when Mr. Franklin introduced us I figured the Captain was going to give me a demonstration of his strength by gripping me real hard.

"Well, I know a trick or two about that and I was ready for him. But instead he shook my hand just like anybody else would, not strong only firm. He stepped back and moved his head from side to side like he was wondering what the hell a man my size was doing on a job as big as this one.

"Neither of us spoke for a minute sort of like we were measuring each other up. Then he looked down at me and smiled, something he didn't do very often and said, 'Well, Jamie'—that's what he always called me—'you must be a mon all right, even though you're only a little one. We'll get along, you and me.'

"And when he said that I knew we would."

Linden's job would be to maintain infrequent and irregular contacts with McParlan and deliver urgent messages in either direction. He could not pretend to be the detective's friend, because Linden was well known throughout the coal regions where, for the past fifteen months, he had been assigned to work with the Coal and Iron Police, although on Pinkerton's payroll.

Instead, Linden would pose as McParlan's enemy, delighted to haul him into custody as often as possible and happy to handle his prisoner roughly in the process. Once they arrived at an "interrogation" room in the Pottsville jail there would be plenty of opportunity for the pair to talk in private. Members of the Coal and Iron Police were unaware of McParlan's role and since they were convinced Linden detested the detective they were sure to shove him around whenever they got a chance.

Should McParlan need immediate help Linden would be capable of rendering considerable assistance, provided, of course, he was around to give it. But these would be rare occasions indeed, and for much of the next fifty-four months the Irishman would be dependent upon his own quick wits and his ability to defend himself.

"I don't mind letting you know now, Jake," McParlan told the older Haas, "I wasn't quite as fearless as I let on. Oh, I knew I could handle myself with two or maybe even three tough guys and I carried a loaded pistol wherever I went. But these were murderous micks I was going to be up against, whole gangs of them, and they were playing for keeps. I'd seen those reports Mr. Gowen had gotten together."

"Did the fact that they were Irishmen and Catholics you'd be hunting down bother you?" Haas asked the detective.

"Never for a single moment. I knew what the Bishop wrote about them and I heard what Father McDermott and other priests had called them. These bastards were renegades. They'd no right to call themselves Catholics because they weren't. They never went to Confession and as far as I was concerned they were just a bunch of killers. I didn't give a damn if they were papes, Jews, Orangemen or Germans. I had a job to do and I was going to do it the best way I knew."

McParlan spent the opening night of his campaign at Port Clinton. From his first drinking companions, a Pennsylvania Dutchman named Timm and an Irishman named Dougherty, all McParlan got in return for his efforts and the cost of several rounds of drinks was the name of a boarding house and a blank stare in response to mention of the Molly Maguires.

"The detective spent the night in a bedroom with six laborers and left after breakfast," reported Major Pinkerton, a painstaking chronicler of details.

The detective paid his bill and, pack on his back, walked toward Auburn along the tow path of the little-used Schuylkill Canal. He paused to talk to everyone who passed, hoping somehow to make a friend of a wandering Irishman who might provide the detective with an introduction to a Molly.

"But the only response I got for my 'hellos' was '*Wie geht es*,'" McParlan told Haas. "There wasn't a mick in the lot—all Dutchmen. I got as far as Auburn that night and stayed at Moyer's Tavern. The owner sized me up when I walked in. I guess he didn't like what he saw and I can't blame him. I was filthy looking and I hadn't shaved for a couple weeks. I thought I was going to get turned away but I pulled out some money. He grumbled but gave me a room.

"I washed up and came down to the bar for something to eat and drink and some conversation. My point was, that if I could only get some kind of a lead before I hit a shebeen which the reports claimed was a Molly hangout, I'd be better off than going into one of those places cold. I knew there wouldn't be many Irishmen in that part of the county but I'd hoped to meet at least one who might know something or somebody. This might be a guy who'd feel friendly to a fellow Irishman because there weren't many of us around. I figured it would be easier this way than going straight into some place where there was nobody around but Irishmen.

"I couldn't get more than a passing word from anybody. I went to a union meeting outside of Schuylkill Haven a couple days later. There were two or three Irishmen and I offered to buy them drinks. I guess I didn't look as though I could pay for one and they figured all I was trying to do was to cadge a shot or a beer from them. So they refused politely and left me to myself."

McParlan drifted about aimlessly for another few days, never quite penetrating into Molly Maguire "territory." Some nights he stayed at wayside taverns and others he spent trying to keep warm by campfires built by hoboes in "jungles" along the Reading Railroad tracks. Once he heard that a few Mollies congregated at Donohue's saloon at Tower City, but the frequenters of this bar treated the detective as coldly as he had been treated elsewhere.

"I didn't get close to anybody," the detective admitted. "Mr. Franklin had a good point in reasoning that nobody would be suspicious of a dirty tramp. He felt this kind of indirect approach, until I really knew something, would be best. We assumed the Mollies would be highly suspicious about a stranger, even an Irishman, who got too curious, and he wouldn't last very long.

"Sure there was plenty of talk about the Mollies everywhere but nothing you could put your hands on. They paraded openly; they only smiled when the police called them Mollies but what went on in private nobody knew and that's the way they intended to keep it. We figured they had their meetings and their secret passwords but how the hell, I asked myself, would a filthy looking tramp find out anything. It was safer, maybe, this way, but I didn't like it. I didn't think it would get us anywhere and I wasn't comfortable in this kind of a performance."

On November 10, the detective left Schuylkill County for a conference in Philadelphia, where he told Franklin and Linden he wanted to change strategy. The Captain said nothing but it was evident from the way he shook his head and frowned that he was not in favor of McParlan's proposals. But Franklin, after warning the detective he would be placing himself in a far more vulnerable position from which there would be no return, agreed to let the operative try a new approach.

The following morning McParlan went to Buffalo, where he was outfitted at a good men's clothing store. Then he spent three or four days perusing current and old Buffalo newspapers. One evening, less than a week later, McParlan, dressed like a dandy, beard and mustache trimmed, hair neatly combed, body clean and fresh smelling, strode boldly into Patrick "Big Pat" Dormer's Sheridan House on Center Street in Pottsville.

Inside the noisy, smoke-filled room, where men were lined up three deep at the bar, the swaggering McParlan pushed his way to the front, pulled out a thick wad of bills from his pocket, peeled off a ten, laid it on the counter and shouted, "I'll buy a drink for any son of Erin in the house and the rest of ye be damned."

The response was immediate and all-embracing. Nobody but an Irishman would dare enter the Sheridan House. It was presided over by a towering, pockmarked Irishman with a record

57

of arrests (but no convictions) for assault and battery on Welshmen, Dutchmen, Englishmen, or anybody else who crossed him, including quite a few belligerent Irishmen.

The Sheridan House, according to Gowen's reports, was a Molly hangout, even though no secret meetings were held there. There was reason to exclude both the Sheridan House and Dormer from direct Molly Maguire activities. Headquarters for the Coal and Iron Police was only a block away and raids without warrants were omnipresent possibilities. Except for Henry H. Dunne's murder in 1866, Molly Maguire violence was neither plotted nor executed in Pottsville.

Dormer himself was one of the three bartenders, and drinks were poured and drunk quickly, patrons edging up to McParlan in their anxiety to get close to a man with a large roll of bills he was willing to spend freely. McParlan bought another round, and the third one was on Dormer who'd been eying McParlan with both suspicion and avarice.

The detective caught Dormer winking at somebody and shortly afterward the tavernkeeper bent down to ask McParlan if "You'd like to get a little action for your money?" McParlan nodded his head and to the bitter disappointment of Dormer's patrons, followed the saloonkeeper into a back room.

"For a couple of moments I didn't know whether I was going to get the hell beat out of me, get rolled, or be invited to join the Mollies. It was nothing like that," the detective recalled afterward.

"'Would you like to join me bhoys in a friendly game?' Dormer asked.

"I looked over the 'bhoys,' a tough-looking bunch of thugs sitting around a big table. '*Friendly*,' I thought to myself. These bastards would be happy to cut my throat.

"But what could I do, so I said 'yes.' Dormer asked me my name and I told him 'Jim McKenna.' He says, 'All right, Jimmy boy, shake hands with some good lads.'

"The cards are dealt and I'm playing stud poker in a dive as bad as anything I'd ever seen in Chicago or Dublin, with six guys I don't know and wouldn't trust any more than I could throw ten of the Queen's Guards. But as it turned out, it was the best break I could have got and it saved a lot of time and maybe a few men's lives. It's damned near forty years ago but I remember every detail of that night as though it happened yesterday.

"I maneuvered my chair so I would be with my back against the wall and I'd face the others with Dormer directly in front of me. There was a window, pretty high, but big enough to let me through if I had to get out in a hurry. I figured if worst came to worst, I'd pull my gun, plug Dormer and one or two others, jump up, and kick over the table while I scrambled out the window.

"I was sweating plenty and thinking to myself, 'Well, Jimmy, you moved into fast company awful quick, didn't you?'

"We start out with small change but pretty soon there's a pile of paper money on the table and I'm the busy little fellow. I'm watching Dormer and the other players for any fast moves and of course I'm watching my cards. The funny part is except for one man I got my suspicions about right away, the game's honest.

"Well, I'm trying to figure out my own strategy—should I take their money, and after a couple rounds I know I can, and make them respect me or should I drop a few bucks and pull out? I decided to hell with them. I'll win and teach them not to play poker with strange little Irish boys.

"They were all well heeled, but Dormer had the most money so I bluff him out of a couple of fat pots and took his heart away. In a little while this guy I'm leery about and me are the only winners. His name, I remember well, was Joey Clarke. He was pretty slick and about every third round, when it was his deal, he stacked the deck. I let him get away with it because I'm not sure what the other boys would do and besides Major Pinkerton was not paying me to trap card sharks in Pottsville, P.A. I did enough of that for him in Chicago.

"But then Big Pat drops a big one to Clarke and you can see he's getting sore because it looks to me then like Clarke must be a regular winner. I watch my chance and it comes. The rest fall by the wayside after a raise or two and there's only Dormer, me and Clarke left. Clarke's the dealer. To this day I recall the hands.

"I got sixes backed up and a pair of ladies showing. Dormer's got a king, ace and ten showing and I figured him for an ace in the hole. Clarke's showing an ace, deuce and jack and I *know* he's got a deuce in the hole. It was the biggest pot of the evening and Clarke had set it up.

"There's no noise at all in the room where we're playing and the sounds coming from the bar are muffled. All you could hear was the players pulling on their clay pipes and Dormer breathing heavy. He'd take a slow peek at his hole card, then at me, then at Clarke.

"Just as Clarke's ready to deal the fifth card I jump up, with my back to the wall and say, 'Hold it, Clarke!' and I pull out my pistol. Nobody makes a move, least of all Clarke. I got my gun pointed right at him.

"I keep Clarke covered and I say, 'This man's a cheat. I'll prove it.' Nobody says anything. I say to Dormer, 'Mr. Dormer, take the deck out of Clarke's hand but don't turn up the cards.' He took the deck. Now I say, 'The next card was yours, wasn't it?' and he nods his head.

"I said, 'It's a king, turn it up.' He did. It was a king. I said, 'The next one's mine. It'll be a high card but it won't pair me.' Dormer turned it over. It was a jack. 'Now,' I said, 'the next card's the dealer's. He's got a deuce in the hole, a deuce showing. The next card's a deuce.'

"Everybody turned to watch Dormer. Clarke was white as a sheet. 'Go ahead, Mr. Dormer,' I said. 'Turn it up.' It was a deuce.

"There was a second or two of silence, then Dormer spoke up, very quiet. 'Take him outside, boys. You know what to do.'

"Dormer looked at me. 'Well, me lad,' he said, 'I don't know what your game is but let's you and me have a drink together upstairs where it's peaceful and quiet and we can talk.' "

With the little Irishman in the lead and Dormer's hand resting heavily on his shoulder, the pair walked up a back stairway into a second floor parlor. Dormer closed the door without saying a word, motioned McParlan to a chair, pulled a bottle from a cabinet, and filled two glasses with whiskey. Both men downed their drinks in one swallow. Dormer turned to McParlan.

" 'Now, McKenna,' he told me, 'keep your hands off your

pistol. If you try anything you'll never get out of this place alive. All I want to do is ask a question. All right?'

"I nodded.

" 'What's your game, McKenna?'

" 'I think I can trust you,' I told Dormer.

" 'What the hell else can you do, McKenna?' he said.

" 'Well, Mr. Dormer,' I answered, 'I'm wanted in Buffalo for killing a man.'

" 'Did you kill him?'

" 'Yes,' I said, 'he was a bloody Englishman. He fired me for having one too many.'

"Dormer nodded agreeably. 'Anything else?'

" 'Why, yes,' I answered. 'I've been shoving the queer.'

" 'Why you dirty bastard,' Dormer said and before I could do anything he had me pinned against the door. 'You mean we've been gambling with counterfeit money? It'll be passed all over Pottsville by tomorrow and traced back to me. I don't want no trouble with the Government. I've got enough with the Coal and Iron Police.'

" 'Take your hands off of me, Dormer," I said as soon as I could get my breath. 'We played with good money. I keep the other separate. And even if I didn't you or nobody else can tell it from the queer.' "

McParlan took a billfold from his inside coat pocket and extracted two ten dollar bills. He tossed them in Dormer's direction.

" 'Take these to the bank tomorrow and see if they know the difference.' "

" 'All right, Jimmy boy,' Dormer said. 'I'll do just that. You'll stay right here.' "

The following morning, while McParlan remained in "protective custody," the saloonkeeper took the money McKenna had given him to the bank. He told the teller he was suspicious of the twenty dollars that had been passed to his bartender the preceding evening by a couple of strangers. The clerk examined the bills carefully, then turned them over to the cashier, who scrutinized them under a magnifying glass. He handed them back to Dormer with a smile.

"They're all right, Mr. Dormer," he said. "We'll take as many of these as you get."

As McParlan tolds Haas, "Why shouldn't they? This was good U. S. cash."

McParlan had become a hero in the eyes of Dormer and habitués of his bar to whom the story of the card game and the counterfeit money was soon spread. The detective remained at the Sheridan House for several weeks. During the day he slept, and at night, as historian William Munsell said, "McParlan literally sung, danced, fought and drunk himself into popularity with the rough men among whom he mingled."

Chapter Ten

McParlan had been able to slip away only once to mail his report to Franklin, and the superintendent became concerned about his detective's safety when five or six days passed and he heard nothing further. Then he learned that McParlan was last seen in the Sheridan House. Fearful that the detective was being held there against his will, he ordered Captain Linden to raid the hotel.

On November 23, shortly before midnight, Linden, leading a dozen heavily armed Coal and Iron Police, burst into the noisy, crowded Sheridan House bar. To the Captain's surprise, McParlan was standing on top of the bar doing a jig while an enthusiastic audience clapped time.

At the entrance of the police, silence fell except for the sound of the detective's heels, which continued to tap. His pistol back in its holster, Linden, arms akimbo, stood watching the performance as McParlan, apparently unconcerned, danced on.

Then Dormer spoke up.

"Where's your warrant, Linden?"

"Don't need any," the Captain answered. "I'm just after one man for questioning. But if you get tough with me I'll arrest you for harboring a fugitive."

"A fugitive? Who's the fugitive?"

With that Linden grasped McParlan, who had not lost a beat, and pulled him from the bar to the floor. McParlan reached for his revolver, but before he had a chance to draw the Captain pinioned the detective's arms and dragged him through the swinging doors.

"Don't worry, I'll be back," McParlan shouted to Dormer, "as soon as I settle with this big ugly bastard."

The next afternoon McParlan, his face swollen with bruises, returned to the Sheridan House.

"There's more than one way to fool a copper," he said mysteriously to Dormer by way of explaining his early release. "But I must get out of Pottsville, the town's too hot for me. Do you know anybody in Shenandoah? I hear it's a good place."

"I do. I do, indeed," replied Dormer, impressed by McParlan's willingness to stand up to Captain Linden and his ability to outwit the law. "I think maybe we could use a man like you. I'll take you over to Shenandoah meself in the morning."

At noon Big Pat and McParlan boarded the train for Shenandoah. When the local stopped at Mahanoy Plane to pick up passengers, John "The Cat" Mahoney of Gilberton joined the pair.

"Mahoney," McParlan told Haas, "was the strangest-looking man you'd ever want to meet. He was young, I'd guess not over twenty, although his hair was dead white. His eyes were slanty and colorless. He had no beard but over his lip there were a few dozen hairs which stuck out just like a cat's whiskers. They say he could see best in the dark and I believe it.

"His fingers were long and skinny and his nails were very sharp; when he shook hands with me I could feel them scratch. His walk was a kind of pad and you couldn't hear him two feet away. They used the Cat when they needed somebody to sneak into a house at night while people were sleeping. He was an albino, and I know he was a Molly. I've met some strange characters in my day but this boy really gave me the creeps."

Dormer's destination was the saloon of Michael "Muff" Lawler, Jack Kehoe's first deputy.

"Lawler," reported the Philadelphia *Press,* "was one of the chief leaders of the Molly Maguires . . . He was bodymaster of the division at Shenandoah. On Wednesday, January 21, 1874, James McParlan was introduced at his home in Shenandoah by 'Big Pat' Dormer.

"Lawler acquired the name 'Muff' from a breed of game chickens he raised which won him fame and money throughout the coal regions. Cock fighting was his favorite sport and famous mains were frequently held in the basement of his house at Shenandoah. He wielded great power. He was a fine-looking man and the most popular in the Schuylkill mining region . . . Lawler was a whole-souled grand-looking giant of a fellow and became a fast friend of McParlan."

Muff was married and the father of seven daughters, three of whom had joined holy orders. His wife, a most attractive woman, was totally unaware of her husband's criminal involvements and was respected by both Catholics and Protestants. As a matter of fact she became "godmother" to one of the first Jewish children born in Mahanoy City, six miles away. Despite Lawler's reputation for geniality and his seemingly open way of life, Muff was deeply enmeshed in Molly Maguire activities.

"Lawler and I hit it up right away," McParlan told Haas. "Big Pat sang my praises, told him about the card game and then how I'd outsmarted Captain Linden. That went over well with Muff.

"'Linden,' he said, 'that big, interfering son-of-a-bitch. I'd like to have my boys lay their hands on him some dark night. We'd fix him. Well, lad, you're welcome at Muff Lawler's. Now what can I do for you?'

"I wanted to stay with Lawler badly because I was convinced this was the place where I'd learn something and maybe if I played my cards right from here on in I might even join the Mollies. I knew Lawler had a reputation to perserve in the community so I had to make sure he wouldn't think Linden would come bouncing in there all the time and raising a fuss.

"Big Pat told Lawler nothing about my 'shoving the queer' or my Buffalo 'murder' so I opened up. Muff was impressed. He asked me why Linden let me go and when I told him there wasn't enough evidence to hold me for extradition and that I wasn't wanted in Pennsylvania, I could see Lawler had made up his mind. He gave me a big smile and said, 'All right, lad, there'll be room for you here. In a couple days we'll have to talk with a friend of mine in Girardville.' I knew he meant Kehoe, the man I wanted to meet more than anybody else."

It was almost a month before the detective and Black Jack

got together. Meanwhile, in order to establish McParlan's respectability in the eyes of Shenandoah residents and to protect his own reputation, Muff got the detective a job at Indian Ridge Shaft where the saloonkeeper had enough influence to make sure his new friend wasn't overworked.

The detective, known as Jimmy McKenna, spent most of his evenings in Lawler's barroom. At times he would drop into other saloons where he was made welcome. Wherever he went the little Irishman would buy a round of drinks, dance a jig or two, and sing a few sentimental ballads. Within a few weeks Shenandoah's newest citizen was its most popular.

During this period McParlan met a lot of Irishmen who he felt could be Molly Maguires and heard many boastful stories of Molly Maguire activities but actually learned nothing more than what was common gossip throughout the coal regions. As for gathering evidence that would stand up in court, the detective's hands were empty. Without arousing suspicion he managed to mail his daily (and meaningless) reports to Philadelphia. He had no further encounters with Linden, who'd been informed of McParlan's whereabouts.

There was no letup in coal region violence. While McParlan was spending his days at Indian Ridge colliery and his nights in Shenandoah saloons, many additional outrages were committed. Edward O'Toole and Joseph Lafferty, two respectable, well-liked Irishmen, were badly mauled a few doors from their homes in broad daylight on a Mount Carmel street corner in the presence of at least a dozen witnesses. There were no arrests. Both victims were members of Father McDermott's parish and had protected the priest from a jeering mob the preceding Sunday a few hours after the cleric denounced the Molly Maguires from the pulpit.

On February 17, Alan Wilson, superintendent of the Baldwin Colliery, south of Pottsville, discharged three men, William O'Neill, his younger brother Patrick, and Michael Kelly, for drinking on the job. On February 18, the Baldwin Colliery was burned to the ground and Wilson shot from ambush. His wounds were serious but not critical. The O'Neill brothers and Kelly were arrested on suspicion but all three were able to establish alibis and were discharged by a Pottsville alderman.

Shortly after the Baldwin fire, a mule stable near Mahanoy Plane was burned to the ground and half a dozen animals perished. Only a few hours before, Llewellyn Jones, the stable boss, had used his whip on "three drunken Irishmen I found sleeping in the hay."

On the evening of February 25, while McParlan was drinking in Lawler's barroom, he overheard a habitué bitterly condemn an English fire boss who "hated the Irish." The threat "He'll get his soon" was uttered. The detective tried to find out who was meant but learned nothing more than the boss's nickname, which was "The Screw." On February 28, John Reed, a foreman at Mahanoy Colliery, was badly beaten and left to die on a back road between Mahanoy City and Wiggans Patch. Fortunately for Reed, a Mahanoy City physician on his way home from a night call saw him, treated his injuries, and took the man home. As McParlan learned later, Reed's nickname was "The Screw."

It was not until March 1 that McParlan met Kehoe. That morning Lawler told his boarder not to report to work. "We've something more important to do today, Jimmy," he said. A few hours later, after riding over the mountain to Girardville in a hired rig, they entered the Hibernian House. They were expected. Kehoe was behind the bar, but as soon as he saw the pair come through the swinging doors, he nodded to them and led the two into the back room. Muff performed the introductions and when his guests were seated Kehoe poured whiskey.

"From the first words he spoke," McParlan told Haas, "I knew this man was going to be difficult to convince.

" 'Well, McKenna,' he said while he looked me over carefully with his piercing black eyes, 'I hear you killed a man in Buffalo.'

"Not knowing what was coming next I jumped up, pulled my gun, and pretending I was angry said, 'That's none of your goddamned business, Kehoe. I don't have to account to you for anything.'

"Kehoe didn't budge from his chair. He looked at Muff.

" 'Cocky bantam you brought with you, Muff, ain't he?'

"Muff grinned. 'He's all right, Jack. I told you that.'

" 'Sit down, McKenna,' Kehoe ordered. 'If your story's straight you've got nothing to worry about.'

" 'You're the one should be worried,' I told Black Jack. 'You were the one on the wrong end of the pistol, not me.' Kehoe smiled.

" 'It so happens,' he went on, 'one of your Buffalo buttys is living in Pottsville. I invited him over. He ought to be here any minute.'

"I didn't know what to do. Naturally, I had no 'buttys' in Buffalo. So all I could do was sweat it out. We had a few more drinks, and then Kehoe's bartender comes in and says to Black Jack that the man he's expecting is outside waiting. Kehoe nods his head and in walks an Irishman I'd never seen before. And I knew he'd never seen me either.

" 'I want you two fellows to meet,' Kehoe said. 'You're both from Buffalo.'

"I turned to Kehoe. 'I never told you or Muff I was from Buffalo.'

" 'That's right, McKenna, all you said was that you killed a man there.'

"It was a good thing I'd studied my lessons in Buffalo.

"This fellow and I talked for about an hour. I rattled off places, names of cops, wanted men, crimes committed there, hinting all the time that I'd had a hand in some of them. I guess Kehoe was satisfied and so was the fellow who really was from Buffalo. When he went away and Muff and I were ready to go back to Shenandoah, Kehoe said, 'All right, lad. We could use a man like you. I'll be in touch with you after a bit. Meantime, I think it would be better if you moved away from Muff's. You might get him in trouble.' "

A day later McParlan left Lawler's to board at the home of Fenton Cooney on Main Street. Unlike Muff, who had a half-dozen boarders, Cooney had room for only one guest at a time. It was here that McParlan made the only close friend he had during his dangerous mission. His name was Frank McAndrew and he was totally unaware of the detective's identity.

McAndrew was McParlan's age. He was married and had two

children. A steady worker who rarely drank, he was seldom without a job. He had never had any trouble with his employers. His active involvement with the Molly Maguires was as much a mystery to McAndrew himself as it was to McParlan.

Cooney was married to McAndrew's only sister, Elizabeth. McAndrew visited Cooney's home several times a week and so became acquainted with their popular boarder. Of the relationship between McAndrew and McParlan, Major Pinkerton wrote in 1877:

"A friendship immediately sprang up between these two men that, notwithstanding the trials and troubles through which both have passed—in fact, danger and adventure seemed to strengthen the feeling—remains to this day unimpaired and unshaken. McAndrew held true to McKenna in his darkest hour."

Chapter Eleven

McParlan never failed to attend Mass, and on his first Sunday at Cooney's he was joined by McAndrew. The pair sat side by side and heard Father O'Reilly bitterly condemn the Molly Maguires and exhort any of his communicants who belonged to this "vicious society" to resign at once. Both men listened in silence. When they left St. Anthony's to stroll along Center Street McAndrew turned to his new friend and said, "The Mollies ain't as bad as the Father painted 'em. Someday you'll find out for yourself."

This last was what the detective had been waiting to hear, but he said nothing and did not press McAndrew to explain. He was shocked to learn that the seemingly gentle, kind and soft-spoken McAndrew was obviously a member of the secret society.

The hopeful conversation between McParlan and McAndrew took place early in March of 1874 and McParlan half expected he'd be proposed for membership any time. But the weeks dragged on and while he saw McAndrew almost every day and drank at Muff Lawler's saloon each night, there was no further direct mention of McParlan's "finding out anything about the Molly Maguires for himself."

He felt that the three days a week he was a mine laborer were wasted, yet he had to have some plausible explanation for his ability to spend money freely. He told Lawler and McAndrew he was going to Philadelphia for a day or two to exchange some of his roll of "counterfeit" bills for good money. He didn't want to "shove the queer" in Shenandoah, he said, because it might get the saloonkeeper in trouble.

In Philadelphia, McParlan met Franklin in a secret session. In view of what the detective reported, Franklin believed McParlan to be close to reaching his initial objective, admittance to the Molly Maguires. The superintendent felt that if McParlan could give another demonstration of his dislike for authority he might convince Muff the time had arrived for McParlan's acceptance as a candidate for membership in the secret society.

When the detective returned to Shenandoah he boasted to Lawler he was "loaded with cash" and suggested that he, Muff, and a few of the boys spend some of this money on an out-of-town spree. Lawler agreed with alacrity and suggested they go to Lofty, a mining village about thirty miles from Shenandoah. "I've got some business to tend to there, anyway, Jimmy," Muff informed McParlan, "and we can kill two birds with one stone at Mickey Coughlin's place."

This was on April 4, 1874. The "spree" was set for April 9, giving McParlan time to lay his own plans.

On the appointed Saturday, McParlan, Muff, and two habitués of Lawler's saloon boarded the Reading Railroad for Mahanoy City. There they changed to the Lehigh Valley and were on the train no more than half an hour when a stop was made at Delano. Here, to the surprise of all members of McParlan's party except the detective, Captain Linden stepped into the coach.

Conversation died down as the big officer strode directly to McParlan and reached over Lawler as though to seize McParlan by the collar. The detective jumped up, pulled a revolver from his pocket, and pointed it directly at the Captain's heart. "If you lay a finger on me, Linden, you're dead. You have nothing on me, and unless you produce a warrant you better let me alone."

Linden looked calmly down at McParlan. Without raising his voice he said, "All right, McKenna. You think you're a big man with your gun. Put it away. If I wanted to take you I'd have walked into this coach with my own gun ready. All I wanted to see was the kind of scum you're traveling with. Now I know."

He looked at McParlan's companions carefully.

"I know you, Mr. Muff Lawler, and I think I've seen these other gentlemen before. They're no angels. But McKenna, you're worse than all of them put together."

McParlan's "heroism" was told in great detail and embellished by Lawler and his companions at Coughlin's Lofty saloon. It was relished by the rough crowd of miners who stood around the bar and slapped the little detective on his back, bought him drinks, and sang his praises. All of them knew and detested Captain Linden.

In the midst of the carousing, which went on far into the night, Muff, proud to be McParlan's sponsor, suddenly motioned to Coughlin who stood behind the bar. Before the pair left the room Lawler winked at the little Irishman and whispered, "We'll soon have no secrets from you, Jimmy boy."

Lawler kept his word. Three days later, on Tuesday evening, April 14, 1874, just after McParlan finished supper, McAndrew entered Cooney's kitchen and they left the house together. This was not unusual, for the pair took a walk for an hour or two along Shenandoah's streets nearly every night. Normally McAndrew would go home, leaving his companion at Lawler's. But this evening McAndrew, too, walked through the swinging doors.

"I'm with you tonight, Jimmy," he told the detective with a smile. "We've a good surprise."

Lawler's was filled with its usual crowd and in addition there were a few men whom McParlan had never seen before. One of these was Alex Campbell, owner of the Columbia House at Tamaqua, where he was both bodymaster and division chief of the Molly Maguires and Kehoe's second in command.

"Campbell," declared the Tamaqua *Courier* in 1876, "was born in Ireland . . . He took an important part in local and county politics . . . the influence he wielded among men . . . and his power to overawe the more timid among his countrymen, made him sought, petted and pampered by the political wire pullers . . . He was a bold unscrupulous man and would go to any length to effect an object politically or otherwise. It was darkly hinted he had been guilty of crime before he came to this country.

"Campbell cared nothing for the innuendoes uttered against him. Campbell is supposed to have been privy to at least ten murders and is a man of strong will."

High as Muff Lawler stood in the ranks of the Molly Maguires, his recommendation was not enough to insure McParlan's admittance into the secret order. Apparently the approval of Campbell, as Kehoe's delegate, was necessary before the detective won complete acceptance.

To Muff Lawler's cordial "shake hands with my friend Jimmy McKenna," the tall, raw-boned bodymaster barely touched the detective's hand and responded to McParlan's pleasant smile with an embittered twist of his thin lips. It seemed to the detective that Campbell was unimpressed and the moment the detective had been striving for would not occur, at least not that night.

Yet half an hour later, when Campbell turned to leave Muff's where he, Lawler, and McParlan had been drinking at one end of the bar, the Scotch-Irishman nodded his head to the Shenandoah bodymaster, said "Good luck, McKenna" to the detective, and strode out of the saloon. With this, a wide smile of satisfaction swept over Lawler's face. He motioned to McAndrew who'd been standing a few feet removed. The latter then walked through the back door and returned with Mrs. Lawler who went behind the bar.

"Taking their cue from Lawler," wrote James Corrigan, whose recent sympathetic history of the Molly Maguires appeared in an official journal of the United Mine Workers of America, "Edward Ferguson—called Fergus—Pete Monaghan, and Thomas Hurley, one by one dropped into the kitchen and quietly ascended the stairway leading to the second floor. McAndrew and McKenna (McParlan) were thus together with the landlady. The former appeared to be acting as a sort of outside guardian of the division. Very few words were exchanged between the two men.

"The thoughts which passed through the brain of the detective at the moment, as he sat listening to the retreating footsteps of the Mollies, may be imagined but he breathed more freely when he saw Pete Monaghan, who made a signal that he should accompany him upstairs, still leaving only McAndrew below."

When McParlan, behind Monaghan, entered Lawler's large upstairs sitting room, the conviviality of the saloon below had disappeared and a group of a dozen or more men stood silently around. In addition to those who had been drinking at the bar a few minutes before were others who had entered Lawler's through a side door and quietly made their way to the second floor. There they awaited McParlan's appearance.

"Behind a small table," continued Corrigan, "Muff Lawler, the bodymaster, stood holding in his hand a slip of paper which at the moment he was studying. The other men were ranged, standing erect with arms folded, around the room, leaving a clear spot of carpet in the center of the floor. Each Molly devoutly made the sign of the cross as Monaghan and McKenna entered. The latter was instructed to similarly bless himself, and promptly obeyed. He was taken to the middle of the room, and, still standing by his side, Monaghan proclaimed all in readiness to proceed.

" 'The neophyte will kneel,' said Lawler.

" 'Now get down on your prayer-bones,' whispered Monaghan; McParlan knelt upon the carpet.

"Here all the members, at a signal from Lawler, drew near the initiate, leaving room for the bodymaster who came also, still holding the mysterious paper in his hand.

" 'I will now proceed,' said the presiding officer, 'to explain the objects of the Ancient Order of Hibernians.

" 'We are joined together to promote friendship, unity and true Christian charity to our members, raising money for the maintenance of the aged, the sick and infirm. The motto of the order is Friendship, Unity and Christian Charity . . . It is the desire to promote friendship among the Irish Catholics and especially to assist one another in all trials. You are expected to keep all matters accruing within the division room a secret in your own heart. None of the workings of the society are to be recalled to those not known to be members.'

"McKenna, still on his knees and guarded by Monaghan, repeated the oath as Lawler read it from the mysterious paper:

" 'I, James McKenna, having heard the objects of the Order fully explained, do solemnly swear that I will, with the help of God, keep inviolably secret all the acts and things done by this Order and obey the constitution and by-laws in every respect

74

. . . I will obey my superior officers in everything lawful and not otherwise. All this I do solemnly swear.'

"Then McParlan was told to cross himself once more, the surrounding brothers doing the same, and the test paper, as it was called, was handed to him by Lawler and still in a kneeling posture, he reverently kissed it and was prompted by Monaghan to rise."

As McParlan pointed out, there was nothing illegal or immoral in any of the indoctrination ceremonies, which were no different basically from those of most American secret societies.

"The fact that part of the oath required me to obey my superiors in 'deeds lawful and not otherwise' would seem to eliminate all of the crimes for which the Mollies were correctly blamed. But this oath was the sheerest hypocrisy. I found that out soon enough. It was put there to conform to the international by-laws of the A.O.H. and the Mollies couldn't have had the local charter, under which they operated, without it.

"I don't know what they did when they got an official 'visitation' from the A.O.H. division chiefs but I guess they covered up and got away with it. We never had an investigation from state or national headquarters while I was a 'lodge brother.'

"The Church, too, had to be deceived. It was opposed to Catholic membership in *all* secret societies including, at that time, even the Ancient Order of Hibernians. But opposition to the Mollies was particularly bitter from Bishop Wood down to parish priests. They all knew how the parent organization had been perverted.

"You had to hand it to the priests. Once in a while I used to sneak away to listen to Father McDermott over in Pottsville where he was transferred from Centralia. It made me proud to be a Catholic and a son of Erin when I heard that tall, skinny Irishman lambaste the Mollies. Often I wanted to go up and talk to him but I didn't dare. If I'd have been seen it would have been the end of Detective McKenna's career."

The transition from Molly Maguires to A.O.H. was observed with bitterness by Bishop Wood and the *Catholic Standard,* official organ of the Philadelphia diocese.

"When it became impossible any longer to bear the odium of being called a 'Molly Maguire,' " said the *Catholic Standard* on October 24, 1874, "application was made to the State Legislature for a charter for the Ancient Order of Hibernians. A *printed* constitution and by-laws had to be presented to the Legislature in order to inform it of the objects of this society. . . .

"A man, who afterward acknowledged the iniquities of the society to the Bishop of Philadelphia . . . and another leader, now serving out a term for inciting a riot against a priest . . . were the worthy (?) Catholics who lobbied the charter through the Legislature.

"After obtaining this [charter], all the Mollies were metamorphosized into Hibernians, and the association assumed the style and title of the Ancient Order of Hibernians—the Mollies did not cease to be bad men, but they became Hibernians and ceased to be Mollies, somewhat after the manner of a wolf ceases to be a wolf after he dons the clothing of a sheep. Because sanctioned and approved of under the seal of the Keystone State, the Mollies became independent of the law of God and threatened any priest with prosecution who would oppose them."

After McParlan's formal initiation was over he was given the "goods," the Molly Maguire's name for passwords, "distress" signals and phrases for mutual recognition. The meeting concluded on an ominous note.

"Just before Muff and I went downstairs to the bar where the others had gone," McParlan recalled, "he turned to me, all friendliness gone from his voice and said, 'You're a full-fledged member now, McKenna, and you'll be given your orders soon. Just be sure they're carried out.'

"Oh, yes. I almost forgot. The initiation fee was $3.00 which I had to put in a box in front of Mr. Muff Lawler."

Highly elated by his first major triumph, although aware of the great dangers that lay ahead, the detective said good night to his friend Frank McAndrew and the others who stood around Lawler's bar, and walked alone to Cooney's boarding house.

"In the cold, silent room, very late that night before retiring," wrote James Corrigan in *The Anthracite News*, "McKenna indicted the most important report he had ever written, minutely detailing . . . every particular of the ceremony attending his initiation into the Shenandoah Division of the Molly Maguires; with the signs, toast, passwords, and other matters of interest. His final sentence was: 'So you see victory is won at last!' "

McParlan, more than anyone else, was to know soon enough that the conclusion he had drawn so optimistically the night of April 14, 1874, had been premature.

Chapter Twelve

The "goods," McParlan told Superintendent Franklin, would be changed four times a year. Those he received the night of his initiation included the password: "The Emperor of France and Don Carlos of Spain unite together, the Pope's right to maintain." The correct response to this, the detective reported, was: "Will tenant rights in Ireland flourish if the people unite and the landlords perish?"

There was also a "quarreling" toast which McParlan said was given to evade an argument rather than provoke one with an unrecognized lodge brother. "Your temper is high" were the words to be spoken, preferably, of course, before the blow was struck, the knife wielded, or the pistol fired. Should the recipient of the toast fail to return the right response, "I have good reason," it was presumably *de rigeur* to proceed "as you were."

The after-sundown password was: "The nights are very dark." It is to be hoped that this, too, would be given prior to an attack on an unrecognized stranger so that the latter had a chance to reply, "I hope they will soon end," and thus avoid mayhem or execution.

A recognition symbol, enabling unknown brothers to establish instant kinship, required manual dexterity and excellent co-ordination.

"The little finger of the right hand," said McParlan, "is placed in the corner of the left eye near the nose while the index finger of the left hand touches the elbow of the right hand."

The correct answer to this demanded technique worthy of a contortionist.

"The right lapel of his own vest is caught with the little finger and thumb of the left hand while the right hand is raised to the left side of the head."

As McParlan said, "If the business hadn't been so damned serious, it would have been funny. As it was, I had a hard time to keep from laughing."

A few weeks after McParlan's initiation he was able to combine business and pleasure at a wedding to which he and some of his new lodge brothers had been invited. The ceremony took place in St. Stanislaus' Roman Catholic Church, Shenandoah, where a Polish-speaking priest served recent East European immigrants, soon to replace the Irish as low men on the employment ladder. In 1874, however, these were only a tiny minority of "greenhorns," amusing to "natives" who'd been Americans for at least two decades.

Following religious services, a reception for the bride and groom was held in the bride's house at Turkey Run, a village on top of the mountain between Shenandoah and Gilberton. For a description of this event we are indebted to Allan Pinkerton's autobiography.

"The bride," wrote Major Pinkerton, "seated herself in the best room which was the kitchen, having a small table near on which stood a steaming pitcher of blackstrap and a tin pot. In the open fireplace blazed pine knots and light wood giving a genial brightness to the place which was devoid of candles and lamps.

"By the chimney, on a log fashioned into a rude stool, sat the aged grandmother of the bride, grey, wrinkled and trembling in limb, but rigged out in a white ruffled cap, and smoking a brand new clay pipe . . . Chairs there were none, except that devoted to the queen of the occasion . . . with hair done up in a knot behind her head, combed flat at the sides, and the whole surmounted by a high tortoise shell comb. She was supplied with dress pockets capacious enough to contain a small fortune in silver.

"Male friends, one after another, came in and saluted her, wished her good luck and helped himself to liquor," added the head of the National Detective Agency (still unable to match pronoun and antecedent).

The beverage was a combination of raw potato whiskey, no less than 120 proof and frequently stronger, and blackstrap molasses to which had been added large quantities of cayenne pepper as well as other pungent spices tossed in recklessly by the chef. The interesting concoction was prepared the night before, poured into a large iron kettle (normally used for the family laundry), and allowed to simmer for twelve hours. Just about the time the reception began, the brew was ready for guests. A violent shudder usually accompanied each swallow, for the scalding beverage seared even seasoned throats.

"Each," continued the Major in an unexpectedly romantic vein, "handed the bride a present always in the shape of money according to ability or generosity. Then he kissed the lady three times. She now placed the cash in her purse and was ready for the next person.

"McParlan watched this part of the proceedings and then walked up, paid his money, enjoyed a small share of the lady's lips and stepped back. Following him was a young lady from Tamaqua. She went to the bride, took a dainty sip of liquor, tendered a bank bill then, her roguish Irish eyes resting upon the detective, suddenly swooped down on him, rested one hand for a second on his shoulder, and before the defenseless man could prevent it, kissed him three times on the cheek. . . ."

Hardly the one to turn down any attractive female, McParlan responded with vigor. His enthusiasm increased when the girl, whose name was Mary Malloy, announced that her sister was married to an important Tamaqua citizen, Mr. James Kerrigan.

His nickname had been "Jimmy." This was changed, one cold morning early in January, 1868, to "Powderkeg," a sobriquet given not without grudging admiration by a group of the gentleman's buttys assembled around a fire some three hundred feet below the earth's surface. All were participating in what is now known as a "coffee break" but was then (and still is) called "eating your piece."

Fatalists all, they were unimpressed by the fact that several barrels of blasting dynamite, enough to blow them into microscopic bits, rested only a few yards away. They drank coffee and smoked their corncobs, pausing now and then almost casually to stomp on a flying ember that had fallen too close to the explosives to be ignored.

"Kerrigan," said Cleveland Moffett in *McClure's Magazine* of December, 1894, "entered into the cold slope when the men were crowding around a huge salamander heated with coals.

"He carried with him on his shoulder a keg of powder. Seeing there was no place for him, he leaned over the circle formed by his comfortable comrades, placed his keg on the red hot coals and remarked coolly,

" 'As long as you boys won't move I'll have to make a place for myself.'

"Men scattered in terror, right and left, whereupon Kerrigan calmly lifted the keg of powder off the coals, lit his pipe and began smoking."

Kerrigan was spawned in a Dublin slum. His mother died when he was an infant, and shortly afterward his drunken father abandoned Kerrigan and four or five brothers and sisters.

Jimmy never spent a day in school but he was intelligent, had an incredible memory, and before he sailed from Ireland could read and write, no mean feat for one in his circumstances. In addition, he acquired enough money to pay for first class passage to America and this was indeed almost unique for an Irish immigrant. Something of a fop, he loathed uncleanliness. When his workday in the mines was done, he scrubbed himself clean, dressed immaculately, and strolled down the streets of Tamaqua, where he lived.

His subsequent actions were contradictory. He never expressed patriotism for his adopted country nor fondness for the Union cause, yet he was one of the first volunteers. He re-enlisted twice and fought at Shiloh, Antietam, Vicksburg, and Gettysburg. He was wounded several times, and once when his platoon was trapped behind Confederate lines, he skillfully planned and executed its escape. When the war ended, however, he refused to have anything to do with his former comrades, repulsed efforts to be enrolled in veterans' and civic organizations, and associated almost solely with Irish Copperheads.

He married a woman of character and seemed to be devoted to her and to his family, supporting them far better than did most of his co-workers. But he spent little time at home. He was a nightly frequenter of a saloon owned by Alex Campbell, but he rarely took a drink. When he did, it was a full quart which he poured down his throat without lowering the bottle from his lips.

Because of his courage and ability to beat men a foot taller and a hundred pounds heavier than himself, he was feared and respected by acquaintances. But he had a sharp, sarcastic tongue, used frequently, which infuriated those who didn't know how to reply in kind, and he was detested. Often the instigator of trouble, Kerrigan was nowhere to be found when it began. His own alibi was always legitimate and could be supported by Tamaqua's "solid citizens," the Welsh and English.

He was on seemingly amiable terms with the community's leading Protestants, whom he visited occasionally in their homes. Nevertheless, Powderkeg Kerrigan "fingered" his erstwhile hosts for out-of-town assassins. Despite this strange admixture of personality traits, he was considered by Jack Kehoe, who rarely made mistakes in judgment, to be reliable enough to become a bodymaster.

His tombstone reads JAMES ALOYSIUS XAVIER KERRIGAN, B. 1833 D. 1901, MAY GOD HAVE MERCY ON HIS SOUL. He had been a miner and a resident of Carbon County ever since he arrived in America about 1850. During these years he acquired a wife and begat fourteen children, an accomplishment which might be considered remarkable by those who mistakenly believe fecundity and stature are directly proportionate. Mr. Kerrigan, in his bare feet, was four feet eleven inches tall.

"That wouldn't be Mr. 'Powderkeg' Kerrigan, now, would it?" asked McParlan.

"It would indeed," replied the young lady proudly.

As the detective told Jake Haas, "This was like holding two high pairs in a game of draw and the dealer gives you a full house. I hated to take advantage of Mary, she was a very sweet and pretty girl about seventeen, but this was too much to turn down. So, after we left the wedding, I escorted her over to Shenandoah where she was staying for a couple days with a cousin.

"I told her I'd come calling when she got back to Tamaqua and she said I'd have to speak with Mr. Kerrigan first. This, I knew, would be my pleasure indeed."

During the next few months, McParlan pressed his friendship with Mary and cultivated Powderkeg. Since his reason for spending so much time in Tamaqua was to court the Malloy girl, Mc-Parlan had a "legitimate" excuse for not being with Muff and the boys in Shenandoah as much as he'd been. This gave the detective a chance to explore another bodymaster's territory.

McParlan and Kerrigan often passed an evening together in Alex Campbell's saloon, drinking and gossiping with Molly Maguires who frequented that barroom.

"I was wonderfully lucky," said McParlan. "Here I was with Kehoe's number one man, Alex Campbell, and his number two boy, Jimmy Kerrigan. You couldn't get close to Campbell—he wouldn't let you, he was cold as a fish—but I got as near to him I think as any man could.

"Powderkeg and I hit it up right from the start. He was a funny little guy, as smart as they come and as brave as they make 'em. But he had a peculiar sense of humor and he could turn vicious in a second.

"We'd be walking along Broad Street in Tamaqua and some important-looking gentleman, maybe a banker or a mine superintendent, would stop us and greet Powderkeg quite formally but you could see that they were glad to talk to him.

"Kerrigan would ask the gentleman how he was and how was his wife and how were his children and how was everything coming along at the bank, or the mine, all very nice and polite. And the gentleman would ask Mr. Kerrigan how *his* wife and *his* children were and why didn't Mr. Kerrigan drop into the gentleman's house some day soon again for a cup of tea and maybe read some Irish fairy tales to the little ones who enjoyed Mr. Kerrigan's company.

83

"By the way they talked you'd think Powderkeg and the gentleman were social equals and members of the same congregation. But the minute the gentleman and Mr. Kerrigan would each raise their hats to the other and walk in different directions and he and I would be out of earshot, Kerrigan would turn to me and say, 'The dirty, blackhearted Protestant bastard. He'll get *his* some day and don't you forget it.

"Like he once did, saying, 'That was Dan Shepp. Owns a couple mines and a mill. I'll blast him to hell some day, see if I don't!' "

McParlan's friendship with Campbell and Kerrigan paid off far sooner than the detective ever dreamed it would. In June of 1874, Dennis O'Keefe, secretary and second in command of the Shenandoah Division of the Mollies, died of a heart attack. Backed by Lawler, Campbell and Kerrigan, McParlan, to his own astonishment, was appointed by Kehoe (albeit reluctantly, because Kehoe never fully trusted McParlan) to replace the deceased "brother." Now the detective, a member of the society less than four months, would be privy to a majority of its secrets.

When Muff Lawler called to order the July meeting of the Shenandoah Division of the Molly Maguires, James McParlan sat at the bodymaster's side. The new secretary, dependent no longer upon his memory, could make as many notes as he wished.

Chapter Thirteen

The Molly Maguires were nearing the peak of their power. They had become so potent a force that for the first time in their bloody history they no longer concealed their membership, although they certainly kept their activities secret. Now, cloaked in the respectability provided them by their recently granted A.O.H. charters (which they promptly perverted), they dared show themselves openly at public gatherings.

On St. Patrick's Day, March 17, "Nearly five hundred members of the Ancient Order of Hibernians from Divisions at Shenandoah, Tamaqua, and Girardville, paraded gallantly through the streets of our borough, waving their flags and singing their marching songs," said the Mahanoy City *Tri-Weekly Record.*

Legend has it that the words and music of the Molly Maguires' theme song were written in the Hibernian House by two transplanted Irish minstrels named Bell, Thadius and his cousin Manus. But which Bell wrote the lyrics and which the tune is anybody's guess. A plethora of Bells adds to the confusion since the inspiration for the song likewise bore the same surname. The story is that William Bell, a native of North Ireland and a justice of the peace in Girardville, bailiwick of Jack Kehoe, had the effrontery to hold three patrons of the Hibernian House on charges of arson. Within minutes of the magistrate's decision, a mob of armed men allegedly swarmed into Bell's courtroom, beat the magistrate and his constables, battered down the cell, and released the prisoners.

At the cost of severe corporal punishment and swift retirement from the Bench, Magistrate Bell can claim immortality by reason of his mention in what subsequently became widely known as "Song of the Molly Maguires." The melody has been lost but the lyrics follow:

> "Pat Dolan, it's my Christian name,
> Yes, and my surname too, sir!
> An' oft you've listened to me sthrane,
> I'll tell you somethin' new sir!
> In Cavan-town, where we sat down
> Our Irish hearts to inspire,
> There's bould recruits an' undaunted yout's
> An' they'r led by Molly Maguire.

CHORUS

> With me riggadum du, an' to hell wid the crew
> Wouldn't help to free our nation;
> When I look back, I count 'em slack,
> Wouldn't join our combination!

> Said Molly to her darlin' son
> What tyrant shall we humble?
> That filthy tribe we can't abide,
> They rob both meek and humble;
> There is one Bell, a child of Hell,
> An' a Magistrate in station,
> Let lots be drew an' see which av you
> Will tumble him to damnation!

CHORUS

> The lot's new cast, the sentence passed
> I scorn to tell a lie, sir!
> I got my chance, it wur no blank,
> I wur glad to win the prize, sir!
> To swate Billy Conny's I did repair
> To meet the parson, Bell, sir!
> At his brain I took me aim,
> Sayin' Come down, you fien' o' hell, sir!

86

Those Orangemen they gathered then,
An' swore they'd kill us all, sir!
For their frien' Bell, who lately fell
An' got a terrible fall, sir!
But Molly's sons, wid words an' guns,
Wid pikes, pitchforks aglancin'
Those bould recruits an' undaunted yout's
Stepped into the field just prancin'.

CHORUS

Those Orangemen, they all stood then,
To fight they they thought it folly;
They'd rather run an' save their lives,
An' leave the field to Molly!
Although I'm in a foreign land,
From the cause I'll ne'er retire,
May heaven smile on every chil'
That belongs to Molly Maguire!"

According to the historian, James Ford Rhodes, the Molly Maguires were at their height during the summer and autumn of 1874.

"They were quick to see what a weapon to their hand was universal suffrage, and, with the aptitude for politics which the Irish have shown in our country, they developed their order into a political power to be reckoned with. Numbering in Schuylkill County only 500 or 600 out of 5000 Irishmen in a total population of 116,000, the Molly Maguires controlled the common schools and the local government . . . in the mining sections of the county."

At about the time McParlan assumed his duties as secretary of the Shenandoah Division, Governor Hartranft appointed Kehoe to be high constable of Girardville (he was elected to this office the following November). Molly Maguires in Carbon and Northumberland Counties were on school boards and in the tax assessor's office and there was an excellent chance of installing their own jury commissioner in Schuylkill County.

87

"They came near electing one of their number, who had acquired twenty thousand dollars worth of property, an associate judge of the Court of Oyer and Terminer. In one borough a Molly was chief of police. In the elections were fraudulent voting, stuffing of the ballot boxes, and false returns; in the administration of these offices, fraud and robbery," Rhodes declared.

Late in July of 1874, two of Bloomsburg Bodymaster Hester's representatives appeared at a meeting of the Shenandoah Division. They needed a couple of men, they said, "to put the fear of God into a blackhearted Irish fire boss," who'd traitorously fired a Molly in good standing at Kulpmont Colliery, near Mount Carmel. "We'll return the favor whenever you need us," they promised. The would-be victim was to be beaten but not murdered. Bodymaster Lawler, presiding, agreed to furnish the required manpower. The date, a week hence, was selected.

Normally, the method of choosing members to do the usual "clane" job was accomplished in the fairest manner possible. Those (whose luck was good or bad, depending upon the point of view) pulling the shortest straws were given the assignment. Since the victim (at least during later days when the Molly Maguires had know-how) was unknown to his assailants, he had to be fingered by "locals." This was done some forty-eight hours before target date to permit a "dry run" and to protect the innocent so that, if humanly possible, the wrong man would not be killed or injured.

In the matter of Jack O'Keefe, who was merely "to get the hell beat out of him," Muff dispensed with formalities and chose two youthful members anxious to see action. Neither was over nineteen years of age.

McParlan, in his role as secretary, made notes which he coolly assured Muff, who watched the detective with a certain amount of understandable anxiety, were intelligible to no one but their author. This would be McParlan's first opportunity to forewarn a victim of Molly vengeance. The detective's ability to live without seeming to work was due, in the opinion of knowing lodge brothers, to McParlan's past great success in shoving the queer and building up a large cash reserve. This gave him the maneuverability he needed.

As the detective and McAndrew, with whom he had developed a close friendship, left the meeting together that night, McParlan said that for a brief moment he contemplated taking this Molly into his confidence. "But the risk was too great," he admitted afterward. "I couldn't take the chance although, in view of later events, I could have won him over to our side. He was a fine boy and was intensely loyal to me."

McParlan determined that any warning to the intended victim must come through Captain Linden. The problem was to get a message to Linden. He was afraid a letter would not be delivered in time.

The afternoon following the assignation, McParlan went to Tamaqua where he called on Mary. "I'm flush," he said. "How about a trip to Philly to see a show? We'll take Mr. Kerrigan with us." Mary and Powderkeg were delighted to accept and the next morning the trio left for Philadelphia. At Reading, when their train made its usual twenty-minute stop to change engines, McParlan volunteered to go into the station and pick up refreshments, liquid and solid. Powderkeg was to remain with his sister-in-law to protect her from rude advances made by gentlemen who filled the crowded coach.

While inside the station the detective first bought sandwiches and beer at the lunch counter, then dashed to the telegraph office to send an innocuous sounding message to Superintendent Franklin at the latter's home, using code names previously agreed upon.

"It was a risk, I knew," recalled McParlan, "but I didn't think it was a very big one. My worry was if the telegrapher recognized me or if Kerrigan decided to come in while I was at the telegraph desk. He was a damned smart man and I'd have been in real trouble. But I was lucky. The telegrapher didn't know me and Powderkeg stayed with Mary.

"When we got moving again I went to the washroom and wrote out a note. All I said was 'Jack O'Keefe gets his big pay Tuesday.' This wasn't much to go by but I figured if I got the message to Captain Linden he'd work it out.

"We got off the train and right away I knew my telegram had been delivered because we were being followed. They played it smart and this time it was Mr. Franklin, himself, I saw about twenty feet behind us. I was pretty sure Kerrigan didn't know him or the lady who was with him. As soon as Mr. Franklin caught my quick glance, he stopped, turned around and the lady who was with him walked ahead and passed us by.

"Now here I had to be damned careful. Kerrigan could see everything I was doing. He knew a hell of a lot of people and it wasn't impossible that he'd met Mrs. Franklin. Well, I 'accidentally' brushed against the lady and knocked down her handbag. I picked it up and handed it back with the note underneath. That was all. The rest was up to Mr. Franklin and the Captain. Kerrigan did not get suspicious."

From the word "big" Franklin deduced that the O'Keefe mentioned by McParlan must hold a supervisory job. By combing the lists of all mine bosses in the hard coal regions, a tedious but not difficult task, three men bearing the name of John or Jack O'Keefe were found to be foremen. Two, one in Luzerne and the other in Lackawanna County where the Mollies had been comparatively inactive, were not considered "candidates." The third was a Kulpmont fire boss.

All this used up valuable time and it was not until the following Monday, the day before the attack was scheduled, that O'Keefe was called into the colliery superintendent's office and told what would presumably take place within twenty-four hours. The Irish fire boss was furious. He was given his choice of having bodyguards or taking a temporary leave from his job. To accept either offer, of course, would have tipped off his would-be attackers that there had been a leak in the Society's system of communications.

O'Keefe refused both offers and said he was perfectly capable of defending himself. He went about his regular duties that shift and the next. He was not molested during daylight hours, so he assumed the attack, if it were to come at all, would take place at dusk, in or near his home outside of Kulpmont.

Late Tuesday afternoon O'Keefe took a short cut over the mountain and reached his house just before sundown. On one pretext or other he had sent his wife and three children to

Shamokin to spend the night with a relative. O'Keefe stood in his yard apparently digging a drainage trench. He'd been working for only a few minutes when he heard someone opening the front gate. Out of the corner of his eye he saw two men approach him holding cudgels.

When the pair was only a few feet away, O'Keefe, tall and powerfully built, whirled around suddenly and raising the sharpened shovel high, brought it down edgewise with enormous force on the top of the nearest Molly's head, splitting the skull almost to his shoulderblades. The other screamed in terror, tossed down his club and fled, never to be seen again in the hard coal regions.

O'Keefe surrendered to police immediately. He was given a hearing and held in five hundred dollars bail, which, old-time residents claim, although there is no proof, was furnished by Father Koch, O'Keefe's pastor at the Church of Our Lady of Mount Carmel. A Grand Jury refused to indict the Irish fire boss, and he never again had trouble with the secret society. Bodymaster Muff Lawler's comments must have been unprintable.

Early in August, McParlan completely failed to prevent a savage attack on Anthony Cheracovich, a Polish "greenhorn," then living in Gilberton. Cheracovich had in some way insulted a member of the Shenandoah Division and the honor of the entire "local" was at stake.

"I knew what was coming three days before," McParlan admitted, "and I couldn't talk them out of it without giving myself away. There wasn't much I could do. Either I had to notify Cheracovich myself and since he didn't speak English and I didn't speak his language, this would have been tough. Chances are I'd have been caught. My other choice was to let them go through with the beating and hope Cheracovich wouldn't be hurt too badly. I did nothing further to stop them and the poor guy was injured so seriously he could never work again."

The rolls of the Shenandoah Division were reduced by the involuntary deletion of one more brother on August 11 when Edward Cosgrove was killed in a fist fight with Gomer James, a tough Welshman. James was a member of the Modocs, an informal group of compatriots banded together for mutual protection against the Molly Maguires, and also to initiate a few lawless acts of their own.

The borough of Shenandoah, oriented to violence, was divided in half by those who loudly defended the murdered man as an upright gentleman and those who called Cosgrove's killer a hero and took up a public subscription to award him a medal for his "courageous act." But one man used the occasion to demand a fair trial for James and to berate his fellow citizens for permitting such desperate acts to become commonplace.

Thomas Jefferson Foster was the only editor-publisher who openly thumbed his nose at the Molly Maguires, and when he decided he had had enough of their violence, he blasted them in every edition of his newspaper, the Shenandoah *Herald*.

On the masthead of Foster's four-page, five-column weekly, appeared the owner's motto—"To Fear God; Tell the Truth; and Make Money." His approach to journalism would have won the admiration of newspaper giants of his day.

"Right from the start Foster took off about the Mollies, or what he first called 'organized lawlessness,'" said Tom Barrett, Foster's journalistic descendant. "I'm inclined to believe his original motivation was that this was a damned good circulation builder. Whatever his reasons were, his was the first, the strongest, the most persistent and courageous voice raised to fight the Molly Maguires. He never let up!"

"It is evidence of a rotten condition of affairs," the editor once wrote, "that desperate characters of this kind are at large and that the law has no terrors for them. We believe our judges' hands are tied by timid or dishonest jurors who perjure themselves by refusing to bring in guilty men . . . because they fear the vengeance of friends of the prisoners . . .

"It is about time law abiding citizens of the area organize posses and take over the functions of officials and jurors too cowardly to act on their own."

Receipt of four "final coffin notices" failed to dampen Foster's zeal and, strangely enough, he was never attacked physically, although his presses and the building which housed them were dynamited and set on fire more than once.

"If Gomer James is to be tried for the murder of Edward Cosgrove in the newspapers of the county and the general public is to be judge and jury, perhaps his friends are right in engaging in a discussion of his case and endeavoring to manufacture public opinion," declared Foster in the *Herald* of August 21. "But if he is to be tried by a jury of his fellow citizens before the County Criminal Court where he is certain to receive exact justice, it is high time both for the cause of law and order in . . . Shenandoah and for the best interests of the parties engaged in it, that this agitation cease."

Gomer James had two trials. The first was in Schuylkill County's Criminal Court at Pottsville where he won a fast acquittal. His second trial, held at Muff Lawler's with the accused *in absentia*, was even briefer: he was condemned to death.

Chapter Fourteen

In mid-August of 1874, the new "goods" arrived. They were passed first to Jack Kehoe then distributed by local bodymasters and secretaries all over the hard coal regions to members in good standing of the A.O.H.

"This time," said McParlan, "the recognition sign was easier to perform. All you had to do was to put your front finger and thumb of your right hand on the bottom of your necktie. If you didn't wear a tie you used the top button of your shirt. The answer was equally simple. You rubbed your right hand across your forehead and touched the bottom of your hair. I admit, for a bald man, this could have created a problem and I'm afraid that those on high who passed down the orders didn't give this any consideration.

"They changed all the rest of the rigamarole including the password which now became, 'What do you think of D'Israeli's plan? He still keeps rule from our native land.' The correct response was: 'But with good swords and men at command, we will give long-lost rights to our native land.'

"Bodymasters were provided with an official toast—'May the President of France, the General so grand, banish all heresy and free Ireland!' "

In addition to acceptance and understanding of the new "goods" and perfection of plans for Gomer James' execution, the regular August meeting of the Shenandoah Division, Bodymaster Lawler presiding, had other resolutions to be voted upon, passed, rejected, or tabled. One was a request from Bodymaster Michael

94

Clarke over the mountain in Mahanoy City to do a "clane job" on Henry Detweiler, a stable foreman who had incurred the wrath of a faithful member of the organization.

There also was a petition from Mr. Hester, in Bloomsburg, to take action against two Centralians who had the effrontery not only to praise Father McDermott's denunciation of the lodge but also to defend similar sermons preached at St. Ignatius by his successor, the Reverend Father E. T. Field. This last was particularly serious, Mr. Hester's personal representative pointed out, because the new priest was winning many converts in the Church's crusade against the Molly Maguires.

"I was in a sweat," recalled McParlan. "Things were breaking so fast I wasn't sure how I could take care of them all and still keep the boys from getting suspicious. I was mailing full reports to Philadelphia as often as possible and trying to get warnings to intended victims in time to do some good, although I missed plenty, I know.

"Even though I was secretary of the lodge I still didn't hear everything that went on. I knew Gomer James was to be killed— that was said in open meeting. I got the name of the Mahanoy City stable foreman who was to be beaten, or murdered if he fought back. But I didn't know who were the two Centralia men."

Many secrets were not revealed at open meetings. McParlan was sure at the time, but admitted he had no legal proof, that word was being passed from Kehoe to individual bodymasters who in turn appointed executioners sworn to absolute silence. This meant that all the facts in many murders and assaults were known to none except Black Jack and those directly involved.

"I'd like to have been able to get over to the Hibernian House at least occasionally" McParlan recalled with regret, "but you didn't go there unless you were one of his regulars or if you were asked. Kehoe didn't ask me. Since he'd become High Constable he was more aloof than ever. I doubt if he ever trusted me fully and I know he didn't like me. However, if that gentleman had ever had any real doubts, I would have been a goner.

"After that August meeting I felt the most important job at

hand was to get word to the stable foreman, Henry Detweiler, a Dutchman. I didn't know where he lived or worked but I was informed he hung out at Triers' corner.

"I couldn't worry much about Gomer. I was sure he'd know, without my telling him, he'd be executed by the Mollies the first opportunity they got. Every man in the lodge wanted that job and they weren't going to ask any brother from an outside division for a 'favor.' But Gomer wasn't taking any chances. He was a tough guy. He carried a pistol he knew how to handle. And almost everywhere he went he had a couple of Modoc plug uglies along."

Although he was aware that Captain Linden was never more than fifty miles away, the detective had no way of communicating with him directly. Unless an emergency arose he was afraid to be "arrested" again because Kehoe, if not Muff or Powderkeg, might then entertain grave doubts about "McKenna's" real identity.

Without showing undue curiosity, McParlan could not find out where Detweiler lived or worked. But the boys talked freely about the fact that the stable foreman was known as a "lady killer" despite his marriage, and that he spent his early evenings loafing at Triers' corner in Mahanoy City.

"Triers' was a neutral spot," said McParlan. "Most of the boys who hung out there were Protestants. Trier was a Jew but he was a good tailor and some Mollies used him to sew their clothes. I knew he made Michael Clarke's suits for him.

"I got hold of a fancy envelope which I scented with perfume I pinched from Kerrigan's pretty little sister-in-law. I wrote down the foreman's name outside but for his address I put: 'Care of Triers' Tailor Shop, Fourth and Center Street.' I slanted my handwriting to look like a woman's. I figured the boys at Triers' who might be standing around when he opened it would figure it was from one of the women Detweiler was playing around with who didn't want the message to get to his home.

"Maybe Detweiler thought so, too, until he opened it up and he must have turned white. Inside I had written a damned grim warning and he couldn't mistake who I meant was out to get him. I don't know exactly what happened but I do know he got wise, quit his job and beat it away fast. Whether he took his wife with him I didn't know and didn't care."

By the time McParlan learned the names of the Centralia offenders marked for execution, it was too late. On August 13, Michael Lanahan was shot to death on the main street of the village almost in front of his home. Two hours later, Thomas Dougherty was ambushed and garrotted on his way from work. Both men were communicants at St. Ignatius' Roman Catholic Church and outspoken admirers of Father Field.

There were witnesses to both murders but no one was willing or able to identify the killers. The Columbia County coroner's jury returned verdicts of "Death at the hands of unknown assailants." No arrests were ever made for either crime. "These murders," wrote Tom Barrett, "were 'shrouded in mystery' but every circumstance pointed with moral certainty to the Molly Maguires as the conspirators and perpetrators."

The Mollies made their first attempt to take Gomer James's life at the Ringtown Fair on September 15, a little over a month after Cosgrove was murdered. The Fair was an annual event at the village of Ringtown, located in a pleasant farming valley over the mountain a dozen miles south of Shenandoah.

Each day as many as two thousand men, women, and children attended the event which, reported the methodical Major Pinkerton, "had its usual attractions, side shows, ugly dwarfs, scrawny giants, slimy anacondas, and a fine display of bullocks, cows, etc. There were foot races, greased pigs, lady equestriennes, music, dancing and a full brass band from a neighboring city."

McParlan was one of eight brethren whom Lawler chose to do the job. Strategy called for one of the octet to pick a quarrel with the Welshman. The others would immediately gather around the combatants and separate James from his friends. In the midst of the scuffle each Molly would plunge his knife into Gomer.

The detective was the only one who knew the plan must fail; he had learned that the Shenandoah "Sheet Irons," another name for the Modocs, would attend the Fair en masse. To prove good intent McParlan protested to his bodymaster that the assassination platoon would not be sufficient to do the job required. But Lawler refused to acknowledge that eight well-armed Mollies couldn't handle any number of Welshmen.

When representatives of the Shenandoah Division, headed by McParlan, arrived at the Fair and strolled through the midway, they got their first glimpse of Gomer James. The big Welshman, stripped to the waist, muscles bulging, was swinging a sledge hammer down upon a wooden knob which, when struck hard enough, sent a heavy metal plug along a trolley wire fifty feet up into the air to strike a bell on top of a tall post. Few men were powerful enough to "ring the bell and collect a five cent cigar" even once but every one of James's methodical strokes was followed in a few seconds by a loud clang.

Giving Gomer plenty of room to swing, yet close enough to prevent anyone from approaching their leader, were at least a hundred brawny men, recognized by the small detachment of Mollies as Modocs. Had McParlan proceeded to carry out his commands, slaughter of the Molly Maguires would have been assured. Retreat was the order of the day and the platoon retired to Shenandoah headquarters.

A few days after this fiasco, Muff received a summons to present himself before King Kehoe and to bring McParlan with him. Black Jack, of course, had been informed both of the intended execution and its subsequent failure. As a matter of fact —and this was what disturbed Kehoe most of all—knowledge of plans to kill James, including the proposed time and place, had been bruited about all over the coal regions and was certainly known to the Modocs. By their inability to dispose of an enemy when and where promised, the Mollies lost face.

Kehoe scornfully berated Lawler and sarcastically belittled McParlan, leader of the "execution" platoon. "I could have done better meself with a blow gun," said the Girardville bodymaster. But Lawler, who accepted the censure which he felt was deserved, pointed out to Kehoe that McParlan was not to blame and that the lodge secretary actually had protested the plan and predicted its failure.

"The chance I took telling Muff beforehand about the strength of the Modocs paid off. Even though he never trusted me fully,

I went up quite a few notches in Jack Kehoe's estimation. I could see that by the way he talked to me afterward," the detective recalled. "Plans for Gomer James's execution were temporarily tabled. 'We' couldn't afford to be laughed at soon again."

Late in September, 1874, the Mollies destroyed the Newkirk Colliery near Tamaqua because Owen Jenkins, the Welsh superintendent, had refused to "co-operate" with the organization.

Jenkins, too old to be of service, was pensioned. "The Mollies, and I *know* they did this job, got rid of their Welsh super," recalled Dan Shepp, "but at the same time they put seven hundred men out of work for nearly five years. A bad bargain I'd say!"

Chapter Fifteen

No one, not even McParlan, could ever hope to know as much about the Molly Maguires as the Roman Catholic clergy whose communicants included not only members of the hated society but their wives, sons, and daughters, who had knowledge of many an untold horror. Their lips sealed by the sanctity of the confessional, these priests were forced to keep their dreadful secrets from public knowledge.

Angered by continuing acts of violence for which they blamed the Molly Maguires, seven Roman Catholic priests, on October 3, 1874, signed a strong statement condemning not only the local branches but the national Ancient Order of Hibernians as well. The group of priests, with parishes in six Schuylkill County mining towns and one in Pat Hester's territory across the border in Columbia County, was headed by Father McDermott. This priest had by then been assigned to a parish in New Philadelphia, site of William Williams' murder and many other bloody deeds.

The "white paper" appeared two weeks later in the *Catholic Standard,* official publication of the Philadelphia Diocese, with this brief editorial preface:

"The Right Reverend Bishop (Wood) has requested us to publish the following statement regarding the A.O.H. It is made by seven most respectable priests. The position of these reverend gentlemen is such as to enable them to form a correct estimate of the character, influence and acts of the unfortunate Association, and their statement is entitled to the fullest credence. May all interested take warning."

The statement followed:

1. Ribbonmen and kindred societies have been, *nominatim,* condemned by the Holy See.

2. A society in America organized on the same basis, holding the same principles, and animated by the same spirit, comes within the condemnation of its prototype in Ireland.

3. When the spirit and principles, as manifested in acts, are the same, it matters little by what name the society is styled.

4. The testimony of members, ex-members, public reports and our experience, compels us to believe the A.O.H. has all the vices of societies, *nominatim,* condemned in Ireland.

5. Experience has proved that no faith is to be placed in the most solemn promises or denials of the A.O.H.

6. It is certain that a fear, terror of the punishment that may, in secrecy, be decreed in the upper circles, compels members to execute the commands given under the countersign, no matter how repugnant to the laws of God and men those commands may be.

7. Men of notoriously infamous character (the constitution and by-laws notwithstanding), have not only been admitted to membership, but elected to office and actually control the society in many places.

8. Evidence sufficient to convince the most skeptical has come to light, that works forbidden by the Commandment, THOU SHALT NOT KILL, are traceable to the A.O.H.

9. The spirit and acts of the A.O.H. are clearly condemned by the plainest teachings of the Decalogue.

10. It is vain to eliminate the objectionable features from the letter of the laws of such a society, while the same spirit, the same traditions, remain, and the same men control it.

Rev. Michael Sheridan, Ashland, Pa.
Rev. Joseph Koch, Shamokin, Pa.
Rev. Jos. Bridgman, Girardville, Pa.
Rev. H. F. O'Reilly, Shenandoah, Pa.
Rev. E. T. Field, Centralia, Pa.
Rev. D. O. O'Connor, Mahanoy Plane, Pa.
Rev. D. I. McDermott, New Philadelphia, Pa.

In areas of Pennsylvania where the A.O.H. enjoyed good reputations, many of the clergy, including the Right Reverend Ordinary of Pittsburgh, came to the defense of the organization. But in the hard coal regions the "white paper" was accepted as truth by devout Roman Catholics, most of whom were innocent victims of the hatred Molly Maguires aroused among Protestants.

While its appearance in the conservative *Catholic Standard* at first stimulated additional anti-Irish sentiment, in the end the statement of these seven courageous parish priests set the climate of public opinion, and so enabled McParlan to achieve his ultimate goal.

At this particular moment, however, McParlan was more interested in saving his own neck than in worrying about general anti-Catholic sentiment. The detective spent the night of October 19 in Tamaqua where he was Mary Malloy's escort at a dance. After the dance he joined Powderkeg in Alex Campbell's saloon. The pair drank heavily while the barroom gradually emptied. Finally, only the detective and Powderkeg remained. Campbell, before going upstairs to bed, placed a bottle of whiskey on the bar and told the two gentlemen to help themselves.

"Powderkeg was a bright man and he'd seen a fair portion of the world," McParlan recalled. "We talked about everything under the sun. It's a funny thing, I never gave a damn about Kehoe —he was easy to understand. If he liked you, you knew it, and if he hated you, you knew that, too. As for the rest, they were easy enough to figure out. Quite a few of them wouldn't have been bad fellows under other circumstances. Heavy drinkers, yet lots of times it was giving the dog a bad name and then watching him live up to it.

"Then there was a hard core of real mean ones. They'd have gone wrong no matter what country they lived in, even if the Irish hadn't been pushed around. They had no right to call themselves Catholics—they never went to Mass or Confession. They didn't mind assaulting a priest. He was just like another enemy to them.

"There were a couple of decent lads, such as my friend, Frank McAndrew. I could even see how a fellow like him with a nice wife and respectable, God-fearing parents might have sought the excitement the Mollies provided, and once he got in, there was no way to get out."

Kerrigan, McParlan admitted more than once, was difficult to understand.

"He was different," the detective continued. "Of all the 'brothers' he was the one I feared most; he was so damned shrewd. Many a time I was convinced he was suspicious of me. Every once in a while he'd say something like: 'Wouldn't it be a terrible thing, now, if a detective ever got into the organization? He sure would bring sorrow to a mess of good men.' Then he'd look at me in a peculiar way and cock his big head and smile.

"He had a strange smile. It could be pleasant and then in a second turn real evil. I often had the feeling he was baiting me and if he ever decided to pull the hook I'd be a goner. Then, again, I almost had an idea he actually was hinting at something he wanted me to catch on to.

"This was one of those times. I don't remember who we were discussing when all of a sudden he brings in the name of Simon Trier, the Mahanoy City tailor."

McParlan knew that Trier was the Tamaqua dandy's tailor and that Powderkeg had spent many hours in the rear of the shop playing euchre with the "regulars." The detective was also aware that Simon's wife, Gertrude, was proud of her reputation for good German cooking and that on a number of occasions Kerrigan had been invited to eat with the family.

"'There's one Jew,' says Kerrigan to me out of the clear," McParlan went on, "'who's got plenty of gold stuck away somewhere in that big house of his. I wouldn't be a bit surprised if one of the boyos took it away from him any day. And maybe gave him and his wife a good shellacking in the bargain.'

"I didn't say anything and a minute later Kerrigan went off on another tack and never went back to that one again. Then, after we finished the bottle, Kerrigan said 'good night' and went home and I walked around the corner to the Mansion Hotel where I had a room for the night.

"The next day I got to thinking. There were three possibilities. First, Powderkeg was so drunk he didn't know what he was saying and wouldn't remember it the next morning. This I doubted although it could be so—we must have polished off a quart that evening, but I drank most of it.

"Second, that Kerrigan was sounding me out to see if I'd be interested in maybe joining him, and the two of us robbing the

Triers ourselves. That I wouldn't believe either, because Kerrigan didn't go in for this kind of stuff; not that I wouldn't put it past him.

"The third thing was, and I was almost afraid to believe it, that Kerrigan suspected who I was and that he was either laying a trap for me or was protecting himself in the event that I was really a detective."

Jake Haas, to whom McParlan told this story, asked McParlan if it weren't likely that Kerrigan's friendship with the German tailor and his wife made him wish to protect them from robbery, assault, and murder. But the little Irishman would have none of this, declaring that any such gesture on Kerrigan's part would have been out of character.

"I'd heard how Powderkeg fingered his Tamaqua 'friends,'" McParlan added. "The man would have cut his mother's throat to save his own neck."

Instead of falling asleep at once, as he usually did despite any worries he had, after Kerrigan's mention of the Triers the detective tossed restlessly in his bed the whole night.

"There was so much at stake," McParlan continued. "I was just getting places with the Mollies and I could throw it all away easy and cost lots of people their lives. But I didn't want to have Trier's blood on my hands either. I decided it wouldn't hurt to keep my eyes peeled. A good spot to watch from was Michael Clarke's in Mahanoy City.

"Michael was the bodymaster there and his saloon was only a short distance away from the tailor shop on the other side of Center Street. As secretary of the division it was easy enough for me to cook up business at Michael's. So for the next couple of nights that's where I was—drinking, joining the bhoys in some sentimental ballads about their mothers and Ireland, and doing a bit of soft-shoe on the bar for their entertainment."

Late on the third evening of his vigil, when saloon hilarity was at its peak, McParlan, from a vantage point on top of the bar, saw John "The Cat" Mahoney at the edge of the crowd. The detective was sure the burglar had just entered. Since this strange, self-conscious character did not drink, and left his Gilberton home only on "missions," McParlan felt certain the Cat's destination for the night was Triers' tailor shop. His purpose in stopping at Clarke's, where his very presence caused cold shudders, was to establish an alibi, McParlan reasoned. Nobody was likely to forget the Cat's presence.

A moment later, when the detective looked again, Mahoney was nowhere to be seen. McParlan smiled, joked with his loudly appreciative audience, and leaped down from the bar. He edged himself through the noisy mob toward a back door which led to the toilet thirty feet in the rear of the saloon beneath a high railroad embankment.

As soon as he was outside he took off his shoes and crept softly around the building and walked along a back alley until he came to Fourth Street, where he stood silently beneath a grape arbor directly opposite the Triers' tailor shop. Except for muffled sounds coming from the barroom, the distant whistle of a slow freight train, and the murmur of the creek which flowed in back of the next alley, all was still.

McParlan stayed there while his eyes adjusted themselves to the darkness. The only light penetrating the gloom was a thin beam which escaped from behind the lattice work of the Union Hotel and cast dim shadows across Center Street.

For perhaps two minutes McParlan saw nothing. Then he caught the faintest motion on the side of the tailor shop, just over a basement coal shute. At the same time his ears noted a slight metallic sound as though the rusty hanging bars across the cellar window were being raised softly.

McParlan waited another few moments. Turning around to make sure he hadn't been observed, he tiptoed quietly across Center Street and stood beneath the eaves of the Triers' front porch. Creeping across the east wing of the house he almost stumbled over the opened basement window. Then he knew the Cat was inside.

If McParlan sounded an alarm, aroused the neighborhood, and awakened the Triers, the Cat would murder both the tailor and his wife to prevent identification. Such action could also lead to a revelation of the detective's true role.

He hesitated for only a second. He turned around once more, peered into the night behind him, pulled his pistol from his belt, cocked it, and eased his way through the window. Soundlessly, he lowered himself into the dusty coal bin. He paused. At first he could hear nothing. Then there came the faintest sound of feet padding up the stairs and in a second the fumbling of a door latch.

It was time for action, McParlan decided. Picking up a small lump of coal, he tossed it lightly in the direction of the steps. The noise at the head of the stairs stopped abruptly and Mc-Parlan could almost feel the Cat turn around and cast his eyes downward to sweep over the cellar below. In a second there was the patter of feet descending so their owner could explore the cause of the disturbance.

"I crouched, hidden in a corner of the coal bin, the butt end of my pistol in my hand," McParlan said. "I could feel, but I couldn't see, the Cat creeping alongside of me, not a foot away. I knew it was nonsense, but I'd been told so often he could see in the dark that I really believed it. And I could almost imagine his whiskers bristling.

"I held my breath while he crawled over the bin and looked up at the window. Just then, the headlight of a passing freight engine swept into the cellar. In that second I could see Mahoney's pale white face like it was daylight. Just as he turned all the way around I swung my pistol as hard as I could on his skull. He gave a little groan and dropped to the ground.

"I dragged him by the scruff of his neck through the window, closed it, and took him back into the alley. I tossed him right in the dirty creek. I didn't care whether he was dead or not. I brushed the coal dust off me, recovered my shoes where I'd laid them, ran to the back of Clarke's, and hopped up on the bar again and did a fast jig. I hadn't been gone ten minutes and I wasn't missed. There were fifty men there that night to provide me with a perfect alibi without troubling their conscience.

"As far as the Trier family was concerned, nobody knew a damned thing about what happened until about forty years later. Then I ran into Charlie out in Denver, Colorado. He hadn't even been born.

"Somebody picked up the Cat the next morning. He wasn't dead but he was useless. He'd lost his nerve and his mind, too.

The last I heard of him was that he was sitting on an Allentown street corner, hat in hand, begging pennies.

"I never broached the subject to Kerrigan even though the boys at Muff's and Michael's were mystified. But one day, a few months later, Powderkeg and I were having a beer together in the Malloy's kitchen. Mary'd gone upstairs to get dressed. Powderkeg, out of the blue, suddenly says to me, 'Too bad about the Cat, wasn't it?'

"Then he gave me a *very* odd look and without letting me answer him, he stood up, swallowed his drink and walked out the house. He never said another word to me about it and you can be certain, neither did I to him."

Chapter Sixteen

Next to cocking mains, the best attended sport in most coal region towns, prior to the turn of the century, was fighting fires. Intense rivalry among volunteers frequently produced far more excitement than the blaze itself. Too often a flaming house or store was ignored while firemen fought it out with fists and clubs to determine which organization had gotten there first and so earned exclusive rights to quell the conflagration.

Each community of any consequence had at least two companies, which owned their own buildings and equipment. And every organization had loyal fans who, more frequently than not, arrived at the scene before their team. Sometimes these eager rooters came in numbers sufficient to bar the enemy from an approach and in this way held the field for late arriving heroes.

In 1874, Mahanoy City, with a population approaching 6000, boasted two volunteer fire fighting companies. Members of the first, "The Humanes No. 1," could be distinguished by their bright red shirts, wide blue suspenders, thick yellow belts, black boots, high-crowned metal hats with wide brims both front and rear, and long tan coats nearly reaching the ground. These last garments, which certainly must have hampered their efforts, were usually saved for parades.

The Humanes were headed by Billie Yost, Freddy Spiegel, Dan Fogarty, and Pat McInerney, Sr., all four of whom had won plaudits for heroism. The rank and file of sixty were recruited from every ethnic group in the town. In addition to having its own physician, Dr. Phaon Hermany, the company owned a piece of equipment, an ancient, hand-drawn hose carriage which the neighboring community of Pottsville had discarded as obsolescent a few years before.

Members of the second volunteer organization, "The Citizens Steam Hose Company No. 2," had equally excellent manpower (although it filled its rolls with Englishmen, Germans, and Welshmen) and no doubt similar verve. Dr. Hermany, a Bible student and wit, used to say that the rival company might well have chosen for its motto Hebrews 1:11—"Faith is the substance of things hoped for, the evidence of things not seen." For the Citizens Steam Hose Company No. 2, at least during the first five years of its existence, owned no equipment.

The first piece of fire fighting apparatus bought by the "Citizens" was a hose carriage steamer (also a Pottsville discard), later christened "Major" in honor of Chief Burgess George Major, murdered, his fellow volunteers claimed, by the Molly Maguires.

On a windy Saturday night, the last day of October, 1874, one long and two short rasping shrieks of the whistle at Kaier's Brewery on the edge of the borough announced that a fire was blazing somewhere in town. A few moments later, the sky was lit up as flames swept through several frame stores and dwellings. Wildly enthusiastic advance supporters of both the Humanes and the Citizens poured out of barrooms or leaped from their beds to clog the muddy, unpaved thoroughfares and await the arrival of their teams.

"The fire," said Tamaqua publishers Eveland and Harris in their 1877 version of coal region troubles, "is supposed to have been started either in the ranks of the Mollies or by someone hired by them to do the deed." Neither Mr. Eveland nor Mr. Harris offered any proof of this allegation.

"While the flames were licking up the buildings the entire fire department, composed of both Americans and Irish firemen," continued Messrs. Eveland and Harris "were on the ground and vying with each other to see which would contribute most to the suppression of the flames. This friendly and laudable rivalry was entered into by the citizens generally, and everybody lent a helping hand.

"The police force was on the ground lending their attendance in preserving order, a very necessary duty on occasions of this kind, the Chief Burgess George Major, as his position warranted, taking general supervision of the whole. When the fire had been gotten under control and the people were congratulating each other, a riot commenced among the roughs . . . Bludgeons and spanners, knives and pistols were freely used, and many of the combatants were severely injured.

"The policemen did the best they could to quell the disturbance, and many of the citizens gave them valuable aid, and the riot was at last suppressed, but not without being attended with tragic effects."

The most seriously injured were two men who had supposedly engaged in a pistol duel. The one was Burgess Major and the other, Dan Dougherty, a member in good standing of the Mahanoy City Division of the Mollies. Major was removed to Dr. Bissel's surgery while Dougherty, a bullet deeply imbedded in his upper thigh, was treated by Dr. Hermany, then placed in protective custody "to prevent a lynching," claimed police.

Open anti–Molly Maguire sentiment raged through the town. Tom Foster's Shenandoah *Herald,* with a large Mahanoy City circulation, added to the fuel by urging formation of "vigilantes to give the Mollies what they well deserved."

Retaliation against the editor was swift. The night after his page one editorial appeared, *Herald* machinery was damaged and barrels of ink poured all over the pressroom floor. An unexploded bundle of dynamite sticks was found in the basement the next afternoon.

McParlan was in Shenandoah when the fire and resultant shooting occurred. There was much talk about the "throuble" over in Mahanoy and the detective soon learned that Dougherty, on the evening of the melee, was armed only with a club. Through Frank McAndrew, the detective found out the man who probably shot Major was McAndrew's wife's cousin, Jack McCann. McCann, a part-time bartender at Michael Clarke's, was a member of the Wiggans Patch Division.

McCann, said McAndrew, was hiding in the home of Mrs. Mamie McDonald only a few hundred feet from the scene of the riot. He had fled there the moment he saw the Chief Burgess drop to the ground. Mrs. McDonald was anxious to get the bartender off her premises. Feeling against the Irish was very high in Mahanoy City as Major lapsed into a coma.

Michael Clarke, fearing that he would arouse suspicion in the town if he or any of his own members were to be seen at Mrs. McDonald's, sent word to Muff Lawler asking that the Shenandoah bodymaster help McCann make a getaway. The detective volunteered to call on McCann to hear his story and Lawler agreed. On the following Monday, just as dusk fell, the secretary of the Shenandoah Division slipped through the back gate of the McDonald home and identified himself to the lady of the house.

A thoroughly frightened McCann, hiding in an upstairs back bedroom, readily admitted it was he who shot the Chief Burgess, claiming, perhaps truthfully, that Major had fired first. The bartender knew Dougherty had been arrested for the crime, but he was far more interested in saving his own skin than in clearing the prisoner. McParlan told McCann he would see what could be done but in the meantime the bartender was to stay where he was.

"If you leave here," McParlan warned McCann, "be sure to let us know where you're going."

From the McDonalds, McParlan went to Dr. Hermany's surgery where Dougherty, much improved, was under police protection. How McParlan did it nobody knows, except that he probably bribed the guard, but he managed to speak to Dougherty in private. To McParlan's astonishment, the wounded man not only knew it was McCann who shot Major but also knew where the bartender was hiding. He told McParlan that even if his own life were in jeopardy he would never "inform."

The detective was now faced with the problem of letting the authorities know where McCann was and also advising them that Dougherty was innocent. He decided to do nothing for the moment, hoping Major would recover. But the following morning the Chief Burgess died. Dougherty, the bullet still in his thigh, was arrested, charged with murder, and moved to the Pottsville jail.

With Major's death, McParlan's difficulties increased enormously, and could be solved only if McCann confessed and surrendered himself to police. There was little likelihood that this would happen. Should McParlan inform authorities that Dougherty was innocent and at the same time reveal McCann's whereabouts, there was better than a fair chance the detective's dual role would be disclosed. If that happened during this critical point in his investigation, everything he had accomplished so far would be lost.

The detective decided the decision was not his to make. He knew Captain Linden was in Pottsville and sent word to the big policeman that an emergency had arisen. Two days later, on warrants sworn to by the District Attorney, McParlan and nineteen other members of both the Shenandoah and Mahanoy City Divisions were taken into custody, charged with being "material witnesses" in the Major shooting.

By noon of the following day all twenty had been questioned and released. Captain Linden had now been apprised of the situation but he would not tell McParlan what to do. "You'll have to wait until I talk to Superintendent Franklin," he said.

Franklin, in turn, passed the buck to Gowen. The answer came down fast—Franklin to Linden to McParlan—"Sit tight."

When McParlan returned to Shenandoah he told Muff he wanted to speak to McCann again. But the bartender by then was a fugitive. "I haven't any idea where he is," Lawler admitted, "but I can tell you this much: McCann promised to let Dougherty know exactly where he'd be so he could be reached if he was needed. What's more, there's somebody who's in a position to make him keep that promise."

Less than a week after Major's death, a Grand Jury indicted Dougherty on a charge of homicide. So strong was public opinion against him that the prisoner's counsel was able to obtain a change of venue from Schuylkill to Lebanon County, sixty miles away.

At the ensuing trial before Judge Kemmerer and a panel of twelve placid Pennsylvania Dutch farmers, defense counsel claimed that when the Chief Burgess was shot, the prisoner was *hors de combat*, victim of a bullet fired by Major's younger brother William. If counsel could prove that the bullet still in their client's thigh came from William Major's pistol and not from the Burgess's, who fired a minute or two later, it could be concluded that George Major died at the hands of an unknown assailant.

But Dr. Hermany claimed the bullet was so deeply imbedded in Dougherty's body that an operation to remove it would probably be fatal. McCann apparently had no intention of confessing; Dougherty had no intention of informing; McParlan, who knew the truth, was nowhere to be found. The prisoner volunteered to submit to surgery. He assumed, since he knew the trial was going against him, that he had little to lose either way, and a scalpel sounded more inviting than a hangman's noose.

The operation was a success; the patient lived; the bullet was removed; it fitted William Major's pistol; and Dougherty was set free.

"Of course it was right that Dougherty should be acquitted, he not being the guilty person," Tamaqua's historians Eveland and Harris declared magnanimously. "But the fact remains," they added, "that Major, an officer in the discharge of his duties, was shot down and died a victim of his devotion to law and order."

What would he have done if the verdict had gone against Dougherty, Charlie Trier once asked McParlan.

"I don't honestly know," the detective answered. "I'd have been in one hell of a spot. Franklin had been told the truth and I don't think he'd have let them hang an innocent man. He'd have worked out something. If he didn't I might have. Not that Dougherty was a saint. He was a damned bad actor. He caused another man's death the next year."

As for McCann, Messrs. Eveland and Harris indulged in wishful thinking once more. "We might predict, gentle reader, by this time [1877] that McCann is in custody."

"Not so," said McParlan. "They never found McCann and he never came back. I can't say I blame him."

Chapter Seventeen

By late autumn of 1874 working conditions throughout the hard coal regions had grown intolerable. Wages fell again, working hours were reduced, and new floods of immigrants were poured into the anthracite counties, swelling the already overfull labor pool. This time a far larger proportion of the men and women coming into the promised land were from the East European countries.

Employers, led by Gowen, would make no concessions to the delegations of miners who appealed to them for relief. During that terrible winter of 1874-1875, very few miners—and this included not only the Irish but the old established English and Welsh miners as well—could keep their families from slow starvation.

On December 4, John Siney, the St. Clair labor leader, called a strike of the Mine Workers Benevolent Association and thousands of men everywhere in the anthracite counties laid down their picks and shovels. The strike was by no means general; there were many pockets of resistance throughout the Schuylkill and Lehigh regions. In the upper coal fields surrounding Scranton workers accepted operators' terms and refused to heed Siney.

From the miners' point of view, this, "the long strike" as it has been called for nearly a century, was to become the most disastrous walkout in all of the hard coal regions' troubled labor history. From Gowen's point of view the strike was a brilliant success. When the desperate, beaten men finally returned to work six months later they came back at terms dictated by Gowen and the operators he represented. The terms were the same as those which caused the strike—twenty per cent reduction in wages, no guaranteed minimum work, no additional safety precautions, and no protection from unjust dockings by ticket bosses.

There could have been no other result. There was little money in the union's treasury and the workers had neither cash in their pockets nor food in their larders. In every anthracite county there were many collieries and mines where Siney's call was ignored, and enough coal was dug and prepared for market to supply a fair portion of the nation's coal needs. The men and boys in the "rebel" areas worked full time every week and there was appreciable leniency in ticket bosses' judgment as at to what was coal and what was waste.

Then, too, Siney never could dissolve completely the suspicions each ethnic group had for the other. As a matter of fact, the M.B.A. chief was unable even to communicate directly with many of his reluctant members, the newly indoctrinated Americans who'd arrived from Poland, Russia, Hungary, and Lithuania.

For a very brief period, perhaps a week, there was a lull in coal region violence. Self-idled miners were waiting to see what would happen and so were their employers. The Mollies, too, at least as far as McParlan could learn, were in a state of quiescence; only a few of their members, and those bodymasters, could stand being out of work any longer than anyone else.

One of the working collieries was Richardson's near Shamokin in Northumberland County. On December 13, according to a report Gowen prepared for the State Legislature, John Taylor, an Englishman and inside foreman at Richardson's, was sent an unsigned note warning him to leave or "you will die." Gowen declared this was sent by the Molly Maguires but neither McParlan nor anyone else ever substantiated the claim. Whether or not Taylor took the hint also is unknown; at least there is no record of his subsequent murder.

The next threatened act of violence, one which could scarcely be related to the strike, although Gowen blamed the action on labor "agitators," occurred at Indian Head Colliery, an independent operation near Sunbury where workers did not go out with the M.B.A.

Shortly before midnight, two strangers dressed in black appeared just as the night watchman was about to enter the shaft to grease the pumps. "If you put your hands in that can of grease you're holding," warned one of the men, "you're a goner and so's Indian Head. That's the fireman's job."

"The two were Irishmen," the night watchman reported to his superintendent and of course the assumption was that they were Molly Maguires. Since the majority of employees at Indian Head were Welsh, English and German, resistance to Siney and his Irish "agitators" strengthened, fed by this rumor, which was promptly dispersed throughout the community.

These were busy days for McParlan. He was not only carrying out his official duties as division secretary but because of his increasing popularity as a singer of Irish ballads and a dancer of jigs, he was spending many evenings entertaining habitués of saloons all over the hard coal regions. Then, too, he was carrying on his courtship with Miss Malloy and continuing to cultivate her brother-in-law, Powderkeg.

"It was a strain, and I didn't know how long I could keep it up," he admitted to Charlie Trier. "But I was young in those days and my whiskey consumption was high. That helped. My main job of working for the Major didn't worry me and I was mailing in my daily reports without any trouble. Mr. Kerrigan's friendship was paying off and I was beginning to tie Mr. Kehoe to a few past and present actions I hoped he'd regret someday.

"It was my side chores that really had me on the run. I started to teach Frankie McAndrew's oldest lad, Billy, how to box, and before I knew it there was a flock of youngsters in my 'class,' two of Muff's and six or seven others. None of it hurt me with Lawler and the boyos from the Shenandoah Division, though that wasn't why I did it. Then, too, I was a bachelor, and every bodymaster and brother in each division had an unmarried sister they'd like me to meet. We Irish always seem to have an unmarried sister around, now don't we?"

The detective was busily engaged in another activity which he reported to no one.

"There was a pretty young Polish barmaid I'd met in Harry Murphy's Oasis Hotel over in Frackville. She took a liking to me and I to her, for the time being anyway. I had to sneak out to spend one night a week with her to keep us both contented.

"My only real problem was with Mary Malloy. She was a decent Irish girl and everytime I kissed her (which was as far as I went) she heard wedding bells."

One problem McParlan did not mention was his inability to warn some potential victims of danger. As a matter of fact, the detective admitted, he often knew only that a vicious assault or murder was scheduled but could learn neither the marked man's name nor the hour and place of the designated attack. During the very early "non-violent" phase of the "long strike," the detective gave Franklin sufficient information to prevent two assaults but failed to stop a third one.

"The first was a foreman at a Foster Township colliery," McParlan said. "Here's how I found out. One afternoon I came into Muff's the back way, like I often did when I was anxious to see Muff alone and didn't want to pass through the bar. There was nobody in the kitchen and up the side steps I went, whistling softly to myself.

"I was at the top and just about ready to push the parlor door open when I hear Lawler's loud voice saying saying, 'No, boys, you'll do it *my* way—don't kill the son-of-a-bitch yet, just give him a good shellacking.' I stood there listening and in another minute I find out who they mean."

Without revealing the fact that he had eavesdropped, the little Irishman tiptoed softly down the stairs and slipped out of the house.

"It was so easy," McParlan confessed, "that I kept thinking it might have been a 'plant' set up to trap me maybe by Kehoe but not Muff, who didn't have that kind of brains. But I had to run that risk. I did, and passed the word to Mr. Franklin. Nothing happened to the foreman, at least as far as I knew.

"Luck was still with me. That same evening a couple of our boyos talked about giving 'it' the next week to a young Irish fire boss. This was to return a 'favor' to the Middleport bodymaster who wanted the lad punished for sacking a drunken brother. We reached him in time and I think I can take credit for saving more than his neck."

One crime McParlan was unable to prevent, because he knew only that an elected official was to be executed but could not learn his name or position, was the murder of Frederick Hesser, Northumberland County coroner. "This one," said Tom Barrett of the Shenandoah *Herald* unequivocally, "was done by the Mollies. As further events showed, there could be no doubt about it at all."

Hesser, besides being coroner, was a night watchman at Hickory Swamp Colliery, a few miles east of Shamokin. At the time of his slaying, he was sixty-nine years old, and had a wife, five children, and twenty-two grandchildren. He was of German extraction and had lived and worked in the hard coal regions ever since arriving from the Palatinate in 1822. Quiet and well-liked, he had incurred the enmity of Dennis Canning, Shamokin Division bodymaster and Northumberland County delegate to the A.O.H.

"To save my life," Canning lamented quite literally a few years later, "I wish I could remember why I was sore at Hesser."

Hesser was accustomed to arrive at the colliery six nights a week punctually at 11:45.

"On the evening of December 18, 1874," reported the Philadelphia *Press,* "Mr. Hesser was last seen alive on his way to work for the night. His duties as watchman were to make an inspection of the breaker several times a night, to guard against fire, and to blow the whistle every hour. On the evening of December 18, the whistle blew for the last time at midnight.

"On the morning of the next day, the engineer and outside boss, on coming to work between six and seven o'clock, discovered the body lying in an engine room near the stove. He was covered up with his soldier's overcoat. Upon examination it was found that his head was cut in eight places and his skull fractured in three. Any one of the latter would have caused his death."

Apparently whoever conducted the inquiry in the absence of Coroner Hesser failed to ask a leading question—"Where was the night superintendent when the watchman's whistle failed to blow at one, two, three, four or five o'clock that fatal night?"

．　　　．　　　．

As Christmas gifts to 27,000 involuntarily unemployed or striking miners and their families in Schuylkill, Carbon, and Northumberland counties in 1874, Gowen and the other operators gave bobtail checks and a complete stoppage of credit at the "pluck me's." The shelves of independently owned grocery stores near Gowen's mine had long since been emptied.

The miners returned the compliment by smashing scores of tool sheds, dynamiting several collieries and engine houses, derailing hundreds of loaded coal cars, and hurling stones against the windows of company bosses.

The pangs of hunger were beginning to be felt even by those used to a lifetime of nearly empty bellies. As midnight church bells in Mahanoy City, Shamokin, Shenandoah, Pottsville, Audenried, and Tamaqua rang in the New Year and early morning choirs sang "Peace on Earth, Good Will to Men," the hard coal regions' most terrible year of violence, 1875, began its tragic course.

Chapter Eighteen

There was no end to fury, sadness, and despair as the "long strike" dragged on. Only a small number of the most violent deeds were reported in the press or reached courts of record to be available to later historians.

The following are only three excerpts (and these on consecutive nights) taken from the lengthening record of daily atrocities committed in every coal region town, village, and patch from Port Clinton, when McParlan began his mission, to Bloomsburg, seventy miles west:

February 1. An armed body of men beat the watchman at Graeber, Kemble & Company's colliery, Locust Gap, and made its first unsuccessful attempt to burn the breaker.

February 2. Houser's Hotel, on the south side of Wild Cat Mountain in Centreville, was dynamited moments after non-union miners from two independent collieries, Smith's and the Buckville, met to map plans for mutual protection against raids from strikers.

February 3. Every loaded coal car at Huntzinger and Ludwig's, an independent colliery in Foster Township, was dumped; Frank Carlson, an engineer, was savagely beaten, and Everett Welsh, the night watchman, was fired at twice.

Hardly one to turn the other cheek, Gowen took countermeasures. He and the operators he represented placed armed deputies on freight and passenger trains, and offered protection to workers recruited from the big Eastern cities. Unfortunately, these willing neophytes did not know how to mine coal, and production dropped while accident rates soared.

Even though they added little to the fast-diminishing stock-piles of anthracite, the imported scabs justified their cost. Their very presence was enough to add to the despair of displaced workers and outweigh the anger and frustration felt by thousands of starving miners.

Strikers retaliated on March 31. Gathering almost spontaneously, hundreds of men paraded from Gordon to Hecksherville. On the way, they commandeered a loaded freight train, drove scores of workers from collieries, fired at several engine houses, and wound up their march at Ashland, where their presence compelled Gowen to reroute several carloads of scabs originally scheduled for Schuylkill County mines.

But this was almost the last sortie of any consequence. The pitifully weak M.B.A., never in any position to cope with the organized power of Gowen and the corporations, gradually disintegrated, and one by one men crawled back to work on empty bellies.

Few newspapers supported the strike; it was less costly to lose the miners' goodwill than to offend Gowen and the operators. One outstanding exception was the Shenandoah *Herald* which may have condemned lawlessness (except that which Foster personally advocated) yet encouraged Siney and the M.B.A. at a heavy loss in advertising. But even Foster was ready to concede defeat.

"The miners and laborers of the Schuylkill Coal Region have made a noble fight . . ." said the *Herald* on Saturday, May 29, 1875. "This is now the end of the fifth month of the lock-out . . . in this region alone over 10,000 men, having thrown down their tools in opposition to what they deem an uncalled-for reduction in their wages, have for almost six months steadfastly maintained their position, subjecting themselves and families to terrible sacrifices . . .

"The funds of the Branches have been . . . used for relief, but it has been impossible, with the limited amount of cash at hand, to give all the aid required. There are families in this neighborhood who for some time back have not been able to get enough to eat . . . We know of men who, if work was ordered Monday morning, are too weak to work . . .

"Every onlooker must add his approval to ours when we commend the miners and laborers for the bravery and manliness displayed by them in the temper in which they have borne the sacrifices they have been called to make."

Then Foster passed softly over recent violence.

"Has a more stoutly contested struggle or one less strained with the excesses arising from excitement and bad blood ever been made, considering the circumstances and the tremendous odds arrayed upon the other side? Do the annals of history present a brighter page of heroic self-sacrifice in a good cause?

"But, notwithstanding all this and much more, the struggle is over . . . and the result is against the men. However much we wish it otherwise, it is useless to deny the fact that we will have to resume on the operators' proposition . . . there is nothing now to be done but go to work."

Foster's pronouncement that "the struggle is over" was premature, despite the fact that increasing thousands of stragglers were already at work. But many other militant miners refused to give up and fought last ditch battles. Under a Mahanoy City dateline, the Shenandoah *Herald,* only four days later, reported one of the most bitter of all fights.

"Intense excitement prevails in this neighborhood today, caused by the appearance of some five hundred miners . . . who marched through the town at daybreak, on their way to stop the workmen who, in the mines, have resumed labor . . . The crowd was armed with bludgeons, and at once proceeded into the several collieries where they stationed themselves to await the coming of the 'blacklegs.'

"On the arrival of these latter, the ringleader of the raiders at once informed them that they could not be permitted to work any longer on such terms, and that any man who attempted to enter the slope would have his brains blown out. The workingmen, thus threatened, returned to their homes, but not before the raiders forcibly robbed them of their dinner cans and ravenously consumed the contents . . ."

The chief of the Mahanoy City Police Department, Captain Elias Whetson, his force of two patrolmen augmented by a dozen hastily sworn-in deputies, tried to block the marchers but were easily repelled. Had a heavy cudgel, hurled at the Captain's head, reached its target squarely instead of striking it a glancing blow, Whetson's tenure of office would have been the briefest in the town's annals. Only the night before, the Borough Council had elected Whetson to the job held by his close friend, the late George Major. This was his first tour of duty.

Whetson promptly called the sheriff, who in turn passed the word on to Governor Hartranft. Ten hours later, two companies of militia marched into Mahanoy City and drove off the rioters with fixed bayonets. This was the last big clash. Except for sporadic violence, this time the "long strike" was really over.

Gowen, flushed with success, stretched out his arms to embrace a reluctant mistress, one who had served him well during the strike. This was the Lehigh Valley Railroad, which, although it had followed Gowen's leadership, still bore a reputation for treating at least its white-collar workers far better than did the Reading. Until restrained by law somewhat later, Gowen managed to buy enough stock in the Lehigh Valley to enable him to merge the two corporations.

"It had been the long custom of the Lehigh Valley to provide its officials and clerks . . . with the company's mid-day lunches," said James Corrigan in the *Anthracite News*. "But on the day after the railroad merger was consummated, the Reading Company bluntly notified each of the officials and clerks of the former Lehigh Valley R.R. that henceforth it would be necessary for each to buy his own lunch.

"An ex–Lehigh Valley clerk, of poetic nature, penned and surreptitiously posted on the office bulletin board the following memento of that historic period:

> '*Quickly following the Reading's coup,*
>   *They cut off dessert, and then the soup;*
>   *The warming broth, the cool ice cream,*
>   *Are things as seen in a fleeting dream.*

> '*And now, they will all have to go,*
>   *(Officials high and Dinkeys low)*
>   *Without the nourishing consommé,*
>   *For which they now will have to pay.*

'*And missed along with loved tureen,*
Are pies and puddings, apples and cream;
They all must go, their weight to lend,
To help the guaranteed dividend.

'*Pennsy isn't in it,*
Reading made the scoop,
Navi doesn't give a pin,
And we are in the soup.' "

Chapter Nineteen

What were the Molly Maguires doing during the long strike? Well, for one thing, they were busy planning a couple of murders. First on the agenda was a project to make the world safer for Brother Dan Dougherty, who said he would be unable to live in peace, or possibly just live, unless William "Bully Boy Bill" Thomas, another friend of the late George Major, was assassinated. The second scheduled event was a matter of honor —the elimination of Gomer James, who had killed Brother Edward Cosgrove so ignominiously.

Bully Boy was the leader of the Mahanoy City Modocs. Over six feet tall and built proportionately, Bully Boy was unlike many of his compatriots, who were generally short of stature. "A parade of the Welsh," said Joe Davies, present editor of the Mahanoy City *Record American,* "might be described as being one mile long and five feet high."

Among the old folks, he was known as Willum ap Frank, "because my father's name was Frank and I am Frank's son," Bully Boy explained. Most of the English-speaking community, however, knew him as William M. Thomas, or more familiarly by his nickname, acquired honestly and obviously. "Had there been more Welsh like Thomas," claimed Joe Davies with a tinge of regret, "there would have been fewer Irish like Kehoe."

Bully Boy Bill was an experienced rough and tumble fighter not unwilling to use his knee in an opponent's groin or an elbow in an adversary's eye if the occasion required it, or perhaps if only the opportunity presented itself. He was also a good professional boxer and a county-wide favorite of sporting gentlemen who preferred the squared circle to cocking mains. Only the preceding April, in the presence of a few hundred blood-thirsty witnesses who themselves displayed considerable endurance, Bully Boy had beaten Francis Britt, "Pride of Ashland," in a match which lasted 134 rounds.

Despite the admiration he was able to elicit not only from the loyal friends he led but also from some of the town's most respectable citizens, the Bully Boy was not a particularly savory character. He had been arrested on numerous occasions for various charges including burglary, assault, and mayhem. In Ashland, scene of his boxing triumph, he was once caught stealing pigs. He jumped bail and fled to Ohio until some prominent Modocs settled the case amicably.

Why he should have joined forces with Jesse and William Major, the late Burgess's brothers, to avenge the chief's death, is something of a mystery. The only time Bully Boy ever spent in jail was at the hands of William Major, who arrested him, charged him with drunk and disorderly conduct, and "sent him down for thirty days."

Thomas and the remaining Major brothers were in total disagreement with the verdict rendered in Dougherty's favor by the jury, declaring on many occasions that if they ever got their hands on Dan Dougherty, they'd "kill the Molly son-of-a-bitch." In violation of his Constitutional rights, Dougherty was being placed in double jeopardy.

Understandably disturbed by the unfortunate turn of events following his acquittal, Dan, still a member in good standing of the A.O.H., complained to his bodymaster, demanding protection. Word was passed to Shenandoah Division headquarters and from there to Jack Kehoe. A few days later McParlan was ordered to appear at the Hibernian House.

"On Wednesday, May twenty-sixth, I was called to Girardville to see Jack Kehoe. It was a damned lucky thing for me I was available. I'd spent the night before up the mountain at Frackville with my little friend and I'd just got back to Mother Cooney's in time to get a message from King Kehoe. I'd have had a devil of a time explaining to this high-minded gentleman what I'd been doing—courting a decent Irish lass and at the same time bedding a Polack.

"Jack was very friendly and asked me if I'd had anything to eat. When I told him 'No' he said, 'Well, come upstairs, and Mrs. Kehoe'll fix you a bite.' So I did. Now Mrs. Kehoe was a fine woman and knew nothing about her husband's activities and wouldn't have believed it anyway no matter if Father McDermott told her. Jack sat with me and had a cup of tea, and then we went downstairs together where we could talk in private."

The detective followed Kehoe to the room back of the Hibernian House bar and the two sat at a table, a bottle of whiskey between them.

"Jack wasn't much of a drinker," McParlan continued, "but I sure needed the hair of the dog—I'd had a rough night of it.

" 'I'm troubled,' he said, 'over the bad state of affairs in Mahanoy City. I was there a couple days ago and the Modocs are raising the mischief. At first I thought I'd call a county meeting, give the boys pistols and challenge the Modocs to a fight. We'd shoot them down in the daytime. Then we'd find out who was boss. But on second thought I don't like that idea.'

"I didn't think for one moment," McParlan continued, "that a man as smart as Jack Kehoe ever had any intention of showing his hand so openly. He was just blowing off steam while I waited patiently for him to come out with what he really had in mind.

" 'I'm calling the meeting, all right,' he said. 'I sent Tom Donohue to Locust Gap to tell Denny Canning to meet all of us in Mahanoy City, Tuesday, June first. But Denny's away, there was a death in the family at Pittsburgh. So you're going to have to take his place as my representative if I can't make it.'

"I wasn't looking this gift horse in the mouth but I did try to figure out why I was getting the 'honor' which belonged rightfully to Muff. The only reason I could see was that ever since the Gomer James schedule was messed up, Kehoe was sore at Lawler and showed it by imposing authority on me.

"I could understand where it was important for Jack to settle this Modoc thing over in Mahanoy. If he didn't, word would spread around the regions pretty soon that the Mollies were weakening. They'd be clobbered by everybody who hated them but were scared to death to do anything as long as our boyos were riding high.

"Kehoe told me to go over to Mahanoy City and find out how many 'good shooters' they'd need to get rid of Bully Boy and at least one of the Majors."

On Friday, May 28, the detective met Michael O'Brien, McParlan's corollary in Bodymaster Clarke's division. If four competent death merchants were furnished, O'Brien was certain a "clane job" was assured. Details of fingering, etc., would be developed, Secretary O'Brien said, at the June 1 conclave.

On Sunday, May 30, after attending early Mass in Shenandoah where he heard Father O'Reilly denounce the Molly Maguires, the detective went to Girardville to report the results of his conference with Brother O'Brien of Mahanoy City.

When he reached the Hibernian House, McParlan found Kehoe in a fury. The Girardville bodymaster had just come home from late Mass and he, too, had been subjected to a tirade against his organization, delivered with considerable effect by Father Bridgman. To make matters worse, King Kehoe said bitterly, "Some of the people I've been feeding and protecting gave me dirty looks after church."

As it turned out Kehoe was able to attend the June 1 meeting himself with nobody in active attendance except bodymasters and other high officers.

"I was in a hell of a sweat," the detective recalled. "I had a big report to turn in to Mr. Franklin and I was getting suspicious of the mail clerk on the Shenandoah branch of the Reading where I'd been sticking my letters. I decided I'd have to go all the way over to Delano and put them on the Lehigh and this is what I did with the one I couldn't wait to get out of my hands.

"So when I got to Clarke's, I was a few minutes late. It was midnight and Mickey had closed the saloon early that evening, so the place was quiet and dark except for one light upstairs. A guard was standing in the shadow of the side door. He flashed his lantern in my face. He knew damned well who I was, but nobody, not even Kehoe, could get by unless they knew the latest 'goods.'

"I gave him the recognition sign—my forefinger of my right hand in the left sleeve and then the password, 'What is your opinion of Tipperary's election?' and listened to his answer, 'I think England broke her Constitution by Mitchell's rejection. He let me in.

"When I got to the meeting room Jack stopped talking for a second to give me a hard look. I shrugged my shoulders and sat down, and then he went on to brief the boys about his plans, to ask them for suggestions and to estimate conditions in Schuylkill County."

Among those supposed to be present was Dan Dougherty. But Dougherty failed to receive a summons and did not answer when his name was called. This inefficiency irked Jack Kehoe, who ordered his bailiffs to find the witness and bring him to the meeting at once.

"Two men," McParlan said, "went right out and fetched Dan, who was sleeping at his boarding house. Dan showed us one or two bullet holes in his coat, somewhere up by the shoulder, and stated that he believed Jesse Major was the man that shot him, and he had come to the conclusion that probabilities were that the Majors were going to kill him. If they didn't Bully Boy Bill would, and the only way he'd have any peace, he said, would be to put the Majors and Thomas out of the way.

"After Dougherty left, Kehoe called for suggestions from the floor. Donnelly said he'd be happy to furnish two men who'd do a 'clane job' on the Majors if he were told where the brothers could be found. O'Brien then reported that the Majors were working the Buck vein in Tuscarora. He warned Donnelly, however, that the Majors were always heavily armed and were rarely alone. Kehoe gave the nod to Donnelly and the assignment was his."

Next on the agenda was the disposal of Bully Boy.

"There was some question about Donnelly handling this one, too," McParlan recalled, "but Donohue objected. He said it wasn't fair—that he and Donnelly would take care of their side

129

of the mountain if we took care of ours. Somebody suggested that a couple of men shoot Bully Boy in broad daylight right on Center Street in Mahanoy City in front of everybody. O'Brien tabled this one and said that Thomas ought to be killed by a pair of men who'd lay waiting for him on the side of the railroad tracks near his home in Shoemaker's Patch just east of the town.

"Canning made the motion that we accept O'Brien's idea, somebody seconded it and it was passed. Then Jack looked down and said it was up to me, Roarity and O'Brien to take care of the matter.

"The usual procedure then would be for us to ask a bodymaster from the farthest place to furnish the men. In this case this meant Canning. He agreed and said that funds to board his boys while the job was being done would have to come from the county treasury."

But Treasurer Donnelly, to whom a public office was a public trust, refused.

"This is light work," he said. "Do it yourselves." Kehoe agreed, thereby closing the discussion.

One small but pressing matter had to be disposed of before the meeting could be adjourned. Jerry Callahan, it was reported convincingly, had stolen a box of cigars from his Cass Township bodymaster.

"There wasn't any discussion about that," said McParlan. "*All the boys were shocked.*"

For this flagrant violation of Molly Maguire honor, it is pleasant to report that Callahan was expelled forthwith and could no longer enjoy the rights, privileges, and protection of the Brotherhood.

Chapter Twenty

The sun had not yet risen on Monday, June 28, 1875, when four men, three dressed in black and the fourth wearing a light poncho, dropped to the ground from a freight train when it slowed down near the east end of Mahanoy City.

From this point they strode purposefully along a narrow path toward Shoemaker's Patch and the colliery from which it got its name. Here the men hid themselves in the mouth of a coal drift. From beneath his jacket, each of the four would-be assassins removed a pistol, cocked it, and waited in the stillness of the early morning. The men were John Gibbons, John Morris, Thomas Hurley, and Michael Doyle, members of the Shenandoah Division A.O.H., Michael Lawler, Bodymaster. Their quarry was the Bully Boy.

Thomas was a hostler and a good one. O'Brien and those who fingered Thomas said Bully Boy would arrive at the colliery stable shortly before 6 A.M. after walking along the road over which the quartet had traveled. But Bully Boy, warned of his imminent danger through McParlan's reports to Superintendent Franklin, had been using a back shortcut. Unseen by his stalkers, he reached his job in safety.

Actually Thomas needed no warning from McParlan or anyone else. He was certain that from the moment he decided to avenge George Major's murder he was marked for execution. He did not hold the Molly Maguires in contempt; he knew very well what had happened to George Major and countless others who had in some way offended a "brother." It was simply that Bully Boy had complete confidence in his ability to protect himself.

Thomas got his first glimpse of the quartet at about 6:20.

"I was leading a horse from the blacksmith shop to the stable," he said, "when I looked over at the drift mouth that was about thirty yards off. There I seen some men sitting quietly but I paid them no attention. I went to the stable and was talking to the stable boss.

"There is a kind of track where the blacksmith shop turns around to the breaker as it goes up. I noticed them coming around. I looked over again. One of them had a whitish coat on and his two hands in the coat pockets. I turned my head and saw the stable boss, and I heard a gun fired and I was shot, and I saw this fellow with the white coat with a piece in his hand, silver mounted.

"I jumped towards him; I had my hands on his revolver when he fired again and I was shot in the fingers. Just then another fellow came up and pulled me and I got two shots in the back."

Bully Boy dropped to the ground, still struggling, and grabbed the legs of an assailant. He was dragging him along the floor when a bullet hit him in the chest; another passed through his arm and still another lodged in his thigh. Thomas loosened his grip and crawled through the straw toward one of the stalls. He placed his arm on a horse's neck and collapsed, although he never lost consciousness completely. One horse was shot in the leg and another was killed by stray bullets.

The stable boss, who had fled through a rear door the moment the men walked in, now returned, summoned additional help and carried Thomas to the surgery.

Gibbons, Morris, Hurley, and Doyle, believing Thomas dead, separated and walked one by one down the streets of Mahanoy City to Mrs. McDonald's boarding house on West Center Street. There they washed the blood from their hands and clothing, ate breakfast, and went to sleep for the balance of the morning and afternoon.

By the time the quartet reached Shenandoah that evening, still thinking Bully Boy was dead, McParlan, officially in charge of the job, had been informed not only of the shooting but also that Thomas was alive.

"It was hard to believe he could have been so stupid. I *know* he was warned, not once but a couple times. I was at Muff's bar having a drink with Frank McAndrew when the fellows came in to report. They thought Bully Boy was gone, and I had to tell them he wasn't.

" 'That tough son-of-a-bitch,' Hurley said, quite annoyed. 'He threw his hat in my face and spoiled my aim. What'll Jack say now?'

"They got sick thinking about Kehoe and wanted to turn around, head for Mahanoy and kill Thomas *and* Dr. Bissel. I had a hard time keeping them back but I told them the place would be filled with militia. I had half a mind to let them go ahead and try it and see if they could be caught red-handed. Then we'd have had the kind of evidence that would have held up in court.

"But I couldn't take that chance, not only because they just might get away with it but because Kehoe would have taken away my authority if I permitted that crazy kind of action. I just told the boys to wait till I found out what the next step would be."

Three days elapsed before McParlan was ordered to report to the Hibernian House bringing John Morris with him. Kehoe did not know Morris.

"On Sunday, July fourth," McParlan said, "I went to Girardville in company with Morris and Frank McAndrew in a buggy and McAndrew introduced Morris to Kehoe.

"Jack told him right off he was sorry the job was not done right, and then to my surprise he said, 'Well, I suppose it was the best you could do.' Jack gave Morris some money for himself and a few dollars for the others and then dismissed Morris and Frank to the bar. I stayed with Jack.

"He didn't say anything for a couple of minutes, then he looked me right square in the eye and said, 'Your jobs aren't so clane now, are they, McKenna?' I didn't answer but I looked him right back. Then he says, 'All right, you can go.' I don't think he really was suspicious yet but I did think he'd be watching me a bit closer from then on. And I knew he wasn't telling me as much of what was planned as he might have. I found that out.

"I didn't know it at the time, but Kehoe was better satisfied

133

that they hadn't killed the Bully Boy. He reasoned it this way, that if Thomas got better, he'd be so scared he'd quit the Modocs and run away with his tail between his legs, and that would be the end of the Welsh. He didn't give Bully Boy enough credit."

Less than five days after he'd been seriously wounded, the hostler was well enough to talk with Captain Linden. Not only did Bully Boy intend to remain in Mahanoy City, he was planning retaliation and hoped to lead twenty armed Modocs into Clarke's saloon and shoot up the place.

Linden urged Thomas to do nothing and said that if Bully Boy tried to retaliate, he, Linden, would be the first to arrest the hostler and the Modocs he led. The policeman was able to elicit a statement in which Bully Boy gave an excellent description of two of his assailants, although he did not recognize either.

The Captain, however, having seen McParlan's report of the shooting, realized that the hostler was describing Gibbons and Hurley. When the time came for an arrest and trial, he knew this would be invaluable corroborative evidence. President Gowen, Major Pinkerton, and Superintendent Franklin, however, had no intention of arresting a single Molly until the net could be spread to embrace bodymasters and other leaders of the secret society as well as brothers who had participated in past homicides and lesser felonies.

If McParlan had any thoughts of relaxing with his Polish barmaid on Sunday night, they were diverted by news of still another brutal attack. This was the murder of a Tamaqua policeman, shot to death by the Molly Maguires because he had had the effrontery to arrest a lodge member in good standing.

The dead man was Patrolman Benjamin Yost, a quiet, conscientious forty-four-year-old Civil War veteran and the father of two sons. Yost's brother-in-law was Tamaqua's wealthiest citizen, Dan Shepp. Included among those whom Shepp considered his friends was Powderkeg Kerrigan, who visited the mine owner's home many times.

About six o'clock on the evening of July 5, 1875, Yost, his supper over, prepared to make his rounds. He first cautioned his two boys to be careful with their "shooting crackers," leftovers from an Independence Day celebration. He put on his long blue jacket and white hat, strapped a pistol to his right side (he was left-handed), adjusted his night stick, kissed his wife, Henrietta, and went out to meet his partner. Although Yost was a German, a Mason, and a Lutheran, he got along well with his partner, Barney McCarron, who was Irish and a devout Roman Catholic, but not a Molly Maguire. The two men made a good team and their presence on the streets of Tamaqua helped to keep the town reasonably free from noise, rowdiness, and violence.

About eight o'clock, Mrs. Yost, with the dishes washed, the kitchen "redded up," and her two small sons in bed if not asleep, sat rocking on the front porch with a neighbor whose husband was a justice of the peace. They had been gossiping quietly for perhaps fifteen minutes when Thomas Duffy passed by. He paid no attention to the women, but they certainly were aware of him.

Until he was out of earshot neither housewife said anything. Then Mrs. Yost fearfully turned to her neighbor and said, in German since neither spoke English, "I wonder what Tom Duffy is doing? I hope he's not out to hurt Ben."

There was sound reason for Mrs. Yost's concern for her husband's safety. About three months before, Duffy had attacked the policeman with a fifteen-inch Bowie knife when Yost attempted to arrest him for drunk and disorderly conduct on the steps of the United States Hotel. McCarron had hurried to his partner's rescue. At the same time, Kerrigan (who, some witnesses said, had been Duffy's companion all evening) declared, "I saw what was happening and tried to break it up. I never liked Yost much but his brother-in-law Dan Shepp's a good friend of mine and I wouldn't want anything to happen to any of his kin."

In the melee that followed, Duffy was badly beaten. As both patrolmen were dragging him to the local lockup, their prisoner turned to Yost and shouted, "I'll get you for this, you Dutch son-of-a-bitch!" Brought before the justice of the peace two days later, Duffy was found guilty of disorderly conduct and resisting arrest, and fined $10 and costs. He paid the levy, glared at Yost for a moment, and strode out, slamming the door hard behind him.

At the magistrate's nod, Yost rushed after Duffy, grabbed him by the shoulders, and pulled him back to the courtroom where he stood in front of the bench again. "You walk out of here and shut the door quiet or I'll send you up for thirty days," the justice of the peace ordered. Duffy obeyed, but not before giving Yost a look of pure hatred.

Duffy's guiding thought for the next few months was revenge. In this he was abetted by both his bodymaster, Alex Campbell, and his friend, Powderkeg Kerrigan. Campbell felt that the only way to assuage the partly-tarnished honor of the local division and restore its falling prestige in the eyes of Tamaqua's citizenry, was to kill the man who had humiliated Brother Duffy. Kerrigan's motives were more subtle. Always a cynic, it is doubtful if he ever cared much for anybody's honor, least of all his own; he had no particular dislike for Yost and probably egged Duffy on simply because he enjoyed mischief-making.

Because the affair was considered regional rather than county-wide, and because Alex Campbell enjoyed autonomy, neither Kehoe nor Muff Lawler, both busy with their own activities, was consulted about Yost's impending assassination. Consequently McParlan never had any "official" information of Yost's impending doom. The detective knew about Duffy's "throuble," of course, and was aware that the indignity would be avenged. But until it was too late he never found out when it would happen. Perhaps if he had not been investigating Bully Boy's attack, he might have saved the patrolman's life. There never was any question that Yost would be murdered. It was merely a matter of proper timing. Campbell had a far better reputation than Muff Lawler for "clane jobs."

Despite the impatient Duffy's constant demands for "satisfaction," Campbell held back until he was sure proper circumstances had developed. When James Roarity, Coaldale bodymaster, offered to "return the favor" if Campbell would handle an execution for Roarity, the deal was made. In exchange for the assassination of John P. Jones, general superintendent of the Lehigh and Wilkes-Barre Coal Company, Roarity would guarantee to dispose of Patrolman Yost.

Campbell, the better bargainer of the two bodymasters, was able to persuade Roarity to complete his part of the bargain before the Tamaqua Division disposed of Superintendent Jones.

Jones had fired one Hugh McGehan for insubordination and had blacklisted him throughout the coal regions as a "chronic troublemaker." Whether Jones's accusation was just was never determined. But when the superintendent called McGehan a "drunken bum" he was being unfair. The twenty-one-year-old McGehan, who supported an alcoholic father, never took a drink of liquor in his life and despite his truculence was a hard worker.

Until his dismissal and subsequent inability to find work, McGehan's reputation was good. But, soon after he was discharged, McGehan applied for and was admitted to membership in the Coaldale Division, James Roarity, Bodymaster.

McGehan, whose family was near starvation, nurtured an ever-increasing hatred for Jones. So when Roarity asked the new brother if he would be willing to help kill a Tamaqua policeman in return for the execution of Superintendent Jones, McGehan acquiesced. As a gesture of goodwill, Roarity himself agreed to become one of the participants.

Campbell, a stickler for details, advised Roarity that the bare minimum for a "clane job" would be three. This did not include Kerrigan, who was delighted to volunteer for the safe and pleasant task of fingerman. The Coaldale bodymaster was to furnish the two actual killers. Roarity chose James Boyle, a steady, loyal young Lansford brother, to team with McGehan as gunmen. James Carroll, a Tamaqua saloonkeeper and potential bodymaster should Campbell move up a step and become county delegate, was named to develop the escape route and perfect alibis if they became necessary.

On the morning of July 5, Boyle and McGehan arrived at Tamaqua in separate railroad coaches. Each man made his own way from the station to Carroll's Union Hotel, where the pair remained in an upstairs room with drawn shutters. During the course of the afternoon, Kerrigan joined them, bringing a fresh bottle of whiskey although he himself drank none.

At four o'clock, Powderkeg peered through the slats of one window and looked down on Lehigh Street. "Here he comes, boys," he said turning to Boyle and McGehan and relinquishing his place to the hired killers. "The one on the inside is Yost."

Powderkeg, his pleasurable task accomplished, left the Union Hotel and walked east. A few moments afterward he saw Yost, McCarron, and Dan Shepp talking together on a street corner. He paused to nod affably to all three, then made his way into the Columbia House where Campbell stood behind his bar. In answer to the bodymaster's raised eyebrows, Powderkeg nodded his head. Understanding smiles, a thin cold one on Campbell's lips, a cheerful grin on Powderkeg's, passed between the two men.

It was nearly ten o'clock before darkness fell on Tamaqua's streets and brought relief from the summer heat. At midnight, Carroll opened the door of the room which Kerrigan had quitted eight hours earlier. Making sure the shutters were drawn, he lighted a kerosene lamp and woke the sleeping men. From his pocket Carroll extracted the murder weapons, his own shiny .32 caliber pistol and Roarity's heavy, black .44 caliber pistol. McGehan chose the lighter weapon, examined it carefully, and thrust it into his pocket. Boyle concealed the other pistol in the folds of his coat.

At one-thirty, Kerrigan returned to the killers' room. Without speaking, he beckoned to the two men. Boyle and McGehan followed, walking softly down a flight of rear stairs into a pitch black alley in the rear of the hotel. Single file—Kerrigan in the lead, Boyle with his hand on Powderkeg's shoulder, McGehan last with an arm stretched out to touch Boyle's back—the trio groped its way through the darkness.

At the first intersection they turned toward Lehigh Street, where a lamp high up on a pole dimly lit the deserted road below. Keeping in the shadows, Kerrigan led the little procession across the intersection. There he turned to the right, the two assassins close behind. A hundred yards ahead Kerrigan stopped in front of the Lutheran Cemetery, opened an iron gate and motioned to Boyle and McGehan to follow.

Hidden behind a Civil War memorial the three had a clear view of Lehigh Street in both directions. Overhead, almost directly in front of them, was a street lamp. Three hundred yards to the right was a second one, and about the same distance from that a third was faintly visible.

"In a half hour," Kerrigan whispered, "Yost will outen the far light. He'll be on this side of the road. McCarron will be on the opposite side of the street, about a couple hundred feet behind. Then they'll both cross over and Yost will patrol the other side while McCarron outens the second light. When they get to the one right here, Yost will climb up his ladder to outen this. It's the last.

"Now come out quiet but mind you keep your backs to the left side of the street because Yost's house is only twenty-five feet away and his wife usually looks out the window to see if Ben's coming home all right. Get him when he gets near the top of the pole. You'll see his face in the light. When he drops, shoot out the light. By the time McCarron runs over to help, Yost ought to be dead and you should be running away. You know where to go."

"What do we do if McCarron sees us before we get off?" Boyle asked.

"Then kill him, too!" Kerrigan snarled.

At this point Powderkeg presumably left for home. But he could not resist the bloody drama he knew would follow shortly and hid behind a tree thirty yards away, where he could escape the moment the fatal shots were fired.

"A little after two o'clock," wrote James Rhodes in the *American Historical Review*, "Yost went to the lamp-post, placed his ladder against it, began to climb the ladder, heard footsteps behind him, and turned around to see who was coming . . . As he turned, McGehan reached up and shot him in the right side. Yost fell off . . . exclaiming, 'Oh my God! I'm shot, my wife!' "

McCarron, a few hundred feet to the rear on the opposite side of the road, heard the first shot break the silence of the night. Before the second bullet was fired, this one piercing Yost's neck, McCarron was only thirty yards away; he saw his partner drop to the ground.

Another shot rang out, aimed at the lamp; it struck the post and the lantern revealed two men dressed in somber clothing, fleeing into the darkness. McCarron fired his pistol at the fugitives, then hurried to Yost's side.

"Are you hurt bad, Ben?" McCarron asked.

"I am indeed," was his partner's reply. "Get my missus right away, will you?"

But Yost's wife was already on her way.

"Leaning out the window," continued the *American Historical Review,* "she saw him climbing the ladder, saw the flash of the pistol, heard that and a second report, the scream of her husband, the sound of retreating footsteps, and, rushing downstairs and out, found him mortally wounded.

" 'Give me a kiss,' he said. 'I have to die.' "

By this time house lamps were going on all around, and within a few minutes the street was filled with men and women, some clad only in bed-clothes. A passer-by woke Dr. E. J. Solliday, who lived only a short distance away, and someone else called Dan Shepp. The physician, Yost's brother-in-law, and Mrs. Shepp arrived at almost the same moment.

Yost was carried to his home. Dr. Solliday stopped the flow of blood; there was little else he could do.

"Can you tell us anything, Ben?" McCarron asked.

Yost shook his head. "Only that Duffy wasn't one of them. There was two, and I never seen either of them before but they looked like Irishmen."

After this the policeman lapsed into a coma. He gained consciousness around noon but spoke only a few intelligible words, in German. Mrs. Yost, who never left the wounded man's side, told McCarron that nothing her husband said made sense. By ten that night, Patrolman Yost was dead.

Chapter Twenty-One

McParlan learned of Yost's murder within hours, but the detective, in the midst of his investigation of Bully Boy's assault, determined to continue with it until he had completed his work, unless Superintendent Franklin ordered him to Tamaqua.

"I stayed right on with the Thomas shooting," he said, "until July fourteenth. Mr. Franklin knew what I was doing and let me alone, although they must have been howling for something on Yost. It took me only ten days to clean up the Thomas case. I had the whole story by then, names, dates, and places and I could tie in Kehoe, Muff, and a half-dozen others. But I didn't know if any of it would stand up in court. I needed corroborative evidence. I had some but I didn't have enough.

"Anyway this was the best and the fattest report I ever wrote, and then, by God, I almost got caught before I got the envelope out of my hands."

McParlan had established his right to considerable freedom, and could move around almost as much as he wanted to. This enabled him to continue sending his reports to Philadelphia from Delano where he dropped the letters in the train at the railroad station of the village, eleven miles east of Shenandoah.

He spent all the night of July 13 in his bedroom at Cooney's writing the most detailed report (forty-four pages) he had ever made. On the evening of July 14, a fat envelope concealed beneath his coat, McParlan left for Delano.

"I got there about ten o'clock," the detective recalled, "about a half hour before the Philadelphia train was due. This is a sleepy little town and by nine nearly everybody's in bed. There's a saloon a couple hundred yards across the tracks run by a fellow named Joey Hennessy. He's no Molly—in fact Delano's a German and English town, with no Brothers. But once in a while some of the boys'll drop in to Hennessy's place so I figured I'd better stay out.

"It's damned dark except for one light in the depot. I'm not anxious to be seen, not that I expect anybody to be walking around, so I'm standing well back in the shadows. I figure I've got about five minutes more to wait for the train and I'm getting a little impatient. So I walk over to the tracks, still in the shadows, and go to bend down and put my ear on the rail and listen.

"Just as I lower my head, I feel something whistling over it and smash into the bushes on the other side. I straighten up, hop to one side, still in the darkness, and the next second some guys jump me.

"I'm no novice at this so I throw one of them over my shoulder and he lands on the track; I can hear his head crack on the rail and he's out. I can't figure how many of them there are so I move toward the light. I see there's only one other. He's a pretty big son-of-a-bitch and he's trying to get his arms around my neck and if he does I'm finished.

"I don't know who he is but I'm thinking he might know me so I don't want him to see my face. I turn around with my back to the light and at the same time I let loose, giving it all I got. I kick him square in the groin and the fight's out of him. He yells with pain, dropped to the ground. I take out my pistol and crack his skull with the butt end and put him to sleep."

By this time McParlan could hear the locomotive whistle in the distance.

"I didn't want a murder on my hands so I ran along the tracks and nearly stumbled over the guy I'd tossed there. He was still out. I dragged him to the light and I almost dropped dead when I saw he was Jackie Leary from Lost Creek, one of Pat Butler's boys. Pat's the bodymaster.

"Jackie knew me well and even if he couldn't read himself, you can imagine what would have happened to me if he'd found the envelope addressed to Mr. Franklin and turned it over to somebody who *could* read.

"The pair must have been drinking over at Hennessey's, then came over to the station hoping to roll a drunk when they saw me in the shadows. I was sure they hadn't recognized me. I pulled the big guy, who I didn't know, back of the station and then I dragged Jackie there. By then the mail train came along and I dropped the report in the box on the side of the mail car. Nobody could see my face so I felt I was safe. But it was awful close."

McParlan arrived in Tamaqua on July 15 and went directly to Alex Campbell's. No sooner had he ordered his first drink when Johnny Murphy, the bartender, winked at him, and bending over whispered, "Do you see that man sitting by himself over at the corner table? You can look now he's not watching."

McParlan turned around for a moment, then faced Murphy; shrugged his shoulders and lifted his eyebrows questioningly.

"He's a detective," Murphy said, and McParlan had all he could do to keep his face expressionless. "Dan Shepp hired him to find out who done the job on his brother-in-law. He don't think we know who he is and the boys have been filling him full of bullshit. Every day they tell him a different story and get some free drinks. Why don't you try it?"

But McParlan had no intention of taking a chance that this stranger might recognize him and inadvertently give him away.

"I wasn't playing games," McParlan said. "I thought the best thing for all of us was to get this fellow off my neck. He could spoil things for me and besides, if the Mollies got tired of playing cat and mouse they'd swallow him alive.

"So I wrote to Mr. Franklin about it and a couple of days later the fellow wasn't around anymore. He was a detective, all right, from Philly, and Dan Shepp *had* hired him. I doubt if he found out anything about the killing but I know damned well *I* did."

Within forty-eight hours, McParlan learned almost every detail of Yost's murder, the participants, and the *modus operandi*. Even though he knew the policeman's slaying was to be followed by another, he could not find out who was to be killed as a "return of the favor." Not even Powderkeg, who proudly showed McParlan the death weapon, would talk on this point. All McParlan could deduce was that the intended victim was an Eastern Schuylkill County or Carbon County boss who had offended a Molly within the past few months. Obviously this covered considerable territory and could have included practically every supervisor in the area.

While McParlan hoped that by now he had furnished enough data to arrest and convict Molly leaders, he realized that much of the evidence he had compiled would not hold up in court without his own testimony. But at no time had he said he would mount the witness stand, a condition agreed to by Major Pinkerton and understood both by Gowen and Franklin.

The detective was afraid his luck was running out. He wanted to wind up his tour of duty in the hard coal regions and get away while he was still alive.

"I'd had two close ones and I wasn't anxious for a third. I sent in my report on Yost to Mr. Franklin and suggested I be relieved. My nerves were pretty good yet but I'd been on this job for over a year and I was beginning to get to the point where if I didn't want to crack up I'd either have to take a little time off or go sour."

But neither Gowen nor Pinkerton was ready to relieve McParlan or give him a respite. Captain Linden was instructed to drop all other duties and stay as close to the little Irishman as he could without arousing suspicion.

Near the end of July, Linden made his presence known to McParlan.

"Late one afternoon Powderkeg, Mary, and I were walking down Pine Street in Tamaqua," the detective recalled. "I was restless and I'd been carrying a feeling of uneasiness for a couple of weeks. All of a sudden, out of nowhere, comes a welcome sight. It's Captain Linden all by himself. He crosses over and stops right in front of us. He pays no attention to me or Kerrigan but takes off his hat and bends down to Mary.

" 'Young lady,' he says, 'I hope you know what you're doing.

These men you're with are about the two worst bums in the county.'

"Mary's getting red in the face and about to speak up in our defense when the Captain stops her.

" 'Never mind any answers,' he says. 'I _know_ what I'm talking about.' Then he turns to Powderkeg. 'Kerrigan,' he says, 'we all know you and you know us and furthermore you know why I'm here. I can't prove it yet but I think you're mixed up somehow in Yost's murder. If you are I'll track you down, I promise.'

"Then he turns to me. 'McKenna,' he says, 'you're a bad actor. I never liked you and I never will. But I want you to know this. I've got my eyes on you and I'm going to watch what you do. Just remember, I'm never going to be far from you from now on.'

"Then he turned around and walked away before any of us could answer. Mary blew off some steam but Kerrigan said nothing and gave me one of his queer looks. To tell you the truth I don't know if he was fooled. I yelled a bit about my rights being abused and that I'd get Linden some day. Inside myself it was good to realize he'd be sticking around. I didn't know how I'd ever be able to reach him when things got too tough but I persuaded myself the Captain'ld find a way. I went back to work feeling a lot better, I can tell you."

There was no lack of work for the detective. On August 12, another Girardville member of the judiciary signed his own death warrant. That day, Squire Thomas Gwyther, an aged Welsh justice of the peace, ordered the arrest of Billy B. Love (an obvious misnomer), charging him with drunk and disorderly conduct.

On August 14, at 3 P.M. Love stepped around a corner onto the town's busiest intersection, pulled a revolver from his pocket and, in the presence of at least a dozen witnesses, fired three shots into the elderly Welshman. Gwyther died at once. Love calmly wiped off the pistol and put it back into his pocket. Then, he walked away; so did the witnesses. Love was never again seen.

Less than nine hours later, a more "important" murder took

place. This one erased an old stain from the Molly Maguire escutcheon. One year and three days after Gomer James killed Brother Edward Cosgrove on the streets of Shenandoah, the Welshman was himself assassinated.

The murder was well planned; and to all who understood the operations of the Molly Maguires, it was inevitable. The only one who thought it could not happen was the victim.

The annual picnic of Shenandoah's Rescue Hook & Ladder Company began early on August 14, 1875, at Heckscher's Grove.

"The clarion tones of the brass band broke the stillness of the morning air," reported Tamaqua historians Eveland and Harris. "Soon the Fire Company, in its gaudy trappings, red shirts and burnished helmets, came out from their quarters and, preceded by the band, commenced their parade; the procession moved through the principal streets of the town and thence to the pleasure grounds, followed by the populace.

"All were intent on a day's enjoyment, full of hilarity, no one dreaming that the day, ushered in under such happy auspices, was destined to close in blood, and bring sorrow to many a heart, through one of the most dastardly murders that ever disgraced the coal region."

By 10 A.M. all the wooden tables scattered throughout the grounds had been "reserved" by large wooden food hampers placed upon them. The aroma of fresh coffee brewed over open fires soon filled the air. There was swimming in a nearby creek which had been damned and during the afternoon contests were run—three-legged races, burlap bag races, a climb up the larded pole, pursuit and capture of a greased pig, and tugs of war.

"The old folks, gathered in groups," continued Messrs. Eveland and Harris, "and watching the merry revelers, seemed to take a retrospect through the dim vista of years and live over again the days of their youth. Those genially inclined resorted to the stands and drank many a health to each other . . .

"The young men and maidens tripped the light fantastic toe to the sweet music of the quadrille band or joined in the game of copenhagen, all vying with each other in the effort to extract as much of pleasure as possible from the fleeting moments."

After supper there were fireworks, and then the women and

children were sent home. The time for serious drinking had begun.

In back of one of the many temporary wooden bars, Gomer James, stripped to the waist, deftly slapped open the spigots of barreled lager, filled seidels of beer as quickly as he could, and almost in one motion slid the shiny glasses of foaming brew over the wet counters to be grasped by eager hands.

Off to one side, in a circle formed by a group of drinkers holding rapidly emptying glasses, talented thirteen-year-old Pat Scanlon danced jigs for enthusiastic spectators. At the end of each number, Pat bowed and his audience tossed him pennies. Then, before he began his next act, Pat stooped down to gather the scattered coins, which he placed in a large leather bag.

"The bag was near full," recalled Pat to Tom Barrett, "and I'm down on the ground picking up a few stray ones when all of a sudden I'm not alone.

"I don't know what's happened so I stand up. I'm the only one around on me feet. The next thing I hear is a shot over by the bar and my God! you should have seen the men scatter. I'm still standing, too scared to move. Then I seen Tom Hurley, a friend of me father's, with a pistol in his hand plug the big Welshman they called Gomer.

"He hits him once, and he hits him again, and the Welshman goes down behind the counter. Then I seen Tom reach over and plug Gomer again.

"Everybody but me is running like crazy or laying on the ground. And I'm standing there like I'm hypnotized. Hurley looks all around, sees me, and starts moving. He gives me a look I'll never forget. Then he says, 'Kid, if you ever open your mouth about what you seen here this day, you're as good as dead.'

"And I never opened me mouth and told what I seen that day for seventy years, Tom, and you'll print nothing of this 'till I've passed on."

Pat Scanlon, a song and dance man in traveling medicine shows for almost three-quarters of a century, died in Shenandoah on December 7, 1948, thus releasing the *Herald's* current editor from a promise he kept faithfully.

Unquestionably Hurley could have used Scanlon's testimony at a Molly Maguire county convention held in Tamaqua a few days after the murder. On the agenda was the award of prizes for brothers who, in the past few months, had done "clane jobs."

Procedure for this important part of the session was handled in accordance with strict parliamentary rules. The claimant, who could usually neither read nor write, first dictated his statement to Secretary James McKenna. The latter, in turn, passed it to Jack Kehoe, presiding officer. Then, if there were no objections from the floor, the Girardville bodymaster certified the brother's deposition, noted the amount due, and turned it over to Brother Donnelly, the county treasurer, for payment. Since no medals were struck all prizes were cash. Their value ranged from fifty cents, presumably for a "messy job," to ten dollars, which signified an award of real merit.

But to his righteous indignation, Tom's claim was challenged a moment after it was presented.

"You're a liar, Brother Hurley!" shouted Lost Creek Bodymaster Pat Butler when he got the floor. "That job was done by one of me own men, Eddie McClain. Stand up, Eddie, and tell them how you done it."

To McParlan's shock, the big, powerful man who arose was the brother who'd attacked him at the Delano railroad station a month before.

"It was a hell of a sensation," McParlan recalled. "I didn't think he'd recognize me but I wasn't sure. Well, he hadn't the slightest idea he'd ever seen me before and since he and his buddy got the worst of that one, I'm sure they never breathed a word to anyone.

"Well, McClain pressed his claim hard and said he'd be glad to produce the pistol that done such a 'nice clane job,' and that he had plenty of witnesses."

Despite the fact that Hurley, in rebuttal, swore "by my dear departed mother's grave" that he really did the job, a motion to withhold payment of the award was passed. Kehoe appointed McParlan and Butler to investigate the conflicting claims.

"We met in Shenandoah one Sunday," McParlan recollected.

"McClain didn't show up and neither did his witnesses. Hurley was there and he brought three brothers who said they saw Hurley shoot Gomer. We sent Tom out of the room and made our decision. The blood money went to Brother Hurley."

Chapter Twenty-Two

Emotions of the brothers were mixed on the evening of August 21, 1875, when Michael Lawler, presiding, called to order the regular monthly meeting of the A.O.H., Shenandoah Division.

Cheers followed the bodymaster's announcement that the Old Man (Governor Hartranft), keeping his promise to Jack Kehoe, had pressured the pardon board into freeing two imprisoned brothers who had held political jobs. Not all members were impressed by the Chief Executive's clemency, however, when it was considered that the crimes for which the pair had been convicted were no more serious than malfeasance, misfeasance, and embezzlement. A prior charge of homicide had been *nolle-prossed* without any aid from Pennsylvania's governor.

But all brothers were united in their fury at Tom Foster. That morning the editor of the *Weekly Herald* began publication of his new paper, the *Daily Herald*. In an editorial, Foster made the first of a series of promises that unless legal means were taken to enforce the law, extra-legal action would be the result. His meaning and the subjects of his ire were clear to Shenandoah's residents.

"Of those members of council," wrote Foster, "who, in the face of events, still stubbornly persist in refusing to organize an efficient police force for the protection of life and property, we have only this to say: If the good name of the borough and the lives of its citizens amount to nothing to them, the end of their rope will soon be reached.

"Already can be heard the mutterings of the storm, and when it bursts in the shape of an organization of 'vigilantes,' their chances for lamp post elevation are fully as good as those of the rest of the murderous villains whom they are encouraging and patronizing."

This was a direct challenge to the Molly Maguires and the friends whom they had elected to Borough Council.

"The boys were damned sore," said McParlan, "when I read the editorial to them in open meeting. Muff had a hell of a time to keep them from rushing out and killing Foster. But even Muff knew that the town was pretty mad about Gomer James' murder and if they tried that, a posse'd form before the night was over. You couldn't tell what might happen then.

"You got to remember a very small percentage of the people were Mollies. When I was in Shenandoah there were eight thousand people, about fifteen hundred of them Irishmen, and only forty brothers. If the others got angry enough they'd tear the boyos apart. And that's what Tom Foster was trying to do."

On Page 1, Volume 1, Number 1 of the *Daily Herald,* Foster declared he would publish a "live paper," and he kept this promise.

Foster must surely have been aware of the existence of "McKenna, the Molly" and the detective certainly knew who Foster was. Yet their paths never crossed officially. McParlan told Charlie Trier that the few times he and the editor saw each other on Shenandoah's streets, Foster looked at the detective with utter contempt. "I felt like telling him who I really was, but naturally I didn't dare. He was all right, I'd have liked to have had his good opinion."

For the next few months McParlan had little time to worry about what anybody except his colleagues in the Brotherhood thought of him. Early on the morning of August 31, the detective was aroused from a sound sleep.

"I didn't hear the door open and before I knew it a candle was waving in my face. I grabbed my pistol from under the pillow and jabbed it into somebody's belly.

" 'Hold it, McKenna!' a voice calls out, and I didn't shoot but afterward I wish I'd let him have it.

" 'It's me, Jim, Jimmy Doyle.' Jimmy's room was next to mine at Cooney's.

" 'What the hell do you want?' I asked.

" 'I'm going over the mountain,' he said. 'It's cold outside and I need a coat. I ain't got one. Loan me yours, will you?'

" 'All right,' I answered and got up and tossed him mine. 'What are you going to do on the other side of the mountain at this hour?' By the other side he meant over Broad Mountain, past Mahanoy City.

" 'We're off to kill a boss,' he says, and with that he dashes out and shuts the door behind him.

"I don't know who he's talking about and I break into a sweat. I figure it must have something to do with Yost's murder but nobody told me anything. I'm not sure whether Muff's beginning to keep things back from me or maybe he didn't even know himself. But I reasoned he had to; Jimmy was one of his boys. And if he knew, why didn't he tell me? I'm getting worried about my own neck. If they're starting to hold out on their secretary, then they're suspicious and I'm cooked."

While McParlan was trying to determine what his next step should be, there was a knock on the door.

"I pick up my pistol again, stand aside where the door will cover me when it opens, and say, 'Come in.'

"Somebody walks in and I step back of him, jab my gun into his back, and whisper 'Don't move!' All the time I'm pushing so I got the wall behind me and him between me and the door. I don't know if the fellow's alone or somebody else is with him. This time I *really* figured it was my turn.

"But the guy I got covered says, 'Wait, McKenna. It's only me, Tom Hurley.' (Tom was the Molly that killed the Welshman, Gomer James.) 'I got a message for you from Jack Kehoe.'

"With one hand I lit the lantern and when I saw he was unarmed and by himself, I lowered my pistol.

" 'What does Jack want?' I asked. Meanwhile I'm putting on my shoes and shirt.

" 'He says me and you are to stick together in case he needs us. He's coming in for a showdown with Foster today.' "

For the next twenty-four hours, the detective, torn by the knowledge that another murder was imminent yet powerless to prevent it, stayed with Hurley in Lawler's barroom. Muff himself had gone to Pottsville on lodge business, his bartender reported, and Kehoe never showed up.

By seven forty-five the following morning, September 1, while McParlan was still waiting for word from the Girardville body-master, the time had already passed for the detective to prevent a double homicide. At eight o'clock, Doyle, Charles McAllister, Thomas Munley, Charles O'Donnell, and his brother, Friday (the latter two both brothers-in-law of Jack Kehoe), burst into Muff Lawler's saloon.

Breathing heavily and covered with sweat they rushed through the barroom toward a back stairway leading to the cellar. Doyle, last of the five, turned to McParlan and Hurley just as the rear door swung shut. "Well, me boyos," he called out, a triumphant grin on his face, "we got one English bastard and we nailed another just for good luck!"

The dead men were Thomas Sanger, superintendent of the Heaton Colliery at Raven Run, and his friend, William Uren, a miner employed at the same operation. Both men were born in England; they had known each other from childhood. The former, a skilled miner and experienced administrator, came to the United States in 1855. Uren, who had not seen his boyhood playmate for nearly thirty years, emigrated to the United States in 1871, got in touch with Sanger and was given a good job under his friend's supervision.

Long before the sun rose over Broad Mountain that morning, most of Raven Run's three hundred residents were awake. Employees at Heaton's, which had a reputation for fairness and decent treatment of its workers, had not joined Siney's union. The lunch pails their wives packed for them were full and the breakfasts they had just eaten were hearty.

Sanger lived in a substantial three-story house at the far edge of the patch, about a half-mile from the colliery. Normally a sound sleeper, he was kept awake half the night by the crying of his month-old son. Married for twelve years, Sanger had five other children, all under ten.

Uren was a childless widower; a quiet, inoffensive man and a reliable worker.

At five-thirty, Robert Heaton, who owned the colliery with

his brother, walked out of his company store and headed home with a dozen fresh eggs which had just been delivered by a Locust Valley farmer. As Heaton passed a loaded coal car, he noticed five men sitting on the ground near the stable. He glanced in their direction, and, assuming they were waiting for the hiring boss, nodded to them.

There was no response from any of the men. Since there never had been any serious disorders or labor problems at his mine, Heaton attached no special significance to the presence of five strangers. In passing, however, he did notice that one of the men "sat in a peculiar and constrained position, with his hands down in his lap and his body bent in a straight line from the hips upward and forward to the head and neck, and no curvature of the back."

At five-fifty, Miss Melinda Bickelman of New Philadelphia patch, a guest in the home of Mr. Dave Wevell, Heaton's outside boss, walked along a path leading from the kitchen door to the outhouse. She, too, noticed the group of strangers, some thirty yards from where she was hurrying but could see only their backs.

At this moment, Dave Wevell was on his way to the colliery to blow the first work whistle. Sanger, a tall, strong-looking man, had just closed the freshly painted gate of his front picket fence. Uren was waiting for him.

Together the pair walked along the empty street toward the colliery. Uren paused in his conversation with his friend to look into the air where steam emerged from the smoke stack, a fraction of a second before the long blast of the colliery whistle would alert all within hearing that work at the Heaton mine began in a half-hour.

Then, three of the five men who had been lounging in front of the stable thirty feet to the right of the road, walked toward Sanger and Uren. When the ten-second blast of the colliery whistle faded, one of the strangers (Friday O'Donnell) forced himself between the two Englishmen and, addressing himself to Sanger, said, "Is there any work around here for some good men?"

Before Sanger could reply, the second stranger (Munley)

pulled a pistol from his pocket and fired a shot into Sanger's groin. As the superintendent fell to the ground, Uren shoved the assailant aside to aid Sanger and was in turn shot in the stomach by the third man (McAllister).

Miss Bickelman, in the Wevell parlor, heard the sound of pistol fire. She peeked through the slats and saw one man lying on the ground twenty feet away and another, whom she recognized as Sanger, struggling to stand up. While she watched in terror, a heavily-built young man whom she had never seen before (Charles O'Donnell) fired two shots into the superintendent's back, and ran in the opposite direction.

The shots were heard by other people, including sixteen-year-old Joe Williams, standing inside his house ready to go to work and saying good-bye to his mother. He jerked the door open and was about to rush out when Mrs. Williams pushed him back into the parlor. She had just seen two strangers run past her home, pausing only to point smoking pistols at her. She got a clear view of both, and later identified them as Doyle and Munley.

Robert Heaton was at home eating some of the eggs he had brought from his store when he heard three shots. In a flash he thought of the men he had seen lounging by the stable. He grabbed a loaded pistol from the sideboard drawer and rushed into the street in time to see Uren lying on the ground motionless, Sanger crawling toward Wevell's home, and four men running down the street.

Heaton leaned over the superintendent, who gasped, "Never mind me, Bob, give it to them."

The courageous mine owner, puffing hard, chased the fugitives, firing his weapon as he ran. But he was soon outdistanced. Winded, he stopped to lean his elbow on a tree stump and fire his last shot. On his right he saw still another stranger rushing by no more than ten feet from him.

"I yelled at him to halt," Heaton said. "He turned around without stopping and gave me a look I'll never forget. I pointed my pistol at him but it was empty and I knew it. He took off and I threw it at him but I missed.

"I only wish to God I'd grabbed one of my hunting rifles from the wall instead of taking that twenty-two. I'd 'a done much better, I can tell you!"

Sanger, assisted by the men and women who poured out of their homes once it was safe to be on the street again, managed to get to the Wevell house. He died in his wife's arms an hour later before a physician could reach him. Uren was already dead when he was lifted from the street. By nine o'clock that morning, Doyle, McAllister, Munley, and the O'Donnell brothers had washed themselves and left Lawler's cellar to perfect already-established alibis.

It was easy to see why Uren was killed, but far more complicated to account for Sanger's death. Even McParlan and Gowen could never solve this puzzle. The little Irishman did hazard a vague guess. He thought perhaps the comparatively "clane job" done on Superintendent Sanger was a simple "return of the favor." Just what the favor was or to whom it had been returned was never really determined to anybody's satisfaction, least of all Sanger's widow.

Chapter Twenty-Three

"The Sanger-Uren murders," said Tom Foster in the Shenandoah *Herald*, September 1, 1875, "adds two more to the long list of murders that remain unatoned for." Then, the editor prophesied, "Retribution will follow the murders, and it will be *swift* and *sure*."

As soon as his paper was "put to bed," it was Foster's custom to spend a relaxed hour with cronies in Luks' Drug Store across the street from the newspaper plant. Here Shenandoah's leading citizens gathered to gossip. On the afternoon of September 1, he took the newest member of the *Herald* staff with him. This was Thomas B. Fielders, whom the *Herald* had stolen from a competitive newspaper, the Pottsville *Journal*, by doubling Fielders' salary of four dollars a week.

Fielders, a native of St. Clair, was then about twenty and had been with the *Journal* for three years. He was an excellent reporter and an effortless writer. "Fielders," said the Bloomsburg *Columbian* in a thumbnail sketch published later, "is a pretty good fellow. He is rather handsome, parts his hair in the middle, thinks he is uncommon smart, and reports for the Shenandoah *Herald*. During a trial, he is as likely as not to comment out loud on the stupidity of juries and courtroom audiences as well."

The *Columbian* either purposely failed to mention or did not know that the star reporter for the Shenandoah *Herald* was extremely near-sighted. This may have had something to do with his loathing for all athletic contests and his poor marksmanship.

While Foster was aware that Fielders never seemed to remove

his spectacles, he could not have known the degree of Fielders' myopia or he would not have trusted him with firearms.

Foster had just introduced the newest member of his staff to the habitués of Luks' when the druggist called the editor to one side.

"Tom," he said, "I just heard the boyos don't like what you said yesterday and today. They're going to tear your place apart tonight. Watch out!"

Forewarned, Foster prepared for the evening's vigil. He told Fielders what might be expected and suggested that the reporter stay away where he would be safe. But young Fielders, who had as much contempt for Molly Maguires as he held for jurymen, insisted on remaining with his editor. Consequently, Foster, after loading a double-barreled shotgun for himself, handed his reporter a pair of loaded Colt .44 caliber horse pistols.

As soon as it grew dark Foster and Fielders sneaked along an alley in the rear of the *Herald* building, walked through a back door of the plant and made themselves comfortable in an alcove just off the pressroom. From here they could cover every entrance to the building.

Fielders, pistols by his side, took the first watch, a quiet one. At midnight Foster, who had been dozing on a couch, woke up and took over. The reporter then stretched out to rest. About an hour later the editor woke Fielders out of a sound sleep.

"Get up, Tom! Get up!" he said. "The boyos are coming!"

The startled reporter reached for his glasses, but in the dark and unfamiliar room, he could not put his hands on them. At this moment there were sounds of muffled shouts and a scraping noise, as though a wooden keg (dynamite) was being dragged along the street.

"Here they are, Tom," yelled Foster, "let 'em have it!"

The reporter, able to feel the large weapons by his side but still without glasses, fired his first salvo. One shot struck the butt end of Foster's rifle, jarring it out of his hands, while the other whizzed through an open door, hit a press, and ricocheted into a metal slug container with enough force to knock it over.

"My God!" screamed Foster in terror. "What the hell are you doing? Are you on their side or mine?"

But Fielders, stimulated by the unaccustomed action, blazed away. He could hear Foster's voice and knew it would not be good policy to fire in that direction. He made a complete circle, and, pointing his revolver directly ahead, fired. This time the bullet smacked into a wall not two inches away from the gun's muzzle. Startled by this unexpectedly close blast, Fielders reversed himself 180 degrees and shot his next one in the opposite direction, the bullet striking the floor less than a foot away from Foster who flung himself on the ground.

"For Christ's sake, stop shooting!" screamed Foster. "I'd be safer with the Mollies in here."

The Mollies, however, had already fled. Still shaking, Foster lit some lamps and glanced around the room to appraise the damage. Then, without saying a word, he took the weapons which Fielders reluctantly handed to him.

For about two minutes Foster stared at his reporter in disbelief. Then he grinned, broke open the pistols, removed the remaining cartridges, and turned back the weapons to Fielders.

"I think Shenandoah'll be safer this way, Tom," he said.

The following morning, Foster, completely recovered from the night's activities and alerted by rumors of more murders to come, ran his second consecutive page one editorial urging "lynch law."

"A reign of terror and bloodshed is about to be inaugurated . . . in Schuylkill County," said the Shenandoah *Herald*. "There is nothing to be gained by longer concealing the fact that an organized secret body of assassins have determined to obtain control of affairs here in the mining business by driving out every boss whom they may dislike.

"A meeting is held, an objectionable boss is made the subject of debate, and if in the performance of his duty he has incurred the enmity of any of this body of murderers, he is marked for death and generally meets this fate.

"Against such an organization our courts have proven themselves powerless to protect us. The men who do the shooting are strangers and cannot be detected."

Then Foster posed a question that sounded rhetorical but was not.

"What remains to be done?" he asked.

He had his own answer, in which he swept aside the Bill of Rights and other Constitutional guarantees.

"Nothing remains," declared the editor, "but to take the law in our hands and drive out the men who are known to be at the bottom of the murders in the district. The county . . . is too small to contain both the respectable portion of the communiy and this band of assassins. One or the other must go. Who shall it be?

"In a single week, a Vigilance Committee could make things so hot here, that we will never be troubled by them again. Let the work commence! Do not wait until another good citizen is murdered by these same bloody hands."

Even as Foster demanded his brand of justice, the Brothers of the Shenandoah Division completed final plans for the dispersal of their direct type of retribution. Meeting above Muff's barroom that afternoon, six Molly Maguires prepared to return Alex Campbell's favor (the murder of Patrolman Yost) by disposing of John P. Jones. Jones, it may be recalled, was the boss who had treated Brother Hugh McGehan so badly.

Among those who sat in during the entire proceedings was the lodge secretary, James McParlan. While McParlan knew that somebody was to be murdered as part of the complicated deal in which James Boyle and James Carroll had killed Yost, he did not know the name of the second victim until September 2, 1875. Then he found himself in charge of the execution squad. His team consisted of his friend Frank McAndrew and Michael Doyle, the latter to be given a second chance to redeem himself by doing a "clane job" after the sloppy one he and his companions performed on the Bully Boy.

McParlan's immediate problem was to get off a report to Franklin at once so that not only might Jones be warned in time but the would-be murderers might be caught red-handed. The detective had no time to mail this important letter from Delano and had to take the chance that he would not be seen in the Shenandoah post office.

He sent McAndrew and Doyle home to prepare their wives for an absence of several days. The trio was to meet in a half hour at the Lehigh Valley Railroad Station in time to catch an evening train. McParlan hurried to Cooney's, locked himself in his room, wrote a brief message to Franklin, sealed it, and boldly walked to the post office. He saw no one he knew and hoped no one had noticed him.

McParlan's next tactic was delay.

"We've time for a couple of short ones," he told McAndrew and Doyle when they got to Mahanoy City, where they were to change trains for Tamaqua. In Ryan's, across the street from the Reading Depot, the three sat drinking long enough to miss their train connections.

McParlan would have liked to have stayed in Mahanoy City for the night, holding up their departure for at least twelve more hours. But he was afraid some of Michael Clarke's boys would see him and his companions and news of this could well be reported to Lawler and Kehoe. So the trio caught the 10:14 train, arriving shortly before midnight at Campbell's saloon where they'd been ordered to rendezvous with Kerrigan, again the self-selected fingerman.

Kerrigan did not keep the appointment. McParlan assumed that Powderkeg, seeing that his trio of murderers was late, postponed the meeting until the following night, September 3. Thus the murder could not take place before September 4. This would give Franklin all the time he needed to put Captain Linden where he could do the most good.

But Powderkeg had plans of his own, and may or may not have ever had any intention of getting together with McParlan, Doyle and McAndrew. On Sunday, August 29, two days before the murders of Sanger and Uren, Kerrigan was in Mount Laffee, a village on the south side of Pottsville. "We've a job for you over in Lansford," he told Jerry Kane, the Mount Laffee bodymaster, "and we'll need two good men."

Kane's choices were Michael J. Doyle and Edward Kelly, the former a cousin of Shenandoah's Jimmy Boyle, one of Yost's murderers.

Doyle's reputation was good. A breaker boy from the ages of seven to nine, when his Irish immigrant father, a shoemaker, managed to get enough money together to allow Mickey to quit work, the child attended Frances Peck Elementary School for four years in Norwegian Township, outside of Pottsville. The birth of several brothers and sisters put a stop to Doyle's education and forced his return to work. Except for brief periods of involuntary idleness, Doyle had never been without a steady job.

Nor was the twenty-four-year-old Kelly's reputation bad, although his picketing activities as a member of Siney's M.B.A. had brought him into disrepute with employers and cost him his job. He had no previous trouble with the law, however, and for fourteen months had been a member of the Pennsylvania National Guard.

On September 1, with two dollars apiece in their pockets (expense monies provided to them by Kerrigan via Kane), the pair took a noon train from Pottsville to Tamaqua. They went directly to Carroll's saloon, arriving there some thirty-four hours before McParlan and his boys arrived. Only Kerrigan was aware of both teams of would-be murderers and their plans, although he had no advance knowledge of McParlan's delaying tactics, which, in the light of events, would probably have been of only academic interest to him.

"I had a letter to Mr. Carroll," Kelly said. "I handed it to him, then me and Doyle gave him the 'goods'—'What do you think of the European War?' and he answered, 'The Turks will lose.' Mr. Carroll shook hands with us and bought us a beer.

"Then he took us around to see the town. Doyle and Mr. Carroll walked together and I was behind."

Among Tamaqua's sights, one which surely would have been of more than passing interest to the would-be assassins was the spot where Yost had been murdered.

"A good clane job," was Carroll's brief but satisfied comment as the trio walked by the Lutheran graveyard.

Then the Tamaqua saloonkeeper, belatedly circumspect about the company he was keeping, turned to his companions and said, "Well, boyos, I'd better not be seen around too much with you. I'll meet you later at my place."

He handed Doyle a dollar and the pair wandered off without their guide, strolled into the Columbia House where they downed several shots of Barbados rum, and returned to Carroll's about half-past five that evening.

"Me and Doyle wasn't there long when Mr. Kerrigan came in," Kelly continued. "He bought a bottle and put it in front of us but didn't drink any hisself. He started to tell us about meeting him early the next morning and I was afraid an elderly gentleman, sitting in the corner, would hear him so I told Mr. Kerrigan about it politely.

" 'Don't worry about him,' says Mr. K. 'It's only old man Lutz. Deaf as a lamp post.'

"To prove it, Powderkeg walks over to this gentleman and yells, 'How are you, you miserable Dutch son-of-a-bitch?' and the elderly gentleman doesn't even look up from his beer."

Doyle and Kelly, a big day ahead, retired early, but not before Kerrigan handed the pair their murder weapons, Roarity's trusty pistol, which had served McGehan so well in the Yost murder, and another .32, which had no recorded history.

Early on the morning of September 2, while Doyle and McAndrew were still asleep at Alex Campbell's and McParlan was pacing the floor hoping Captain Linden would somehow send him word, Kelly and Doyle were slowly climbing to the top of Storm Hill, near Ashton, with Kerrigan carefully noting landmarks on the path that was to be their escape route the next day.

As they approached their destination they were joined by another man who apparently had been waiting for them at the juncture of the two diverging paths. This fourth member of the execution squad was Brother Condy Trimble of the Summit Hill Lodge. Trimble's function was merely to point out the mine boss's home. Kerrigan would exercise his prerogative of fingering, a task he refused to share with anyone.

It was a warm day and Doyle grew thirsty. He asked Condy if there was any place around where he could get a drink.

"Only milk," answered Brother Trimble. "See that little house over there? That's Maggie Murphy's. She'll give you some. Me and Powderkeg'll wait here."

Mrs. Murphy recalled the incident well.

"They were very polite. One of them was wearing a kind of conductor's cap and he took it off when he talked to me. I gave 'em each a bowl of milk. When they got finished one of them said, 'Thank you, Ma'am. How much is it?'

"And I, thinking the poor lads are out of work, say, 'That's all right, boys. I keep a cow. You can have the milk for nothing.' "

"After a little while," Kelly said, "Condy left and me and Doyle and Mr. Kerrigan peeked from behind a high bush where we could see the super's home Condy had showed us. A couple minutes after out walks a tall, gray-haired man.

" 'That's Jones,' says Mr. Kerrigan. 'Once you see him tomorrow don't let him out of your sight for a second. But don't kill him until he starts for the railroad trestle where he always goes when he's heading for the big house. You'll have plenty of cover there.' "

The trio then returned to Tamaqua. Kerrigan went home to prepare his alibi and the others to Carroll's where they spent their second night, hoping to be seen by no one. But Kerrigan, a well-known Tamaqua figure, a fact he most certainly knew, was noticed not by one but by several men and women during those few moments he walked along the streets of the town accompanied by a pair of strangers.

Long before sunrise on the morning of Friday, September 3, Kerrigan, Doyle and Kelly were trudging back to Storm Hill to begin a brief vigil behind the high bush.

"We were there ony a couple minutes," said Kelly, "and Mr. Kerrigan says, 'Is everything all right?' and I say, 'Yes.' Then he says, 'Watch it now, boys. As soon as Jones heads for the trestle, get him. You know where to meet me afterward. I'll be on my way back to Tamaqua.' With that he goes away."

Powderkeg had no intention of returning to Tamaqua at once. Instead, he paused a few hundred yards away and hid himself behind a thick oak rising from a slight promontory, where he stood waiting with a clear view of Doyle, Kelly and the old railroad trestle. Unfortunately for Powderkeg the bloody arena was moved out of his line of vision.

"Instead of Mr. Jones walking toward the trestle like he was supposed to," Kelly said, "the super heads for Lansford and we follow him. We're only about fifty feet behind. Just as he gets over the top of a hill he turns around and gives us a look.

"I say to Doyle, 'I think he's got a suspicion against us,' but Doyle says, 'No. All bosses look at people that way.'

"Then Mr. Jones starts for the big house but before he reaches it we see him go inside the telegraph place talking to some men. He waves good-bye to them and walks out again."

The hands of the large clock in the telegraph office window showed 6:54. Death was only a minute away for Mr. Jones.

There was little to distinguish Jones's murder itself from so many others. The crime was committed in broad daylight in full sight of fifty witnesses. The superintendent's name was called; he turned around, and was shot, first by Doyle, next by Kelly. When the victim fell to the ground, Kelly and Doyle each put another bullet into him.

The last three shots were unnecessary. Doyle's first bullet pierced Jones's heart. "Death," said the coroner, "was instantaneous."

The big difference between the murder of John P. Jones and other Molly Maguire homicides was that this time the killers were caught.

Chapter Twenty-Four

A master carpenter, and a chute boss, both employees of the Wilkes-Barre Coal Company, arrived at the murder scene in time to see two men, pistols in their hands, fleeing in the opposite direction, and fifty or more men and women scattering as fast as they could.

The master carpenter ran to Jones's body, bent over, and decided that the victim was beyond mortal help. He shouted to the chute boss, looking after the fugitives, "Come on, Jack. Let's get 'em! They can't be far off."

Although the men were unarmed, they rushed toward the spot where Jones's killers were last seen. The moment they began the chase they were joined by twenty others, the pursuing mob swelling each minute.

Neither fugitive was in sight when their pursuers reached the point where the path split. There they paused. The narrow road to the left went down hill to Pottsville; the path to the right led over the mountain to Tamaqua.

"They must have took the one to Pottsville," said the chute boss. "It's easier."

But Mrs. Murphy, in her backyard, had heard the gunfire. She rushed to the front of the house just in time to see two men run up the steep path leading to Tamaqua. She recognized them as the pair to whom she had given bowls of milk the preceding day.

Nobody knows what Mrs. Murphy's exact words were when she responded to the question, "Which way did they go?" but there is an irresistible temptation for the historian to claim the lady replied, "They went thataway."

The posse was off once more. Tom Fielders, piecing together bits of information, reported the chase in the Shenandoah *Herald*:

"The assassins ran up the Pipe Line in the direction of Old Number 4 Tunnel," wrote Fielders. "There the third man signaled them. They went up through the deep woods, entering the old cut, about two hundred yards east of the No. 2 slope. They attempted to get up the right side but failed and did get up the left side.

"Here they were seen by Henry Murphy from a distance. In two minutes Captain Williams, one of the Coal and Iron Police, stopped at Murphy's blacksmith shop and was told the direction they had taken. The murderers kept on in the direction of Spring Tunnel, passing between the houses and the side of the hill, and going down on the old Foster's Tunnel Railroad, leading through the swamp.

"There they took to the woods, up through Dry Hollow, and followed the side of the mountain to the Little Schuylkill, which they forded."

Here the forest ended. As the pair broke into a run across an open field and fled up the side of a hill, they were seen by William Fenstermacher, a farmer. Five minutes later, the posse, with Captain Williams in the lead, passed the same spot but by then the trail was lost.

"The murderers," continued Fielders, "kept on their desperate flight, knowing they were closely followed. They went on the side of the hill at Donaldson's Shaft, passing between the houses and the woods, and entered the woods a short distance west of the shaft.

"No one saw them again until they emerged. Then they were observed but only for a moment, climbing up the side of a mountain where they were once more lost to sight."

By then, news of the murder and the fact that the killers were on their way to Tamaqua had been telegraphed from Lansford. The town of Tamaqua was in a flurry of excitement and armed posses were being formed. Word of Kerrigan's double-cross reached McParlan as he and his pair of would-be assassins, McAndrew and Doyle, stood around Carroll's saloon. Carroll, behind the bar, grinned at the reports.

"They'll be all right," he promised. "Powderkeg's too slick for 'em. By now I'll bet he'll have his boyos, whoever they are, hiding up in Cemetery Hill."

With this McParlan turned to McAndrew and Doyle and said, "I'm going outside to see what's doing. You fellows wait here 'til I come back."

At considerable risk to his person, since Tamaquans were sure he was a leading member of the Brotherhood, the detective rushed into Lehigh Street toward the Reading Depot, where he hoped he might catch sight of Captain Linden near the telegraph office.

Meanwhile the crowd at Broad and Lehigh streets was expanding by the minute and growing more and more unruly. Cries of "Kill the Mollies! Lynch the bastards!" could be heard. The detective slipped past the mob and reached the station.

There, just as he had hoped, was Linden, off to one side of the building near the freight office, talking to Dan Shepp. There was also a third man with a pair of binoculars slung over his shoulder.

"The Captain saw me out of the corner of his eye and motioned me to go 'round the back," McParlan recalled. "I took one hell of a chance that somebody'd see us together. But I was damned burned up that Kerrigan had outsmarted me.

"Well, I didn't have much time for a social visit with the Captain but I managed to tell him how Powderkeg had pulled a fast one. Then I said, 'It that a pair of field glasses that young fellow with you has slung on his shoulders?'

" 'Yeh,' he answered. 'What about them?'

"Then I said, 'If you can take him where he could get a view of some place called Cemetery Hill, I think you might catch sight of Mr. Kerrigan and the boyos.'

"I turned around and rushed back to Carroll's. I got there all right, without being torn to bits like I might. That crowd was getting uglier all the time."

The man with the binoculars, a young Tamaqua law student, went to the roof of the Reading Depot with Captain Linden and Dan Shepp. Each swept the mountain top but could see no sign of the fugitives. Then, followed by scores of armed men, they climbed to the top of Tamaqua's North Mountain, where they commanded a view of Cemetery Hill and the surrounding area.

"At the Odd Fellows Cemetery," continued Fielders, "with a spy-glass scrutinizing the territory, they had the satisfaction of seeing two men come out of the woods near what is called the 'Gums' and join another who seemed to be waiting for them.

"Word was immediately sent to the scouts, who gradually closed in towards Tamaqua. Meanwhile bodies of men had left Tamaqua and were working hard to discover any traces. At last their desires were crowned with success. Near the baseball grounds, a hundred feet from Cemetery Hill, three men were discovered and two of them answered the description of the murderers.

" 'Hold up your hands,' was the order given by the leaders of the party.

"The three men at once complied. Their names are Michael J. Doyle, Edward Kelly and James Kerrigan. Kerrigan is a man well known in the neighborhood, works there, and he it was who met the other two when they broke cover. Kelly is a stranger to every man in Tamaqua . . . Doyle says that he was born in Pottsville and that he wished he had stayed there, and we have no doubt that he does."

Word of the capture was telegraphed to Lansford and Raven Run asking that anyone who had seen the murder come forward and identify the killers.

"Then," said the Shenandoah *Herald,* "the prisoners were marched to the lock-up under the protection of a large body of men, all heavily armed, and their protection was required, for had the crowd reached them, the prisoners never would have required a trial . . .

"On reaching the lock-up they were secured in separate cells and taken one at a time to a room in the second story of the lock-up and examined. The wisdom of questioning them singly was demonstrated by the different tales they told, one contradicted the other on the most material points, and their complicity in the murder was made more certain every moment.

"After the examination, Kelly and Doyle were placed in a room together, and the parties who had seen the shooting were brought in, one at a time, to identify them . . . What must have been the feelings of the two men when a miner would walk into the room, take a long searching look at them, and say, without the shadow of a doubt, in a strong voice, *'Those are the men.'*

"You could see a ghastly pallor creeping over their faces as man after man uttered the words just written. Their eyes had a wild hunted look in them and when their examination was finished they both uttered a sigh of relief.

"Kerrigan is known by everyone in Tamaqua, so that he was not brought forward for identification. He seemed to think that the precaution of keeping him in a cell was altogether unnecessary but appeared more cheerful when he was told that he was a good deal safer in the cell than out of it, and so he was in several respects."

Powderkeg's first visitor was his friend, Dan Shepp.

"This arrest is ridiculous," he told the mine owner. "I had nothing to do with poor John Jones's murder. I knew the man well and thought him a fine fellow."

"Well, then, what were you doing up on the mountain with Doyle and Kelly?"

"Doyle and Kelly? Is that what the rogues' names are? Now would you believe it, Dan, I never laid eyes on either of the rascals before in me life?"

Chapter Twenty-Five

Even though Kerrigan, Doyle and Kelly were lodged safely in the strong new jail at Mauch Chunk, no one, least of all the prisoners, believed the trials of the alleged murderers would be anything but perfunctory. Precedent in Schuylkill, Northumberland, Carbon and Columbia counties offered no evidence to the contrary.

Certainly citizens throughout the area where the Brotherhood's terror had been felt for two decades were now voicing their anger, but such was still the power of the Molly Maguires that men and women everywhere in the hard coal regions were convinced that even if the case were ever to reach the courts, few of the scores of witnesses who saw Jones murdered would be willing or able to testify. Acquittal would be inevitable.

Kehoe, Campbell, Lawler, Clarke, and two dozen other bodymasters were untouched, and their ability to deliver swift death was as yet not challenged. People knew this only too well. And no one who understood the workings of Pennsylvania's politics could forget that the "Old Man," Governor Hartranft, owed his incumbency to the Molly Maguires. Hartranft had not only the power of reprieve but also the ability to pressure the courts and their representatives.

But there were factors pushing toward the destruction of the Brotherhood. There was the detective, McParlan—Secretary McKenna to his colleagues—whose work was nearing completion. There was the mounting anger of the Church of Rome and the continuing bravery of her official representatives, the parish priests.

And there was Editor Foster, openly dissatisfied with due process of law and screaming loudly in every edition of the Shenandoah *Herald* for the formation of vigilantes.

"We were born and raised in Schuylkill County and here we shall stay," he promised. "We thoroughly understand the nature of the disease which affects this district, and we know as well as we know anything that *the law cannot reach the evil.*

"The incarnate fiends who plan the murders are the parties that must be wiped out. They live among us and are known to us, but there is no evidence that can be obtained to punish them under the laws. What more then remains to be done than to drive them away peaceably if we can, forcibly if we must?"

Rebuttal from the Molly Maguires came fast. When Foster and Fielders returned to Shenandoah at about four P.M. on Saturday, September 5, after covering Sanger's and Uren's funerals in Girardville; they found the following "coffin notice" nailed to Foster's desk:

Mr Edtore wie wil give ye 24 hurse to go to the divil
out this ye son of A Bitch R we wil send ye After gomer
Ja mes and Mr. — and som more Big Bug with ye
F molley
we aint done Shooting yet

Foster could not wait to reply to this threat. He sat down at once and penned his page one, column one, answer, although since the *Herald* published no Sunday edition, it did not reach avid readers until Monday, September 7.

"It is all folly and waste of ink and paper to send us 'coffin notices,' " declared Foster. "We have to laugh when we read the concluding paragraph, 'We ain't done shooting yet.'

"To be sure you are not. But we are willing to bet that the one-sided feature of the shooting business is now and forever ended!"

Ostentatiously carried in open holsters were Foster's twin .44's. Fielders, who packed his weapons just as ominously, was the only one who knew the revolvers were not loaded.

Father McDermott, from his pulpit in Pottsville's St. Patrick's Roman Catholic Church, Father O'Brien, from Shenandoah, and all the rest of the Roman Catholic clergy throughout the coal regions took up the cry. It should be said, however, that the means they recommended to restore order were more in keeping with their own religious tenets and the Constitution than ideas urged by Foster.

That these parish priests (still threatened and still molested) kept gaining strength among their parishioners is evidenced by the increasing volume of letters Foster received from bitter but hitherto silent Roman Catholics. One of the many communications, this one signed "Americus" and mailed from Girardville, reached Foster, September 10, and was printed the following afternoon.

"We had a sermon preached us last Sunday morning by the Rev. Joseph Bridgman, pastor of the Roman Catholic Church," wrote "Americus." "He condemned . . . in unmeasured terms the devils who had been revelling in blood in our county, and said that it was well known to what party they belonged, and that he was ashamed to acknowledge that he was an Irishman since a few of that nationality had brought such odium and disgrace on that race.

"He further said that unless all good people combined to punish these murderers there would be such an intense feeling excited against the Irish, both guilty and innocent, that there would be an uprising of the people against them and they would all be driven from the country. . . ."

Almost immediately after Jones's funeral, coffin notices were sent or delivered personally to many citizens who might have witnessed the executions of Jones, Uren, Sanger, Yost, or James. The majority of recipients kept these unwelcome communications to themselves and several left the area at once. But a few who received coffin notices spoke out freely and openly defied the senders. One of the latter was Robert Heaton, for whom both Sanger and Uren had worked.

"Leave this county peaceful, Heaton, or you will be dead within twenty-four hours," read a notice that the mine owner found in his office September 10. On the top of the letter was a crudely drawn death's head and the usual symbol, a pistol and the signature "a Molly Maguire."

Heaton answered the threat swiftly, in a manner which met

173

Editor Foster's approval. The mine owner armed himself and a score of friends, and posted a public notice to the effect that if he, Heaton, or any employee was menaced, the *suspected* felons would themselves be shot to death.

He concluded his warning with the statement that "Everybody who reads this knows who I mean. Take care! Robert Heaton."

Such was the state of affairs in the hard coal regions that the sheriff, the police, and other public officials who certainly saw Heaton's threat to take the law into his own hands, permitted the three-foot-square warning to remain nailed to the outside wall of the Lansford railroad depot for months. Neither the mine owner nor his employees were ever again molested by the Molly Maguires.

Citizens everywhere in Schuylkill, Carbon, and Northumberland counties, particularly those who agreed with Foster's published philosophies, were ready to take action. Obviously nobody counted the number of weapons in the possession of angry men, but it would be reasonable to assume that a fair percentage of adult males carried a loaded pistol or gun if they could get their hands on either.

It would not have taken much to turn the streets of any hard coal town into the site of a bloody civil war with definite religious overtones. Of this fact, the Shenandoah publisher surely was aware. One example of Foster's advice being taken was the borough of Summit Hill's fast response to a *Herald* editorial.

"The law," said Foster, "was never calculated in its ordinary course to successfully cope with a secret organization over a thousand strong in this county alone, composed of bad and desperate men determined to set it at defiance.

"In an emergency such as the present it is only a hindrance to justice, and the opinion we hear expressed on all sides by good citizens, representing all classes of society, is that for the next few months the law of the courts should be set aside and that of Judge Lynch be substituted for it.

"The remedy proposed to be applied is a terrible one—but so is the disease which must be cured. No one, however, doubts its effectiveness. The silent, swift and sure action of the 'vigilantes' with a single example of their power would strike terror into the hearts of every evil doer in the region and make Schuylkill County the quietest and most orderly section of the state. . . ."

Two days later, the Shenandoah *Herald* published, without comment, the following dispatch from Summit Hill:

"Your editorial last evening has echoed the feelings of every heart in our place—that is of respectable citizens—and our people are determined to wait no longer on the actions of tardy officials.

"An example of the strong feeling existing may be shown in the fact that about half-past nine o'clock last night a pistol shot was fired in front of Samuel Green's saloon, and in about a half-minute fully fifty citizens, well armed, were at the scene . . . Had the party found anyone at the time, an example would have been made of the offender in short time."

Although the Molly Maguires must have been concerned over mounting anger at Brotherhood activities, they determined to "fight fire with fire." McParlan's reports to Franklin now carried almost daily warnings to mine owners, superintendents, workers, and witnesses to any recent murders. The campaign of violence was stepped up.

"It was impossible for me to keep up with a quarter of what was going on," said the little Irishman. "On September 10, we got word from Kehoe to put the fear of God into a Shenandoah saloonkeeper named Jimmy Riles.

"Now I knew Riles. He wasn't a bad fellow; I used to see him at Mass regular. He had a little place in the bottom of Jimmy Tobin's house on the west end of Center Street. He tried to keep it respectable and he never liked to see any of our boyos there.

"Kehoe tells him he's to furnish an alibi they need for one of the Girardville brothers and Riles says 'no' he don't want to get in trouble. There's more pressure and Jimmy still refuses. So we get our orders to put him out of business.

"I got word to Mr. Franklin right away. I know Captain Linden's in Shenandoah most of the time, now, and he's never far away from me. So I figure he's warned Riles. First we send Jimmy a coffin notice but he pays it no attention. Then Muff tells me to take a couple boys with me and beat the hell out of him.

"So I take two of the brothers with me one night hoping

Jimmy's expecting us and he is. We can't even get close. There's a couple Coal and Iron Police on the corner and they look mean. But the next afternoon Jimmy gets it from Tim Murphy, who shot him in the arm when Riles went out to take in a keg from the brewery wagon."

This time Riles had had enough. His departure from Shenandoah was noted by the *Herald*.

"Riles leaves his all in Shenandoah for a new sphere. Everybody knows the reasons for the shooting and who did it. Everyone who loves his country and every man who lives his life . . . should do all in his power to wipe out that foul blot upon the good name of our country . . . the association known as the Molly Maguires."

The next prospective victim of Brotherhood vengeance was August Gable, boss carpenter at Gowen's West Shenandoah Colliery.

"Gable," recalled McParlan, "fired two of the boyos and one of their friends; I disremember their names. So Muff said to me to drive the son-of-a-bitch out of town. First I mail in my report on Gable to Philly. I'm not free a minute now and I hardly ever see my Polish friend or Mary any more.

"And it's getting tougher all the time to get to Delano so all I can do is take my chances and get my reports in the mail at the Shenandoah depot. I got to worry about a couple things there. That the brothers don't spot me and that when I'm walking out of Cooney's late at night the good citizens of Shenandoah don't see me and string me up. They're damned near ready for that, I can tell you.

"But I do know, even if I don't see anybody around and the streets are dark, that Captain Linden is somewhere nearby and that's about the only thing that makes me feel good."

Gable received his first coffin notice on September 16 and a second one two days later. Contents of both were the same— "Boss Carpenter Gable . . . I will let you know that you Should leave This Town or we will be after you with pistols and guns. Inshure your life." The usual sign and signature followed.

"I don't intend to leave," Gable told Tom Fielders. "I work for the Philadelphia and Reading Company and as long as there's a job for me to do I'll do it. You can put it in your paper that I know who the three men are and I can lick a dozen like them."

Gable got no more threats.

"It wasn't that the boyos were scared Gable could lick a dozen of 'em," McParlan said. "It was just that the Captain strung a bunch of hard-looking Coal and Iron Police everywhere you could see around the colliery. And he stationed a twenty-four-hour guard at Gable's house. Every place Gable went there were a couple of Linden's boys by his side."

A few days later the detective saved one more life, this time at the expense of another.

At Audenried, site of both the Langdon and Smith murders, James O'Brien, a miner and part-time bartender, was marked for death because he had quarreled with Charles McCool of the Mahanoy City Division. Four of Campbell's men were to do the job and McCool was the fingerman.

The execution was scheduled for Saturday, September 24, at N. D. Fowler's Audenried Hotel where O'Brien worked several evenings a week. But when Campbell's boys arrived they found the hotel filled with guests, including a number of priests in town for the Sunday dedication of Father Marron's new Catholic Church. It would have been embarrassing to kill somebody in the presence of so many members of the clergy so the murder was postponed until the following day.

The squad waited in front of O'Brien's home for hours. When he did not appear, his would-be executioners and their fingerman returned to the hotel. There they found O'Brien, seated in the lobby, pistol in his hand. They did not see Fred Brink, a Coal and Iron policeman, standing behind a curtain.

O'Brien fired first. His bullet struck McCool. Then, to the bewilderment of the five Mollies, Brink pushed aside the drapes and stepped into the room. In one hand was a revolver and in the other a billy. Simultaneously shooting and clubbing, he dropped one of Campbell's boys with his night stick and wounded at least one other.

The fight was over almost before it began. The four Tamaqua Mollies were placed under arrest, although there is no record of the final disposition of their case. Information about McCool's fate, however, is available. According to the Mauch Chunk *Coal Gazette,* "Charles McCool, a miner from Mahanoy City, died in the arms of Father Marron last Sunday. McCool was nineteen years old. . . ."

McParlan was more certain than ever before that his dual role would soon be uncovered by the Brotherhood.

"I was afraid of that Audenreid business. Campbell *knew* I'd heard talk about killing O'Brien and here his boys go to do a 'clane job' and instead they find a policeman all ready and waiting and one of their boys gets it. Then Kerrigan was in jail and you never could figure out what he'd be liable to do. I *never* was convinced I'd fooled Powderkeg.

"I heard nothing from Mr. Franklin, so all I could do was keep plugging, watch my step all the time, and hope that Linden would be close when the going got rough."

Chapter Twenty-Six

On September 26, McParlan received instructions to lead a small detachment of Molly Maguires into Tamaqua, there to intimidate, if not kill, two men who had seen Jones murdered. The plan of attack was different from the usual run. This time a fire was to be started in a home near the witnesses, who lived a few doors apart. When the pair rushed to the street, as they undoubtedly would, they would be beaten. If they resisted, they would be shot to death. During the ensuing excitement, with both of Tamaqua's rival fire companies battling the flames and each other, it would be easy for the Mollies to escape unnoticed.

McParlan got his report to Franklin in time, although he could do nothing to prevent the arson without revealing his identity. The witnesses stayed inside (in the company of Coal and Iron Police) while a blaze burned down a neighbor's house.

"I was a bit worried about Mr. Kehoe's reactions to the Tamaqua deal," said the little Irishman, "so I stopped off in Frackville for a bit of fun before proceeding to the business at hand in Shenandoah. When I walked into Muff's nobody said anything about what happened in Tamaqua. I said nothing in return. And that's the way we left it."

Foster renewed his appeal to the citizenry on October 2.

"While as a public journalist it hardly becomes us to recommend lynch law, and while we do not wish to be misunderstood, there is no mistaking the temper of the people, and bad and guilty men in this neighborhood might as well commence making their last wills and testaments."

A few days later, irked by rumors that a Reading Railroad employee in a position to know was reporting Molly Maguire activities to Foster, Kehoe appeared in person at the station.

"Jack Kehoe," said the *Herald,* "went to the depot yesterday and called out Mr. E. S. Steltz, who is employed at the station, and accused him of writing to the *Herald.* He said he and some more members of his society had concluded it was Steltz who wrote them, and he advised him to stop it or he might get himself into trouble.

"We wish to inform Jack that Mr. Steltz does not write these letters and we further wish to inform him that should any harm come to Steltz, as he has intimated, that not only will harm come to him, but to a half-dozen others of his worthless gang. Intimidation and shooting on your side without retaliation is played out, Jack."

Foster posted the following "public notice" on the front window of the *Herald:*

If any harm befalls any person connected with this paper, either at Girardville or Shenandoah, the vengeance that will be exacted of certain parties, who are well known to the public, will be as terrible and complete as it will be prompt. It is only by the greatest exertion that hundreds of men are now prevented from taking the punishment of crime into their own hands.

Should a spark be set to the powder, hell itself would be a safer place than their own homes for certain people. This is a free country; free speech and a free press are among its privileges, but if murder and murderers cannot be safely denounced until there has been some bloodletting, the quicker it comes the better.

Men and brethren, ARE WE RIGHT?

Thomas Jefferson Foster

There was no let-up on either side. Two days later, a huge rock smashed the *Herald*'s window and battered the notice to shreds. Foster replaced the glass and the warning. On October 5, the Locust Gap breaker owned by Dan Shepp was burned to the ground by incendiaries. On October 8, two foremen at Gilberton Colliery were badly beaten on their way home from work.

But all this was nothing compared to the night of October 9, 1875, when armed mobs took over the town of Shenandoah and for twelve hours terrorized its 10,000 inhabitants. Before the sun rose the following morning, three men were dead, scores wounded, a dozen houses burned to the ground, Muff Lawler's saloon torn apart, and Tom Hurley, Gomer James's murderer, saved from lynching only by McParlan's quick wits.

A NIGHT OF TERROR was the headline on Tom Fielders' story.

"Shenandoah," wrote this reporter, "has just passed through an ordeal, which in a civilized country appears simply awful. The lawless proceedings which occurred will never be forgotten by those who were witnesses.

"How strange and incomprehensible it must appear to those who do not understand the state of affairs here, when they read that a town in such a State as Pennsylvania was rendered unsafe for any respectable citizen, by lawless characters, who ranged the streets, flourishing revolvers and firing them off without the slightest provocation, keeping the peaceful portion of the community in a constant state of terror and giving the town the appearance of a place under siege."

Much, if not all, of the ensuing violence might have been averted had police jailed the first rioter, John Heffron, who shot up the barroom of the National Hotel at seven o'clock in the evening.

"Several borough constables . . . ran into the hotel and arrested Heffron, and took the revolver from him," continued the *Herald*. "They brought him before Burgess Connors, who ordered him to pay a fine of five dollars, when the pistol would be returned to him. As no money was forthcoming, Heffron was allowed out."

Pistol back in its holster, Heffron returned to the National Hotel and to the astonishment of the owner, who thought he'd seen the last of this unruly customer, continued where he'd left off before police interruption. He was joined by a dozen companions, encouraged by Burgess Connor's tolerance for firearms.

When there was nothing and presumably no one left to shoot at in the National Hotel, the mob moved on to Sampson Couch's saloon at the corner of Chestnut and Coal Streets. Here, a few regulars were quietly drinking beer served by Roberta Couch, the proprietor's wife. Richard Finnen, wielding a shillelagh, offered token resistance to Heffron and his mob, and was promptly shot to death.

"The shooting was credited to William Knuckey," continued Tom Fielders. "How the report was circulated that Knuckey was the man who fired the shot, we were unable to discover, for after questioning several parties who were in the saloon when the shooting occurred, no one was able to swear he saw the shot fired.

"It seems perfectly unaccountable that one of a crowd should shoot a man without the action being noticed by anyone . . . When the news of the shooting of Finnen spread there was intense excitement and the prevailing impression seemed to be that the trouble had only begun. Danger was in the air."

A half hour after Finnen was murdered, another shooting proved the correctness of Fielders' observation.

"We were proceeding in the direction of the *Herald* office," the reporter went on, "but before we reached it we were startled by a thundering knocking at the United States Hotel. We at once ran that way and having made an entrance through the dense throng that crowded the passage found that a man by the name of James Johns had been abused in a brutal and awful manner . . . His throat had been cut from ear to ear . . .

"The crowd of excited men in and about the saloon were becoming more dangerous every minute, threats of vengeance on the murderers and their kind were heard on every side. Revolvers were in the hands of nearly everyone . . ."

Soon there were two armed mobs roaming the streets of Shenandoah, chasing each other from saloon to saloon and shooting at anyone who happened to get in the way. A fire at Jardin and Lloyd streets, where several houses were destroyed by arsonists, offered less violent distractions, but only temporarily. Shortly afterward a third man was critically wounded by a stray bullet which struck him as he stood in front of Luks' Drug Store.

"News of this last shooting," said the *Herald,* "spread like wildfire through the town. Crowds of men who were on every corner, not satisfied with their numbers, woke up their sleeping friends, until in a short time, hardly an able bodied man in the town was in his home.

"Men who upon ordinary occasions are cool, became perfectly wild and rushed about looking for an excuse to wreak vengeance on some one, it scarcely mattered whom . . . About half-past two o'clock, as a body of men were going down Center Street towards the Philadelphia and Reading Depot, a man came out of Michael Cassidy's house and fired a shot. The crowd immediately returned the fire.

"For the space of perhaps a half an hour there was quiet, but just as we were beginning to hope that the trouble was over twelve or fifteen shots, in rapid succession, were heard in the direction of East Coal Street . . . The house of Michael Lawler had been fired into . . ."

Fortunately for the Shenandoah bodymaster, he and his family were attending a wedding in Kulpmont, twenty miles away.

"He was lucky," said McParlan, "and I was too. I saw what was happening and got the hell off the streets. So did most of the brethren. The mob that shot up Muff's and then broke into his barroom and tore it apart was led by Reese Thomas. He was a tough Welshman and a friend of Gomer James.

"I was in my room at Cooney's and could hear everything that went on outside. All of a sudden somebody yells out, 'Get Tom Hurley! String him up!' I didn't want the mob to take him. He was an important link in my evidence. He was worth more to me alive than dead.

"I don't have much time, because that screaming mob could rush Hurley's house any minute, drag him out of bed, and kill him. The streets weren't safe for anyone that night, let alone a Molly, and I don't know what might happen to me if I go out myself. So I tell Mrs. Cooney to wake up Joey, her twelve-year-old, who's sleeping through all the excitement.

"I say to the lad to tell Tom to climb over his roof to Muff Lawler's and hide upstairs. Muff's place is only three doors down from the Hurleys and the mob's not going to return to Lawler's any more that night. It'd be the safest place in town. To protect Joey, I tell Mrs. Cooney to give him a medicine bottle to carry and if he's stopped he can say he's delivering a prescription.

"Well, it worked. They did stop Joey but when they saw the bottle they let him go. He got into the Hurleys' and Tom got away just in time. Thomas and his boys banged on Hurley's door a couple minutes later, pushed aside his mother and searched the place from cellar to roof."

The long night finally ended. To prevent a recurrence, the sheriff of Schuylkill County issued the following proclamation:

"All citizens are notified to be in their respective homes by half past nine (9½) each evening until further notice. An efficient *posse* has been appointed to preserve peace and they will be obeyed and respected accordingly. Shenandoah, October 10th, 1875."

But Tom Foster was by no means placated. Almost every day his cries for vigilantes grew louder. His strongest plea for mob action came a short while later, when he reprinted a "Know Nothing" editorial which appeared in the Lebanon *Daily News* under a one column head, THE MOLLY MAGUIRES. He followed this with his own postscript.

"There is a band of outlaws with the above name infesting Schuylkill County, who if justice were meted out to them, would today be hanging higher than Haman . . ." said the Lebanon newspaper. "When these foreigners come to this country and undertake to tamper with our free institutions, as they did when they sent a notice to the Patriotic Order Sons of America to discontinue that glorious organization, it is then time for an uprising on the part of the people . . . for the purpose of exterminating these brutal and ignorant scoundrels.

"The hanging of a few dozen of these rascals for an example would be a blessing and heralded with joy by the more respectable portion of our people. If this won't do, declare them banditti and 'string up' every mother's son of them, and that for the sake of justice, law and order only, and thus rid the county of a scourge worse than the Asiatic cholera."

To this appeal for a juridical shortcut to the Constitution's long way round, Thomas Jefferson Foster added his hearty approbation.

"Are you free born citizens going to allow yourselves to be cowed and murdered by a set of cutthroats, whom it would be an act of justice to shoot down at sight?" he asked his readers who now numbered thousands all over the hard coal counties.

184

"Will you allow your wives and children to be terrified, when you are at home, lest some miscreants enter and murder you in cold blood, or when you are absent, lest they see your corpse brought home and find themselves thrown, without a protector, upon the cold charity of the world?

"No! You are men and will act like men. Show the ruffians who have caused you all this trouble that you have at last become alive to the true state of the case and what remedy is necessary. Show them in such a decisive manner that no room for doubt will be allowed them as to what they may expect. Do this and the reign of terror will soon be over."

It did not take long for the pack to respond and end this year of violence on a fitting note.

Chapter Twenty-Seven

Early on the evening of December 9, a rumor swept through Mahanoy City that Robert Heaton and two witnesses to the Sanger-Uren murders had been shot to death by an "imported" executioner. Crowds of Welsh and English, some Modocs, others merely sympathizers, began gathering on street corners cursing the Irish in general, the Molly Maguires in particular, and the Wiggans Patch O'Donnells specifically.

It was an open secret that Jack Kehoe's brothers-in-law, Friday and Charles O'Donnell, were largely responsible for the deaths of the two Englishmen, although except for McParlan, who was not yet ready to reveal his information, no one could have proved it.

There was more than a slight basis for the belief that Heaton and the others could have been murdered by an overseas killer. Currently visiting his American cousins, the O'Donnells of Wiggans Patch, was Patrick O'Donnell, of Mannaclady, County Donegal. Known throughout the British Isles as "The Avenger," O'Donnell had been recognized in the Reading Railroad Depot by a former member of the Queen's Constabulary who had become a Philadelphia detective. Word was passed to Superintendent Franklin to be on the look-out for O'Donnell, last seen boarding a train for the hard coal regions.

Whether "The Avenger" had come to Schuylkill County to deal with informers or to investigate Jack Kehoe's growing unease that a detective was planted somewhere in the ranks of the Organization was never revealed, although it is probable that his trip to Wiggans Patch was merely social. Eight years later "The

Avenger" was hanged in London for the murder of an informer, whom he shot to death on the steamer *Melrose*, near Port Elizabeth, South Africa. O'Donnell's widow, a domestic in a Philadelphia home, refused to discuss her late husband's affairs.

It is unlikely that the mob, slowly gathering in Mahanoy City near Trier's corner, was aware just who the Wiggans Patch visitor actually was. But they had heard there was a stranger in the village and had been led to believe, perhaps deliberately, that he was an Irish gunman and organizer.

"I knew nearly everything about Patrick O'Donnell," said McParlan. "I knew when he got to Wiggans Patch and I knew when he left. At first I thought maybe it was me he was after but then I figured if Jack Kehoe ever found out who I really was he'd have wanted to do the job himself.

"Jack *was* getting leery. I could feel it every time I talked to him, and some of the boyos didn't seem quite so friendly as they used to. All but Frank McAndrew. I could count on him. No, as far as Pat O'Donnell was concerned, that boy had one real interest—the freedom of Ireland, and there were few ways he could promote it up in Schuylkill County.

"What I think happened was he was paying a social visit to his cousins and it could be Jack Kehoe talked over his problems with them. But I'd bet that's as far as it went. Anyway, the night the Modocs turned on the O'Donnells, Pat wasn't around. He'd left for Denver two days before."

Shortly after two A.M., December 10, 1875, the mob in front of Trier's had swollen to perhaps fifty men. Some of them had been drinking, most of them were armed, and all of them were in an ugly mood. Shouts could be heard—"Lynch the O'Donnells! Get Heaton's murderers!" "Drive the bastards out of town!"

A leader whose name has been carefully concealed for more than three-quarters of a century sprang up and the march was on! Down Center Street past Michael Clarke's, down through the end of the town and on to the dirt road leading to Wiggans Patch tramped the grim paraders, silent now but for the beat of their heavy miners' boots and the swish of their leather jackets.

A few hundred yards east of the gloomy hovels, dark except for what light was cast by a moon rising over the towering black colliery at the end of the village, the mob halted.

"Does anybody know which the O'Donnell's house is?" somebody whispered. And somebody else answered, "Yeah! It's the second to the left on the St. Nicholas side."

Then each man pulled a large red or blue polka dot handkerchief from his pants pocket and tied it over his nose and mouth. "All right, boys, let's go!" ordered the leader.

"This morning about three o'clock, a party of men broke into Mrs. O'Donnell's house at Wiggans . . . and shot her daughter, a Mrs. McAllister, dead in her bed, and took her son, Charles, outside and put seven balls into him, killing him instantly," wrote Tom Fielders in the Shenandoah *Herald*.

"Just before the dawn of day a body of men, supposed to number between forty and fifty, entered the patch. The majority of them spread themselves over what they supposed to be the most advantageous positions while six or seven of their number broke in the back door of Margaret O'Donnell's house. Mrs. O'Donnell is a widow and keeps a boarding house.

"When the house was broken into it contained the following inmates: James McAllister, Charles O'Donnell, John Purcell, Friday O'Donnell, James Blair, Thomas Murphy, Mrs. Margaret O'Donnell, Charles McAllister, and Ellen, his wife. Ellen, a bride of six months, was eighteen years old.

"The door that was smashed opened into the kitchen, back of which was a bedroom, occupied by Charles McAllister and his wife. The two latter were awakened by the noise and McAllister at once jumped out of bed and, telling his wife to lay still, he opened the cellar door and prepared to descend.

"His wife, however, did not heed his request and arising, went to the door of her room and saw the men just entering the kitchen. Before she had time to speak, one of the parties fired, the ball entering the nipple of her right breast. Saying 'I'm shot,' the unfortunate woman fell dead."

McAllister, perhaps braver under more favorable circumstances, turned tail.

"Seeing his wife fall, McAllister ran into the cellar and from there escaped into the next house which is occupied by Mrs.

Cassidy," continued the Shenandoah *Herald*. "Mrs. O'Donnell, on hearing the firing, jumped out of bed and going to the door of her room was met by two men, one of whom clapped a revolver to her cheek. His companion knocked it up and then gave her a terrible blow upon the right temple which knocked her down.

"The other room . . . was then entered by the men, who found there Charles O'Donnell, James McAllister, James Blair and John Purcell. Tying Purcell to the bed posts . . . they placed ropes around the necks of the other three and led them downstairs. Arriving in the open air, Blair was asked what was his name and when he replied, was told to go that he wasn't wanted.

"Two shots were then fired, one of which took effect in the breast of Charles O'Donnell and the other in the right arm of James McAllister. Both of the men then broke away and in spite of a number of shots fired at him McAllister escaped in the woods.

"O'Donnell ran about eight feet when he was brought down by a volley, just as he reached the western corner of a Polander's house . . . A number of the party then ran up and placing their firearms close to his body, fired, killing him instantly. They then decamped and no sooner had they disappeared than the terrified inhabitants of the patch came forth from their houses and were horrified at what they were compelled to look upon."

And where was Friday O'Donnell (murderer of the Englishmen Sanger and Uren) when the mob invaded his home, killed his brother and sister, and beat his aged mother?

"Friday," said the historian Dewees, "sought safety in instant flight."

An inquest was held December 12 in the front room of the O'Donnell home at Wiggans Patch. In one corner of the room were two beds, each one containing a body.

"Dr. Phaon Hermany, the Coroner, arrived from Mahanoy City and at once empanelled a jury," wrote Tom Fielders. "After clearing the room of all parties, excepting the jury and the *Herald* reporter, an examination of the bodies was made and as the cause of death in both cases was so plain Dr. Hermany said it would not be necessary to hold a post mortem.

"Mrs. Margaret O'Donnell, mother of the two murdered parties, was the first witness and was duly sworn. At this moment John Kehoe, of Girardville, entered the room and going to the side of the bed on which lay the dead body of Mrs. McAllister raised the covering from off the face and kissed it; he then went over and kneeling upon the floor he kissed the face of Charles O'Donnell and then standing up he raised his right arm and said, 'Dr. Hermany, this business is going to be settled in another way!' "

At this Mrs. O'Donnell shuddered visibly and glancing first at the body of her daughter and then her son, turned to Kehoe. "There's been enough blood shed around here, Jack," she said. "Let's have no more."

Then she told her story of the night's horror, adding little to what was already known.

"Upon the question, 'Do you know any of the men?' " continued Fielders, "just as the witness was about to answer, John Kehoe stepped up in front of her and said in a loud tone of voice, 'I order you not to answer that question!'

"Dr. Hermany said, 'Kehoe, you have no business in this room and I will hold you accountable for this.' Kehoe replied, 'It doesn't make any difference; I order her not to answer that question. This business will be settled in another way.'

"Witness then said, 'I won't tell, I can't tell; the men who entered the house were both big and small; the man who struck me was not tall . . . to the best of my knowledge there were six men upstairs. They all wore overcoats. They killed my daughter and then they killed my son.' "

Kehoe, who had subsided and was sitting quietly between his remaining sister-in-law and a friend, suddenly saw Fielders, whom he had not noticed before.

"Throw that son-of-a-bitch out!" he shouted. "If it wasn't for his dirty paper my sister would still be alive."

Then he made a lunge at the reporter but was held back by Charles D. Kaier, a husky brewer and a member of the panel.

For all the useful information the coroner's jury was able to extract from scores of witnesses, the six members of the panel might better have employed their time elsewhere. The verdict

in the slaying of Ellen McAllister and Charles O'Donnell—
"Death at the hands of persons unknown."

The funeral was held the next morning.

"Between eight and nine o'clock two hearses, containing the bodies of Charles O'Donnell and Ellen McAllister, left Wiggans Patch for Mahanoy City where they arrived a short time after nine o'clock," wrote Fielders.

"The bodies were taken to the Catholic Church and the funeral service performed by Father Ryan. Between eight and nine hundred people attended. The hearses, containing the bodies, were accompanied by six pall bearers."

One of Ellen McAllister's pallbearers was her brother-in-law Jack. As Father Ryan tossed a clump of grass into the open pit and intoned his prayer, "Dust thou art . . ." Kehoe, his face pale, eyes red-rimmed and wet with tears, turned around, fists clenched, and muttered, "It's not over yet, by God! There'll be plenty of dead men to show for this!"

For the record, it should be noted that Heaton and the two witnesses, whose rumored deaths were the cause of the Wiggans Patch slaying, died natural deaths many years later.

Chapter Twenty-Eight

By instinct, ability and experience, Franklin Benjamin Gowen was best equipped to direct the Commonwealth's offensive against the Molly Maguires, and his leadership was acknowledged by hard coal region district attorneys. Ever since Major Pinkerton sent McParlan on his dangerous assignment, it had been Gowen's strategy to try no Molly until the detective wound up his mission and gathered sufficient evidence to hang or imprison all ring-leaders. From this ex-prosecutor's point of view, the arrest of Doyle, Kelly, and Kerrigan was unfortunate; to try the prisoners quickly would be poor strategy.

As far as the President of the Road was concerned, McParlan's job was far from complete. In the first place the detective had failed to tie a single bodymaster to Siney and other union organizers. (As a matter of fact, McParlan wasn't able to uncover even casual contact between Molly leaders and labor "agitators.")

While Gowen certainly wanted to destroy Molly Maguirism, and fought bitterly to that end, pure justice was hardly his motivation. He wanted a provable connection between the Organization and the Unions. McParlan couldn't produce this link and refused to manufacture one. Then, too, despite frequent, voluminous, and detailed reports, the detective had not succeeded in obtaining the corroborative evidence Gowen needed to prosecute Kehoe, Campbell, Lawler, et al., effectively.

To be sure, McParlan's dispatches made fascinating reading. They also must have been highly frustrating. To know, sometimes in advance, how murders were plotted and by whom, yet be forced to sit by idly, unable to prevent them or arrest their perpetrators, would have tried the patience of almost anyone.

The only man in a position to offer corroborative evidence was McParlan himself. Major Pinkerton, however, had blocked this possibility during his first conference with the President of the Road. Gowen, aware that McParlan's days as an undercover agent were numbered and still lacking the evidence he needed so badly, kept pressing Pinkerton to withdraw previous objections and order McParlan to testify in court. The Major refused; he had no intention of signing his operative's death warrant. Besides, he felt McParlan would say no; the Irishman was a brave man but not a fool.

"Nobody had to tell me," McParlan said, "but I figured Mr. Gowen would want me in court when I finished gathering evidence. I wouldn't have taken the job in the first place if that was part of the deal. Of course, I had the right to refuse. Anyway, things were getting tougher and tougher and I'd been on the job over two years.

"Somehow the boyos in Shenandoah and Tamaqua had a feeling a detective had joined the Order. Nobody suspected me, except maybe Kerrigan. But it gave me a damned uneasy feeling to be sitting in on a meeting taking notes, and hear the brothers talk about what they'd do to the 'son-of-a-bitch' if they ever found him, and then wondering out loud who he could be.

"What I really was afraid of most of all was that Powderkeg would talk. He was a strange guy and I didn't trust him at all. He might squeal to the District Attorney and bring my name in as an undercover man, or he might get the word out to Alex and Jack that I was an informer. Either way I was a goner.

"I was in touch with Campbell all the time, although I didn't see much of Kehoe. I knew him and Alex were anxious to delay the Jones trial as long as they could. They needed to raise a defense fund and they weren't sure how much weight they'd have to be putting on witnesses."

The Molly Maguires were not the only ones uncertain of the pressure required to still the voices which could place Doyle, Kelly, and Kerrigan at the scene of the Jones murder.

"It is thought by many," said the Shenandoah *Herald,* "that to deter the reputable citizens of this place from giving evidence against Kelly, Kerrigan, and Doyle, at present in Mauch Chunk, a citizen or two might be murdered shortly, in cold blood . . .

"This, it is said, the Mollies think will keep witnesses away from the trial, and assist in securing the release of the murderers, which is confidently counted upon."

Even had the Commonwealth been able to persuade enough witnesses to put on a convincing show, there was no guarantee that resultant verdicts would please all "respectable" citizens of the hard coal regions.

"The murderers may be acquitted—such things have happened before—but the blood of Yost and Jones calls for vengeance," said one such citizen, who signed himself "Vindex" and whose letter to Editor Foster appeared in the Shenandoah *Herald.*

"Vindex," in a forum provided by Foster, furnished the answer should the courts fail to do their duty.

"Before the grass of next springtime grows upon the graves of Yost and Jones, the debt will have been wiped out—if not through the agency of the law and the courts, then, and more surely and swiftly, independent of that agency," promised Vindex.

"Our best citizens, our most consistent church members, and the men who have heretofore been the first to protest against any deviation from the strict paths of law, are rapidly 'hardening' so that even a failure to convict Kelly and Doyle, not to think of another murder, will turn them into very angels of death in their mission of vengeance and retaliation.

"Then, look out for those not only known to be Mollies but also those who associate with, harbor and encourage them!"

Other disturbing news came from the Mahanoy *Gazette,* which hinted darkly that "somewhere in these parts there would soon be a jail break and three important prisoners let loose."

Not so, declared the Shenandoah *Herald.*

"The jail is a massive structure, built of freestone, with a wall about twenty feet in height surrounding it. The main entrance is a very heavy looking door lined with a heavy sheet of boiler iron.

"You step inside and from the appearance of the walls and doors you become fully satisfied that the building is quite strong enough to hold even more dangerous men than Kelly and Doyle. The jail is well guarded . . . At night there is a guard of two men inside the building, with a good sized arsenal . . . there are two more men on the outside and two more inside the walls. With the six police who parade all day, that is all necessary to keep in safety any person committed to their charge."

While Gowen and the Molly Maguires shared a common desire to delay the trials of Doyle, Kelly, and Kerrigan, although for opposing reasons, the public continued to demand blood and the pressure was becoming irresistible. Gowen, hoping all along that Pinkerton would change his mind and permit the McParlan to testify or else dig up an informer, urged his Carbon County colleagues to accept all defense moves for postponement.

There were procrastinations while a change of venue was debated and finally denied. Then defense counsel requested separate trials. Fielders covered these lengthy hearings, Judge Dreher presiding. The courtroom was jammed.

"All kinds of classes are represented," declared the Shenandoah *Herald*, "the b'hoys making a specially strong turn and among them we noticed several well known and *respected* members of the Molly Maguire Association.

"Having seen the prisoners at Tamaqua when they were alarmed at their position and fatigued after their long chase we were astonished at the change in their appearance. All three looked fleshier and healthier . . . Kelly seems to be improved by his imprisonment and has lost the hunted look he wore at Tamaqua.

"As soon as Doyle's mother saw him she left her seat and rushing over the rail which separated them, leaned over and putting her arms around his neck kissed him on both cheeks. The emotion raised by this act of devotion and love was clearly visible to those who sat near.

"As they were being led from the courtroom, Doyle turned around and looked toward his mother and sister, nodded his head, tried to smile a farewell, but the effort was more than his spirits were capable of. Doyle seems to be endowed with more feeling than either of the others.

"Kelly sits and looks straight ahead but does not let a word that is said on either side pass unnoticed."

The only nonchalant member of the trio was little Powderkeg, still an enigma to his wife, children, counsel, and colleagues.

"Kerrigan," continued Fielders, "does not seem to bother himself much about the situation . . . Asked how he liked the state of affairs, he answered, 'Oh, first rate. I can get used to anything,' and if he cannot, his looks belie him. He seemed to be perfectly composed and continually amused himself by stroking the short chin whiskers he has grown since his confinement."

The prosecution was still uncertain of Powderkeg's role in the oncoming trials. True, he had been indicted and held without bail on a charge of homicide, but only a few witnesses were able to place him near the scene of the crime and he certainly had no ostensible motive for killing Jones. Jones's widow, who knew Kerrigan by sight and was aware that her late husband had a speaking acquaintance with him, refused to consider Kerrigan a murderer.

Kerrigan continued to deny that he had ever before seen Doyle or Kelly, claiming that his juxtaposition with the pair when all three were captured was purely coincidental. Since neither Kelly nor Doyle confessed to any part of the crime, and so did not negate Powderkeg's story, it was barely possible, the Commonwealth thought, that Kerrigan was telling the truth. Quite a few of Tamaqua's most prominent citizens, including Dan Shepp, half-believed the fellow.

Shepp was puzzled by all the seemingly contradictory evidence about the man whom he still considered a friend. As a matter of fact, the Tamaqua mine owner, baffled in his attempts to discover who murdered his brother-in-law, Patrolman Yost, used to ask Kerrigan to try to solve the crime. And Powderkeg, Shepp said later, always answered with a straight face, "You know me, Dan Shepp. If there's anything I can do to help a friend, you can count on me."

When Judge Dreher handed down his decision granting each prisoner a separate trial, Carbon County District Attorney Edward Siewers chose to begin with Doyle, to be followed by Kelly and finally Kerrigan. The twenty-six-year-old Doyle, whose past reputation was spotless, was not the first Molly Maguire to be charged with a capital offense. Two members of the Brotherhood had been tried in Columbia County for the murder of Alexander Rea, a mining superintendent, in 1864 and both were acquitted; the case against Pat Hester, indicted for the same slaying, was *nolle-prossed*. Another Molly Maguire discharged of murder by a jury of his peers was Dan Dougherty, accused of killing Chief Burgess George Major of Mahanoy City.

But this was the first time in over two decades that the chances of convicting a Molly Maguire of homicide were reasonably good. From the prosecution's point of view, the cases against Doyle and Kelly, if not Kerrigan, were solid. Should Doyle be convicted, the probability was that Kelly, too, would be found guilty.

In addition to witnesses who, if they dared, could trace the prisoners' movements for a full thirty-six hours before the crime, the Carbon County district attorney held other invaluable data, passed on to him from Gowen. To be sure, without corroborative evidence such information from McParlan, whose identity was unrevealed even to Siewers, was basically only of "shock" value. It would be used mainly to startle the defendants and their counsel by disclosing the innermost secrets of the Brotherhood and to cloak the prosecution with an air of omniscience. Properly timed, its psychological effect could be devastating and might cause at least one of the defendants to break. That is what Gowen hoped for.

The defense was not without ammunition. Nobody yet had proved the Molly Maguires even existed. True, there were groups of men all over the hard coal regions belonging to the Ancient Order of Hibernians. While this Society may have been disliked by most non-Catholics (and a considerable number of Catholics as well) in other parts of the United States, it was not castigated there; and its Constitution, by-laws and code of Christian ethics were above reproach. Unless it could be shown that local members had perverted the A.O.H. so thoroughly that it functioned in the anthracite regions only as a figurehead for murder, and that the defendants were active members, there would be no demonstrable motive for Jones's murder.

The trial of the Commonwealth *vs.* Michael J. Doyle began

197

on Tuesday, January 18, 1876. Doyle and his colleagues had been in jail for more than four months, a long time to await court action on a non-bailable offense in those days. Judge Dreher, an elderly, amiable, and fair, if undistinguished, member of the Bench, presided in an atmosphere bearing no resemblance to a carnival. While the population of Carbon County was far from homogeneous, the dominant ethnic group, particularly in the farm lands which nearly surround Mauch Chunk, was placid Pennsylvania Dutch. As a matter of fact, "low" German—Plattdeutsch—rather than English was the common tongue.

Every seat in the large courtroom was filled but there was no overflow into the corridor. "Dutchmen" peering through the door and observing that space was not available did not try to push into the chamber. Instead they walked away quietly, hoping *soll mer's erscht mol* (they should have more luck) the next day.

Relatives of Doyle, Kelly, and Kerrigan—and there were many of them—sat in the front rows behind scores of witnesses. Few, if any, of the women associated with the prisoners by birth or marriage had the slightest idea of their kin's guilt. Most of these daughters, mothers, and wives were pale and careworn, but here and there was a dark Irish beauty, perhaps as lovely as the dead Ellen McAllister.

A good half of the audience were women. Strategically scattered throughout the large chamber were Molly Maguires, hard, young, and aloof, uneasy in the presence of so many hostile faces, and unsure of the role they might play in the drama about to be unfolded.

Up front, to the right of His Honor, sat the prosecutor and his regular staff, augmented by three of Pennsylvania's most distinguished members of the Bar, on loan to Mr. Siewers "for the duration." One of the trio was Major General Charles Albright, veteran of the Civil War. He attended every session of court in full military regalia although there were times when the portly gentleman's sword got into his way. In civilian life, Albright was chief counsel for the Lehigh and Wilkes-Barre Railroad.

To the General's left was Mr. Allen Craig, Yale '29, former Northampton County district attorney but currently head of the Lehigh Valley Railroad Company's legal department. To the

General's right sat Mr. Frank W. Hughes, elected by the Reading Company Board of Directors to fill the position vacated when Franklin Benjamin Gowen ascended to the presidency of the Road. Albright was the orator, Craig, "learned in the law," but the white-haired aging Hughes, suave and still handsome, was the courtroom strategist. His tactics had been planned well in advance, during many sessions with the former Schuylkill County district attorney, Franklin B. Gowen.

Mr. Siewers, nominally in charge of the prosecution, was middle-aged, competent, and friendly. He spoke Pennsylvania Dutch as well as he spoke English—as a matter of fact his English had an unmistakable flavor of Pennsylvania Dutch. On occasion, and this usually delighted the panel, he was known to lapse into Plattdeutsch to make a point. It must have occurred to him that should he win this important case for the People, the People just might elect him to the Bench.

Chief defense counsel was Mr. Linn Barthelemew. In the words of Tom Fielders, "Mr. Barthelemew is an orator. He speaks with energy, rapidity, pointedly. He conducts the examinations for defendants and does considerable talking. He is well-known all over the state, as much for his social qualities as his eloquence."

Supporting Mr. Barthelemew were a pair of very expensive members of the Schuylkill County Bar, John W. Ryon, former judge, and Congressman John B. Reilly. Gossip had it that for every day these gentlemen spent in court, the fee was ten dollars apiece. There was some question about the Congressman's charges and it may well be that he was "returning the favor" to Mr. Jack Kehoe, who helped move Mr. Reilly from Pottsville to Washington, where he represented Pennsylvania's Fifteenth Congressional District. In any event both gentlemen were ready for action.

"Mr. Ryon," said the Mauch Chunk *Coal Gazette*, "is a man of medium height. His face is of the round English pattern, and it is covered with short bristling iron gray whiskers. He has a full, resonant voice which is very powerful. At first sight one would take Mr. Ryon for a heavy, dull lawyer, but it would be a great mistake. He is as droll as he looks solemn, and he adds greatly to the effect of his sharp, dryly pungent thrusts by the grave manner of his delivery.

"Mr. Reilly has the reputation of being one of Pennsylvania's handsomest congressmen. He is a brilliant young lawyer and a fluent talker."

Two members of the Carbon County Bar, Daniel Kalbfus and Edward Mulhearn, completed the defense staff.

Except for the prisoner, waiting to be led in chains from his cell to the dock, the courtroom atmosphere, at least in the area of counsel, was pleasant enough. Since nobody ever hanged a member of the Bar for losing a capital case, this was understandable. "'Lawyers on both sides get along well together," reports the *Coal Gazette*.

There is a sudden hush in the high-ceilinged chamber as Judge Dreher enters from a door leading to chambers. "All rise!" shouts Adam Wagner, Clerk of the Court, and the audience dutifully obeys. The Judge is seated.

"Hear ye! Hear ye! . . ." intones Mr. Wagner, and the case of the Commonwealth of Pennsylvania *vs.* Michael Joseph Doyle begins.

"At eleven minutes of eleven o'clock," said the Mauch Chunk *Coal Gazette*, "Doyle is arraigned by District Attorney Siewers for the murder of John P. Jones, at Lansford, on the morning of September 3, last past, to which indictment the prisoner pleads not guilty. The customary advisory document was then read to him by the clerk, and he having elected to be tried by 'God and his country,' nothing remains but the selection of the jury for the trial to proceed."

If the pattern of choosing the first two jurors had held, a panel would have been completed before the day ended. Within a half hour a pair of jurymen were seated in the box. But it was not until late Friday afternoon, when, as the *Coal Gazette* phrased it, "the dusk of evening was coming in," that the twelfth panelist was approved by the Commonwealth and the defense. He was Craig H. Long, a Lehighton harness maker. Mr. Long, like the eleven who preceded him, "had no conscientious scruples against capital punishment, had heard and/or read of the case but never formed an opinion, and could enter the jury box unbiased for or against the prisoner." Scores of other Carbon

County citizens had been examined and rejected, peremptorily or for cause.

Even those who won acceptance were not without minor handicaps. One juror admittedly was "slightly deaf" and several others were forced to make mental translations from English into their mother tongue before they fully comprehended what was being said. Obviously both the Commonwealth and defense counsel, each in his fashion, hoped to turn these shortcomings into advantages.

On the night of Friday, January 20, ten inches of snow fell in Carbon County and the next morning, the jurors, locked up for the night in the American Hotel, had difficulty walking to the courthouse, a block or two away. Court, in rural Pennsylvania, usually convened at seven A.M., an hour which came as a fearful shock to visiting members of the Philadelphia Bench who were accustomed to arriving in chambers closer to eleven o'clock.

Judge Dreher, a punctilious gentleman, arrived a few minutes late, for which he duly apologized to counsel. The stormy weather had no effect on attendance. Again every seat in the courtroom was occupied, certainly a tribute to the indomitable Carbon County citizens, including hardy farmers who had to plough their way through high drifts from as far off as Lehighton.

Among those not present was James McParlan, appointed by Jack Kehoe to head a drive for defense funds. This assignment took him all over the anthracite regions, tapping, jigging and singing sentimental ballads for barroom habitués, who tossed their coppers to him; persuading bodymasters to contribute generously; and running dances, one in Wilkes-Barre, another in Hazelton, and a third in Palo Alto.

He managed to send daily reports to Franklin while maintaining contact with Lawler and Campbell to "help" provide alibis for Doyle, Kelly, and Kerrigan. But even if he had had time, it is more than likely that the detective would not have been a welcome visitor at the trial. "Most people thought McParlan still was that scoundrel named McKenna, the most vicious Molly of them all," wrote Schlegel in his biography of Benjamin Franklin Gowen.

McParlan did get to see Mary Ann and Mrs. Kerrigan at least once during the first few days of the trial. Powderkeg's wife looked more troubled than ever since her last conversation with her husband. The pair had talked at some length in the Mauch Chunk jail.

"I'm afraid of what he might do next," Mrs. Kerrigan told McParlan. "I think he's scared."

This news was communicated promptly to Franklin and pressure applied to Powderkeg, who merely laughed when told he would be better off to confess if he wanted "to save his soul." At that point Kerrigan's neck was of more interest to him than dubious immortality in a questionable hereafter.

Meanwhile the trial went on. From nine-year-old breaker boy Oswald Moser, who spoke only Pennsylvania Dutch and needed an interpreter, to aged David Livingood, railroad watchman, witness after witness, unafraid of the consequences, mounted the stand and told the truth as they saw it. Through their eyes the fascinated panel was able to follow Doyle and his companions in death from the moment they left Tamaqua for the first time when Jones was fingered, to their subsequent return to Lansford where the mine superintendent was shot, and on to their flight and capture.

While defense counsel ripped into testimony and frequently was able to reveal great discrepancies, the Commonwealth gradually established the power and solidity of its case.

Of course, this was only one side of the story. The defense had a hundred witnesses on call, each prepared to swear under oath that the murderer could not possibly have been Doyle (or Kelly or Kerrigan) because the prisoner before the Bar and his colleagues were forty miles away when Jones was killed.

Chapter Twenty-Nine

Kerrigan, who, with Kelly, was brought into court only after a jury had been selected, seemed interested and occasionally amused by the proceedings. Except for his leg shackles, which could not easily be seen, he appeared to be more spectator than prisoner. He raised his eyebrows in mock disbelief when a witness recounted the chase over the mountains, shook his head sadly as Mrs. Murphy described Doyle's tattered clothing, and smiled admiringly when the Tamaqua law student explained how his binoculars had been used to pinpoint the fugitives.

One bit of testimony caused Powderkeg to chuckle out loud. He could not restrain his merriment when Manfred Nealy, a Summit Hill saloonkeeper, related Kelly's attempts to pad the expense account.

"The pair of them walks into my hotel," testified Nealy, "and orders two beers. I serve them and the bigger fellow hands me a dime an' when I give him his change he takes out a piece of paper and a pencil stub. He licks the stub and writes down something and the other fellow looks over at what he's writing an' says, 'Why are you charging for our supper? You know we ain't payin' for it.' That was the truth. I serve the biggest free lunch in Summit Hill.

"Well, the bigger man says, 'Shut up! I'm ony chargin' a dime,' and the other guy says, 'That ain't honest.' "

(Later, when the expense account was produced, the supper charge had been crossed out. Whether this was due to Doyle's innate honesty, since he *was* born on Washington's birthday, or fear of County Treasurer Donnelly's fish-eyed scrutiny, never was learned.)

Kerrigan appeared slightly troubled when he was led back to his cell late on the afternoon of Wednesday, January 26, nine days after the trial had begun. The last witness, Mrs. Margaret Griffith, who owned a truck patch just outside of Tamaqua and knew Kerrigan well, told the Court she had seen Powderkeg with two other men whom she clearly identified as Doyle and Kelly walking toward Summit Hill early on the morning of Jones's murder.

"It's a full moon and it's almost like day when I seen him and the others," recalled Mrs. Griffith. "I says, 'Hello, Mr. Kerrigan,' and he says, 'Hello, Maggie. What are you doin' out here at three o'clock in the mornin'?' And I tell him I'm after lookin' for me cow which has pulled out her tether.

"Then *I* says to *him,* 'What the hell are *you* doin' out at three o'clock in the mornin'?' And he says, 'Why Mrs. G., me and my friends are lookin' for a goat that's broken off its tether.' At first I think he says 'ghost' and I'm believin' poor Powderkeg's gone daft. I say, 'There ain't no ghost around here.'

"And he answers, 'I said goat, Maggie, but you may be right at that.' Then he says, 'Good night, Mrs. G., or good mornin', take your choice,' and with that the three of them are off and that's the last I seen them until this very day in court."

The endless parade of witnesses for the Commonwealth rolled on the following morning. The display of prosecution strength apparently impressed everyone in the courtroom except Kerrigan, who recovered from the setback Mrs. Griffith had given him, and continued to view all proceedings as a spectacle produced solely for his enjoyment.

From time to time, as defense counsel rose to cross-examine a witness, raise an objection, or file an exception, Powderkeg would lean toward Mr. Barthelemew, Judge Ryon, or Congressman Reilly and smile approvingly as if to acknowledge his appreciation for an apt line well read. Even the fact that the Commonwealth seemed to hold all the cards didn't faze Kerrigan. When General Albright, District Attorney Siewers, or Mr. Craig made a skillful play, they could count on drawing voluble murmurs of approbation from Powderkeg.

Late that afternoon Kerrigan lost both his equanimity and

temper, during the testimony of the assistant jail keeper, whose brother was sheriff of Carbon County.

"One day in October," said the jail keeper, "the prisoners in the upper tier were unusually noisy and I went out to quieten them. Then I snuck down to the lower block where we kept the three murderers.

"I was listening quietly at the register and I hear Kerrigan tell Doyle that next day the lawyers are going to take their statements to Mount Laffee to make them gee with their own witnesses."

Since it was from Mount Laffee that defense counsel expected to produce alibis, Powderkeg's meaning was obvious. An anticipated objection from defense was overruled. The witness went on.

" 'Is zat so?' says Doyle, and Kerrigan says, 'It is. The lawyers are afraid I'll squeal.' Then Doyle asks if any of the prisoners are over at the register or heater listening and Kerrigan tells him they ain't.

"Then Doyle says, 'What would you squeal about? You don't know nothin'.' And Kerrigan says, 'Oh, I don't, don't I? Maybe if I want to talk I wouldn't have to stay in this place ten minutes.'

"Then Kelly curses Kerrigan and Doyle tells them both to shut up and they do."

At this assault on his integrity, Kerrigan lost his poise; his face reddened and he growled furiously. Finally he could bear it no longer.

"Kerrigan, a small man," said the Mauch Chunk *Coal Gazette*, "sprang to his feet. 'You're a liar!' he shouted. 'You're trying to swear my life away.' "

The reason for Kerrigan's anger was clear. It was not that Powderkeg believed the testimony would aid the prosecution: what he feared was that the assistant warden's words would give ideas to brethren in attendance, in which case his life, even in jail, might be in considerable danger. When Kerrigan was led back to his cell at the close of the day, he was a deeply troubled man.

Kerrigan, like the rest of the prisoners, was permitted one visitor for a maximum of fifteen minutes after the session was over, no matter what the hour. Mrs. Kerrigan rarely missed seeing her husband. But on January 27, when she knocked at the jail door, she was told that Kerrigan did not want to talk to anyone. She walked away, extremely unhappy, and instead of spending the night in Mauch Chunk, rode directly to Tamaqua.

It took her nearly four hours to cover the twelve miles separating the two towns. When she arrived she went to the Mansion Hotel, where she knew McParlan was making his headquarters while collecting alibis. He had just returned from Mount Laffee when Mrs. Kerrigan entered the room.

"Jimmy wouldn't see me tonight," she said. "I'm afraid of what's coming. I don't trust him and I never did and if the little son-of-a-bitch informs, I'll kill him meself."

"Who'll he squeal to?" McParlan asked.

"There's only one man," she answered. "His 'friend,' Dan Shepp. There'd be nobody else."

McParlan was as much concerned as Mrs. Kerrigan. If Powder-keg suspected that the detective was playing a dual role, and he was inclined to believe he did, McParlan's position could become untenable. Should Kerrigan, and subsequently Shepp, talk freely, and word reach Campbell, Kehoe, or any other bodymaster, McParlan would be in imminent danger. There would be no protection from Captain Linden unless the detective pulled up stakes and left the area immediately.

At that hour, McParlan had no one to turn to for instructions. Whatever the decision, it would have to be his own. He decided to gamble on Shepp's discretion; there was no question about the mine owner's integrity. When he assured Mrs. Kerrigan he'd do what he could and sent her home, McParlan slipped out of the hotel and trudged through the snow to Shepp's big home at the end of Lehigh Avenue.

"My grandfather, Dan Shepp," recalled Mrs. Isabelle Wilford, "was used to all kinds of shocks. Once he was hunting in Wyoming and his party was attacked by the Indians he'd thought were friendly. He was a forty-niner, too; he found gold and he lost it. He came back east, built a big breaker and one morning he got up and learned it was burned to the ground.

"But he often told mother the biggest shock he ever got was

the night he heard somebody banging on the front door and when he went down in his night clothes, lantern in one hand and pistol in the other, found 'McKenna the Molly' standing there.

" 'What the hell do you want, McKenna?' my grandfather asked.

" 'I want to come in and talk to you,' he answered.

" 'At this hour?' and when he nodded his head, my grandfather said, 'All right. Put your hands over your head and walk in but don't try any tricks. I'd just as soon shoot you as any other rat.' "

It took McParlan a while to convince Shepp that he actually was a detective and not "McKenna the Molly." Shepp was an intelligent, courageous man, but in his effort to track down Yost's murderers, he had made one mistake in hiring a detective whose identity was discovered almost at once. McParlan did not want him to make another error.

Despite Mrs. Kerrigan's fears, there was no assurance that Powderkeg would reveal anything, or that if he did decide to inform, he would ask for Dan Shepp. Nor was there any way to be sure in advance just how much Kerrigan would say. As for price, both McParlan and Shepp agreed that what Powderkeg would want in payment was his life, whatever that might be worth once it became known he was an informer.

Should Kerrigan decide to talk to Shepp, the strategy he and McParlan developed would be to convince Powderkeg that his information was not as valuable as it might have been, because he was not the first to "squeal." If Powderkeg were to question this, Shepp was to give Kerrigan the latest "goods," which Mc-Parlan revealed to the mine owner to use as evidence that someone had beaten Kerrigan to confessing. But in no way was Shepp to disclose to Kerrigan, the district attorney, the sheriff or anybody else, McParlan's identity. The detective knew only too well the speed with which prison "grapevine" news travels.

"My grandfather," Mrs. Wilford continued, "offered McParlan a drink, his hospitality, and protection for the night. McParlan took the drink but said he'd better get back to the hotel before he was missed.

" 'Aren't you kind of scared?' Grandfather asked.

207

" 'I guess I am,' McParlan answered. But he grinned (and grandfather said you couldn't help but like him) and said, 'Good night, Mr. Shepp. Thank you,' and he was off into the dark all by himself."

At midnight when Sheriff Breneiser, making his nightly rounds, passed Kerrigan's cell, Powderkeg whispered, "George, I want to talk to you."

Breneiser flashed his lantern into Cell Eight and looked down at Kerrigan who was standing next to the bars. The prisoner put his index finger over his mouth and at the same time nodded in the direction of the adjacent cells, which held Kelly and Doyle.

"What is it?" asked the sheriff softly.

"Not here, George," Powderkeg answered. "Let's go up to your office."

With that, Breneiser, who had been instructed by Siewers to listen carefully when Kerrigan had anything to say, opened the door.

"Don't try nothin'," he warned Kerrigan. Placing his pistol against Kerrigan's neck, he marched him to the rear of the cell block, unlocked a door leading to the sheriff's quarters, relocked it, and walked to his office, Kerrigan still in front of him.

"Sit down," Breneiser ordered, "and tell me what you want."

"I want to see Dan Shepp. I got something to say to him."

"It's after midnight, Powderkeg. Dan'll be asleep. Wait 'til morning."

"Wake him up then, George. What I got to say won't wait that long. I could be dead by then!"

By the time the sheriff's brother drove his one-horse sled over the dangerous icy road to Tamaqua, awakened the mine owner, changed his animal for a fresh one, and returned to Mauch Chunk with Shepp, it was 5 A.M.

Kerrigan, who had fallen asleep on a couch in the warden's office under the watchful eyes of Sheriff Breneiser, awoke when Shepp entered. Smiling cheerfully, the prisoner stood up, clasped the big mine owner's hand, and greeted him with considerable warmth and no embarrassment.

"I've a few things to tell you, Dan," he said, "but they're just between us two old friends."

Shepp glanced at the Breneiser brothers, who nodded their heads, walked out of the office, shut the door, and left Kerrigan and the Tamaqua mine owner alone.

While court was convening that morning, Kerrigan and Shepp were still talking. At first, Kerrigan would do no more than talk, refusing to allow Shepp to make notes. But by eleven o'clock the mine owner had Powderkeg's signed confession in his pocket.

Kerrigan, in this first of many subsequent confessions, cleverly avoided direct involvement in any murder. His role, one which he never dropped, was that of an almost innocent bystander, drawn unwittingly into the Brotherhood, afraid for his life and that of his family if he should reveal secrets of the Molly Maguires or any of their crimes, or resign from the Order.

His duplicity was incredible, his humor excellent. He grinned knowingly when Shepp denied that McParlan was, as Kerrigan had long suspected, a detective. When Shepp uttered the current password, Kerrigan, in return, gave the mine owner the latest recognition sign by placing the tip of his right forefinger on the bridge of his nose. As Shepp responded promptly by putting his left thumb in the corner of his right eye, Kerrigan nodded his head patronizingly. "Well done, Brother. You'd make a good Molly."

Kerrigan's crowning delight came when he asked Shepp, torn between disgust at Powderkeg's treachery and amazement at his effrontery, whether he knew the current drinking pledge. Shepp was forced to say no. (McParlan had not thought to teach him this one.) Then Kerrigan, who could hardly contain himself, clinked his coffee cup against the mine owner's and between bursts of laughter gave the toast. To anyone else in the prisoner's peculiar position, this might have proved embarrassing.

"Here's to every honest squealer that went upon the stand,

"That swore the truth, and nothing more, may he prosper in this land."

Shepp had promised Kerrigan nothing except his pledge to impress the district attorney with Powderkeg's "sincerity" and perhaps "a return of the favor." While Kerrigan talked freely about the Yost and Jones murders, he politely refused to discuss anything else. "I know a great deal more," he said, "but I want to see where I stand first."

Shepp then called Sheriff Breneiser, who summoned the district attorney and Mr. Hughes, and handed them Kerrigan's signed confession, a portion of which follows:

> Mauch Chunk Jan'y 28/1876 James Carrigan volentarily makes The following Statement and Says he will reveal all he knows in regard to the Murder of B. F. Yost and John P Jones and Says Hugh McGuighen of Summit Hill and James Boyle works at No 5 are the Men that Murdered B. F. Yost on the night of the 5th of July 1875 James Boyle is a Man not Much taller then I am wares a dark Mustash Hugh McGuighen keeps a Salloon on Summit Hill I did not See the Shooting but those Men told Me themselves Thos Duffy was to pay Boyle and McGuighen for Shooting B. F. Yost James Carrall gave the Pistol to Shoot Yost with. Thos Duffy Stayed all night at Jas Carrall's house you Mind the time B F Yost prosecuted Duffy I told him I did. Well John Slatty Came to You to Settle it I told him yes.

The moment Siewers and Hughes read Kerrigan's statement they knew that a break, perhaps the "big" one, had come. They would not be able to use Kerrigan in the Doyle case because Powderkeg, a defendant charged with homicide, could not be called as a witness for the prosecution. Although they might be able to introduce his confession, it would entail calling Shepp to the stand; since the mine owner was not a disinterested witness, the defense could tear him apart on the question of "intent."

Siewers instructed the sheriff to keep Powderkeg in the warden's quarters under twenty-four hour protection. Then, as soon as the Doyle case was over, they could work out a "deal" so satisfactory to Kerrigan that the informer would be willing to tell more. The district attorney and Hughes returned to the courtroom, and the trial, which had been recessed briefly, continued.

Whether the leak was planned or accidental, word of Kerrigan's confession had swept through the courtroom. Doyle's face was a dead white and Kelly, who had behaved stoically for the past ten days, broke down and sobbed, no one knew if from sadness, anger, or frustration.

The Commonwealth called only one more witness, George Purnell, a "gandy dancer" who had noticed red shale on Doyle's shoes when the fugitives were captured. The shale, Purnell testified, was used for tamping rails a few yards from the point where Jones met his death. But under cross-examination Purnell admitted that similar dust could be found almost anywhere in the northeastern part of the United States.

When the railroader stepped down from the box, Siewers declared that the Commonwealth's case was closed. Then to the astonishment of His Honor, the jury, the courtroom audience, and the seventy-four witnesses who had been subpoenaed to provide the prisoner with an alibi, Reilly arose and said simply, "The defense rests."

There is no one around to ask why the defense decided to call it quits at this point; a re-reading of the trial record provides no clue. It is possible the knowledge that Kerrigan "sang" influenced Mr. Barthelemew and his colleagues. But considering the fact that Powderkeg's confession was not made part of the record and that its existence was unknown to the jury, this premise does not hold water.

The American historian James Ford Rhodes has a plausible explanation:

"The defense was a carefully manufactured alibi," wrote

Rhodes in 1909, "but as it was evident that the Commonwealth stood ready to prosecute for perjury as well as for murder, counsel for Doyle, either too timid or too honorable to put upon the stand men who they knew would swear falsely, did not call their witnesses and let the case go to the jury on the evidence of the Commonwealth."

By mutual agreement the Commonwealth would make three speeches and the defense two. There was no time limit set for each appeal. Mr. Craig opened for the prosecution.

"At eleven minutes past two o'clock, Mr. Craig rises amid almost oppressive silence, begins his plea," reported the Mauch Chunk *Coal Gazette*. "He feelingly appeals to the individual judgment of the jury and the sympathies of all good men and women in the audience. Many a tear is shed as he refers to the 'anguish of the widow, and the shrieks of the orphans so suddenly bereft of a loving father.'"

Four hours later, the dignified, white-haired, and confidence-inspiring Mr. Hughes followed the Northampton district attorney. His appeal was without passion and his approach almost professorial.

"During delivery," said the *Coal Gazette,* "he reviewed the whole chain of evidence from whose meshes he constructed a web to escape from which will be found a difficult task . . . Mr. Hughes was cool and collected—in fact the whole was delivered in such an . . . unostentatious manner; so unsensational as to disappoint those who had expected an entertainment of that kind."

Court's recess for the night interrupted Mr. Hughes' grim recitation of the facts. He continued the following morning: his talk lasted four and a half hours.

The briefest speech of all was made by chief counsel for the defense, Mr. Linn Barthelemew. In the single hour he allotted himself, Mr. Barthelemew attacked the value of purely circumstantial evidence which, he said truthfully, was all the Commonwealth had to offer. Next he stressed the theory of "reasonable doubt" and laughed at prosecution testimony, comparing it to "the warming pan and stewed tomatoes" in *Pickwick Papers.* Then he defended the Ancient Order of Hibernians.

"Referring to the A.O.H.," said the *Coal Gazette*, "Mr. Barthelemew claims it is a lawful association and attempts to dispel the theory of Molly Maguirism . . . He ridicules the idea of Kerrigan being a captain, and Alexander Campbell one of the high contracting parties in the assassination of Jones. . . ."

Mr. Kalbfus followed. He opened his defense with a prayer.

"Dear God," said Mr. Kalbfus as reported in the *Coal Gazette*, "put into the hearts of these twelve a little of the charity that covers a multitude of sins."

Throughout his lengthy address, in which he tried to destroy the credibility of Commonwealth witnesses one by one, Mr. Kalbfus had occasional lapses into Pennsylvania Dutch. He would stand in front of the box, pausing now and then as if unable to find the right English word, and be forced to rely on a Pennsylvania Dutch substitute to express himself. The jury, with similar problems, seemed to empathize.

After a speech lasting seven hours, Mr. Kalbfus closed with a quotation in Latin, as incomprehensible as English to several members of the jury.

"Fiat justitia, ruat caelum," thundered Mr. Kalbfus. (Fortunately, for the benefit of future historians, the anonymous reporter for the *Coal Gazette* gave both translation and source.)

Mr. Kalbfus' speech was long, but the prosecution's anchor man went him two hours better. General Albright, his Civil War uniform freshly pressed, his medals polished, began to speak at 3 P.M., Saturday, January 29. The Sunday recess interrupted him after he had talked for slightly more than an hour. He began anew at 7 A.M. Monday, January 31, his sword gleaming first as the morning sun shone through the tall windows, then from the reflected rays of kerosene lamps, lighted when night fell.

He stressed the credibility of all the Commonwealth's witnesses and reviewed every bit of prosecution testimony, then tied them all together. He excoriated the Molly Maguires and lavished praise upon their enemies. From dawn to dusk General Albright ran the emotional and literary gamut. He quoted the Bible, Shakespeare, Swift, Goldsmith, Dickens and Thackeray, without mercy and seemingly without end.

It was not until 5 P.M. that this military gentleman concluded his speech with a supplication to his Creator, with Whom he appeared to be on intimate terms.

"I know God will bless this jury," assured the General, "because it will do its duty like men."

Judge Dreher's charge was thorough and damning. He made no reference, however, to the Molly Maguires, the Irish, or the Church of Rome, all three of which had provided constant background music played by the prosecution for the panel of a dozen stalwart Protestants.

His Honor began with what might be the understatement of that centennial year.

"The question of whether Michael J. Doyle is guilty or not," declared the Court, "is a vital question to Michael J. Doyle."

Then Judge Dreher explained the various degrees of homicide and outlined the case for the Commonwealth.

"The prosecution charges that John P. Jones was willfully, premeditatedly, and wantonly killed by Doyle, Kelly and Kerrigan . . . and has called a large number of witnesses to sustain the charge. The defense has produced none. The law presumes every man innocent until he is proven guilty, and, therefore, the burden of proof rests on the Commonwealth.

"The defense not calling witnesses is no evidence that Michael J. Doyle is guilty of the killing of John P. Jones."

He continued this expository phase of his charge with a statement which must have struck the jury with considerable impact.

"To be sure, by not calling witnesses, the evidence produced by the prosecution remains uncontradicted . . . If the guilt of Doyle is proved by this evidence, the presumption of innocence is overcome and no longer shields him."

The Court touched lightly but firmly upon the testimony of many of the Commonwealth's witnesses, from the first to the one hundred seventeenth man or woman who swore "to tell the truth, the whole truth and nothing but the truth."

As to the value of circumstantial evidence, the only kind produced by the Commonwealth, Judge Dreher had this to say:

"You have been cautioned by counsel for the defense of the danger of conviction on circumstantial evidence; that men have been convicted and hung when innocent. The same thing has happened in positive evidence, and yet because men have been hung when innocent, persons convicted on circumstantial evidence, they should, should be cleared.

"If men cannot be hanged on circumstantial evidence, then they cannot be on positive evidence. All the circumstances proven in the case form a chain connecting the prisoners with the killing. Where circumstances are clearly proven, and can be reconciled, they are superior to positive evidence."

Night had fallen on the mountain village of Mauch Chunk by the time the jury retired. The last minutes of the trial of the Commonwealth *vs.* Michael J. Doyle began at 8:30 A.M. Tuesday, February 1, 1876.

"Long before the hour announced for the opening of the court," said the *Coal Gazette*, "the portico was thronged with people waiting to procure seats. Many were pleading with the Court Crier, Mr. George Markley, to be allowed to enter by a rear door, but the official remained firm in his refusal, and the expectant ones took their disappointment in good humor.

"On the entering of the jury, the Court made the usual remarks in regard to expressions of approbation or disapprobation manifested in the room. The jury were called and answered to their names," said the *Coal Gazette*.

Judge Dreher turned to the panel.

"Gentlemen," he asked, "have you agreed upon your verdict?"

"We have," answered William Bloss, Jr., foreman.

The Court glanced at the defendant. "Face the jury," he ordered. The prisoner obeyed.

"In the case of the Commonwealth joined in issue with Michael J. Doyle, what is your verdict?" asked His Honor.

There was a moment of silence while Doyle looked up at Bloss. But whatever hope the prisoner might have had was demolished by the stern faces of the foreman and the other eleven men.

"Guilty of murder in the first degree," said Bloss.

Doyle staggered backward as if struck and would have fallen to the floor had not Mr. Siewers and Mr. Barthelemew, standing on either side of him, grasped him by the shoulders and waist.

"There was but little excitement in the courtroom," concluded the Mauch Chunk *Coal Gazette*. "No demonstrations were made and apparently relatives of the convicted man were not present, as no expressions of grief were heard at the reporters' desk.

"District Attorney Siewers then moved that the Court proceed to pass sentence on the prisoner.

"Mr. Reilly moved for the arrest of judgment, in order to file for reasons for a new trial .... The Court decided to delay the sentence until the adjourned term of Oyer and Terminer."

With praise from the Court ringing in its collective ears, the jury returned to the American Hotel for a delayed breakfast which the Judge assured them would now be provided. The prisoner was led back to Cell Twelve from which he could share the grim news with his neighbor, Edward Kelly, in Cell Ten. Cell Eight was still vacant. Mr. Kerrigan was upstairs, professing a renewed desire to continue his song, interrupted by the final sessions of the Commonwealth *vs.* Michael J. Doyle.

Chapter Thirty

News of Doyle's conviction and the realization that a Molly Maguire had been found guilty of murder in the first degree swept through the hard coal regions like brushfire. That 117 men and women were willing to stand up in court, with or without fear of reprisal, and testify against members of the Brotherhood, was even more shocking than the knowledge that Kerrigan had turned informer.

However, the six or seven hundred remaining brethren were by no means ready to disband. The Organization was still intact and Kerrigan could be "taken care of" before he completed his song. Then, too, there was hope for a new trial that would give members ample time to renew pressure on defiant witnesses who might be persuaded to change their minds and testimony if shown adequate reasons. Finally, it had to be remembered that the Old Man up in Harrisburg, Governor Hartranft, owed Jack Kehoe and his constituents a few favors. Should all else fail, this was the hour to call for their return.

Even the increasingly strong suspicion that a "spy" had been planted in the Organization and had climbed to a position of authority was greeted without dismay. The ranks were closed. No new man could enter and no old one leave. The detective would be discovered; "dead men tell no tales"; and whatever the spy had learned would be buried with him in his grave.

The pragmatic Kerrigan had no such illusions. Far shrewder and more realistic than his colleagues, he sensed the turn of the tide. He did not have to be told by Dan Shepp or anyone else that "McKenna" was a detective. He had felt, long before, that this well-heeled, gregarious fellow was not a true Molly.

It was no accident when Kerrigan passed McKenna information that Simon Trier was to be robbed and by whom. When the Cat was found lying unconscious in Mahanoy Creek the following morning, any doubts Powderkeg might have had about his sister-in-law's suitor were dispelled. Even if McKenna were to be executed at once, Kerrigan knew it would be too late. The game was up. In Powderkeg's opinion, there was only one neck worth saving and that, of course, was his own.

"I want to talk to Dan Shepp again," Kerrigan told Sheriff Breneiser on February 3, two days after Doyle's conviction. "Tell him to bring Mr. Siewers with him."

The Carbon County district attorney was eagerly awaiting this summons. As soon as word of Powderkeg's first confession reached Gowen's ears, the President of the Road called a strategy conference in Philadelphia. It was attended by Siewers, George Kaercher, district attorney of Schuylkill County, George Farquhar, one of Kaercher's special assistants, General Albright, Superintendent Franklin, Captain Linden, and probably Major Pinkerton.

To feed Siewers with knowledgeable questions that would stimulate Kerrigan and jog his memory Gowen culled material from McParlan's voluminous reports. Out of these, the railroad president listed hundreds of points needing corroboration. Not for one minute did he or any of the other skilled prosecutors believe evidence furnished solely by Powderkeg would be sufficient for convictions. Since McParlan was under no obligation to appear in court (and Major Pinkerton continued to deny that he would change his mind), it was unlikely that the unsupported word of an informer, out to save his own skin, would be taken seriously by any jury. Not even to this discreet group of gentlemen did Major Pinkerton or Gowen reveal McParlan's identity.

What Gowen and those destined to work with him in the prosecution of the Molly Maguires wanted from Kerrigan was evidence sufficient only to establish *prima facie* cases against as many members of the Organization as could be rounded up and brought before a Grand Jury. The Commonwealth was prepared

218

to pay any price for this. "Promise him anything," Gowen advised Siewers, "including his worthless life. If the State doesn't hang him, the boyos will."

Comfortably established in the sheriff's quarters, well fed by Mrs. Breneiser, protected round the clock by Coal and Iron Police, and cheered by the prospect of immunity, Kerrigan sang his song to Shepp, the Carbon County district attorney, and a stenographer furnished by the Reading Railroad.

"You couldn't stop him once he started," said Shepp. "If he wasn't such an utterly miserable son-of-a-bitch who surely had a hand in the murder of my brother-in-law (although he never once admitted direct participation in any killing), you had to admire his gall.

"He talked to Siewers and me as though we were old friends sitting around a bar reminiscing. He'd slap himself on his knees and laugh when he'd think of something funny like the 'goods.' Once in a while the stenographer would say, 'Wait a minute, Mr. Kerrigan, you're going too fast for me.' And Kerrigan would say 'Pardon,' and stop 'til he caught up.

"He spoke as calmly about murders, dynamitings, cutting out a man's tongue or slicing off his ears as though he was ordering another beer. He even told me who burned down my own breaker. He went back as far as killings and beatings as old as fifteen years before—Langdon over at Audenried, Alexander Rea up in Centralia, and so on. He gave us names, dates and places. Of course, many of the Mollies he mentioned were long since dead and others had left the regions forever.

"Lots of it was only hearsay and wouldn't be enough even for a Grand Jury. But I knew Siewers was happy and I was sure Mr. Gowen would be too, because there was plenty of men still around that Powderkeg gave us."

Throughout his confession Kerrigan continued to maintain an air of innocence. He was the good-natured fellow who couldn't say no to an old friend, a man caught in a trap, forced by circumstances to become an unwilling witness to crime—but never an actual participant.

A limited edition of Kerrigan's confession, one which its publishers, Eveland and Harris, admitted was "stripped of its obscene and profane verbiage, and condensed so as to be readily understood by the general reader and retained by the ordinary mind," was published in 1876.

"The only part in it I know for sure was a lie was where Powderkeg elevated himself to the rank of bodymaster," Shepp said.

While this abridged version of Kerrigan's "song" contains words and phrases not likely to have been used by Powderkeg, Shepp, certainly in a position to know, vouched for its basic authenticity.

"I am a member of the Molly Maguires," declared Kerrigan in the Eveland and Harris publication. "I joined the Order when it went under the name of the Ancient Order of Hibernians; the names are synonymous. I was made a Molly in Tuscarora by 'Yellow Jack' Donohue; he took me down into a cellar and put me on my knees and read a paper to me, which I had to kiss, that was the oath administered.

"The obligation of a Molly Maguire is to the effect that he will obey his superior officers in *all* things . . . I became acquainted with all the principal Mollies in the County of Schuylkill and also in adjoining Counties; I became an officer and attended a great many of their Conventions; I was intimately connected with nearly all of their plots of deviltry. . . .

"As Body Master I felt the want of an education; but I have a good memory as some of them know to their sorrow . . . Aleck Campbell is the biggest villain in the whole gang; he was cognizant of the murder of Yost, and it was for the purpose of having Jones killed that *he supplied Carroll with the men to kill Yost.*"

A contrite Kerrigan withdraws from the bad companions of his youth, acknowledges his iniquities, weeps for "Auld Lang Syne," and pleads for understanding.

"I will have no more to do with the Mollies; I'm tired of hunting up men for people to kill. I am blamed for squealing; everybody has gone back on me, even my wife. I was always good to her, yet she has joined the ranks of my enemies but if people knew all, they would not treat me harshly."

Where praise is due, a saddened Kerrigan renders it with humility.

"I am well treated and that's sufficient for me; yet I am very lonesome as none of the prisoners will speak to me; I don't know what will become of me after the other prisoners are tried. I got a new coat, pants and hat from the authorities; I guess I wanted them, for my old clothes were torn off my back running through the brush . . . guiding Molly Maguire murderers to safety."

There is a measure of the old fight, a touch of Uriah Heep, and a clue to his personality in Kerrigan's conclusion.

"When I fell, the whole fabric of Molly Maguirism tumbled down with me. You see, though I was a small man, I proved a very Samson to these Philistines."

Chapter Thirty-One

Gowen was ready to take further action. With Kerrigan's 210-page confession (most of which supported the secrets McParlan had revealed) in his hands, the President of the Road ordered District Attorney Kaercher to swear out and serve seventeen murder warrants.

At three o'clock on the morning of February 5, 1876, Alex Campbell was awakened from what must have been a troubled sleep by loud banging on his front door.

"Open up, Campbell! Police!"

Campbell leaned out of his front window.

"Go away," he called into the night. "Come back in the mornin'. Let a man get his rest."

But there was no sleep for Alex Campbell that night or for many more to come. Heavy boots smashed open the door, and moments later three Coal and Iron policemen, pistols drawn and lanterns flashing, burst into Campbell's home, pounded their way upstairs, and seized the bodymaster. His terrified wife was brushed aside while Campbell was put in heavy shackles, dragged down the front steps, and thrown into a van waiting to cart him to the Pottsville jail.

Before the sun rose that morning, six more Molly Maguires were seized in similar fashion and removed to the Schuylkill County prison, where they were placed in separate interrogation rooms. In addition to Campbell, who was charged with being an accessory before the fact in the slaying of John P. Jones, other members of the Brotherhood taken into custody on February 5 included James Roarity, Hugh McGehan, James Boyle, James

Carroll, and Thomas Duffy. All five were charged with the murder of Patrolman Benjamin Yost.

There is no explanation for the delay, but on the following afternoon, when police attempted to arrest five more Molly Maguires on charges of homicide in the murders of Sanger and Uren, all had fled. These were Thomas Munley, Thomas Hurley (final winner of the contested $10 prize for the murder of Gomer James), Jimmy Doyle (not to be confused with his cousin, Michael J. Doyle, convicted in the Jones slaying), Charles McAllister (who may be recalled as the man who dashed down the cellar steps while his eighteen-year-old wife, Ellen, was shot to death by the Modocs), and Friday O'Donnell, another hero of the Wiggans Patch riot who had run next door as the mob killed his brother and sister.

Furious at this turn of events, Captain Linden, in charge of the arrests although blameless for the delay, which originated in the district attorney's office, recalled that McParlan had once told him about a Molly Maguire hideaway in Gilberton. This was the now unused storeroom of John "The Cat" Mahoney, whom McParlan had caught inside Trier's tailor shop in August, 1874. It was a few doors from Munley's home where he lived with his parents.

On the evening of February 6, Captain Linden broke into the unlit Mahoney storeroom. Here he found Munley, pistol in hand, standing beside a small arsenal. With his huge fists he knocked Munley's weapon down and put handcuffs on the fugitive. Then he looked underneath a table loaded with stolen goods. There, still in character, was Charles McAllister, cringing in a dark corner. Both men were taken to Pottsville in shackles.

But Jimmy Doyle had vanished and was never seen again. Hurley was likewise missing. He adopted an alias and fled to Colorado, escaping discovery until August 17, 1880, when he cut his throat and bled to death rather than submit to a fugitive warrant charging him with four additional Schuylkill County murders.

To the complete bewilderment of Gowen, Kaercher, and almost everyone else, Kehoe chose that day to swear out a warrant for the arrest of George Weinrich, a Mahanoy City butcher, charging him with the murders of Ellen McAllister and Charles O'Donnell. Kehoe, a high constable, made the arrest himself and brought the butcher before a Pottsville alderman. The latter promptly discharged the prisoner for lack of evidence and a mob of Mahanoy City friends of the butcher threatened to lynch the Girardville bodymaster. Kehoe, however, pointed his revolver at the leader's head and calmly walked away unharmed.

Kehoe's derring-do was more than sheer bravado and a display of utter contempt for his enemies. It was to serve as a grim warning that the Organization which the Girardville bodymaster headed was very much alive, fully armed, and led by a man with courage.

To Captain Linden, Kehoe's actions meant something else. Added to the Girardville bodymaster's meaningful gesture of defiance were snatches of a conversation between Boyle and Duffy, overheard by the big policeman. "Jack found out who the spy is," said Boyle, "and he's going to handle it hisself." The time had arrived, Linden was now more certain than ever, when his friend, Jamie McParlan, should quit before he was murdered.

Not knowing or caring what his superiors would say, Linden set out to warn the detective, pick him up, and take him to Philadelphia and safety. But McParlan was not at Fenton Cooney's, where the Coal and Iron officer had intended to place him under "arrest," nor could he be found in Muff Lawler's barroom or any of his usual Shenandoah haunts. Linden had no idea where he was, for the little Irishman, under the surveillance of some of Kehoe's close followers, had been unable to mail his report for more than two weeks. As far as Captain Linden was concerned, McParlan might already be dead.

McParlan was, however, very much alive. While the big policeman was searching for him at one end of Schuylkill County, the detective was at the other, where he had moved into the Kerrigan household. Here, as far as the Shenandoah brethren were concerned, Secretary McKenna was sent to find out from Mrs. Kerrigan just how much her husband was likely to "spill" and whether Bodymaster Lawler would be involved in Powderkeg's confessions.

Mrs. Kerrigan hadn't the slightest idea what Powderkeg would say, she told her guest, and, furthermore, she'd heard gossip that Mr. Kerrigan wasn't the only one who'd be talking.

"They do be sayin' you're a spy, Jimmy McKenna," she blurted out. "But me and Mary Ann don't believe it at all."

"Now where did you hear that wild one?" asked McParlan, knowing of course that there had been rumors about the revelation of his true identity, but until this moment unaware that the report was so widespread.

"From Aleck Campbell, hisself," she said, "before they took the poor lamb away. But Frankie McAndrew was with him and Frankie said it was a lie, that you were the best Molly of them all. I don't know if there is a spy and I disbelieve it. *Nobody* could fool Jack Kehoe. But I'll bet you that if there's any more informin' done, it'll be done by Muff Lawler. You can take my word for it. I know him from the 'ould sod.' "

McParlan believed there was a fair chance that Mrs. Kerrigan had judged Muff's courage correctly and that if pressure were applied and immunity promised, Powderkeg might not be the only informer. The detective was determined to pass this information to Superintendent Franklin and remain "McKenna the Molly" until he was certain Muff had been taken into custody.

Mrs. Kerrigan had one more suggestion.

"Let's pin Ben Yost's murder on Jimmy," she said. "I could get a dozen good boyos to swear he did it hisself and he's only squealin' to save his own worthless skin. I already spoke to a couple and they're ony waitin' for the go-ahead signal."

After assuring Mrs. Kerrigan he'd consider her suggestions seriously, McParlan said good-bye to Mary Ann and his hostess for the last time, mailed his final report to Superintendent Franklin, and boarded the next train for Shenandoah.

The minute he walked into Muff Lawler's and talked to a few members of the Organization, the little Irishman sensed a change in their attitude. Instead of the friendly greetings he was accustomed to, a half-dozen Mollies standing around the bar hardly answered his salutation and refused his offer of drinks. This last, more than anything else, alerted the detective that the "word" had been passed.

"For the boyos to turn down a free whiskey was a damned suspicious act in itself," said McParlan. "Well, I had a couple shots myself, which I needed all right. Then I went up to see Muff Lawler. He was a sick-looking bodymaster but he wasn't sore at me, just gave me a kind of funny stare. I had the feeling he wanted to do some serious talking with me. But all he said was for me to get over to Pottsville right away; that there was a *habeas corpus* hearing for Tom Munley and I might be needed as a witness. I was to see Mr. Ryon who was hired to defend Tom and Charlie McAllister.

"So I go right over to Pottsville and I'm in the courthouse standing around waiting for Mr. Ryon. I don't see any of the brothers but all of a sudden in walks Frank McAndrew.

" 'Jimmy,' he says, 'thanks be to God I caught up with you. The news is out you're a detective. I just come from Frackville and Florence Mahony is takin' bets you're gonna testify in court this very day against all of us.'

" 'Don't you believe it, Frankie,' I says to my friend, and all the time I'm feelin' like a dog, lyin' to this decent Irish lad who's tryin' to save my life. But what could I do?

" 'I don't care what the hell you are,' he answers. 'You're me friend. You don't have to tell me anything you don't want to. But you better skin out of here fast. Florence says if he catches up with you he'll beat the livin' daylights out of you hisself.'

"Now this got my dander up. I decided I'd stick right with it. Nobody, least of all any boyo named 'Florence,' was gonna give *me* a shellackin'. And nobody was gonna order me to get out until I'm good and ready myself. Meanwhile I'm thinkin' I can't give myself away to Frankie yet but maybe if I don't get scared off until the job's finished I can save his neck."

While McParlan was waiting to be called into the Munley hearing, a member of the Raven Run Division entered the courthouse lobby and informed the detective and McAndrew that the case was postponed until the following day when McAllister would join in the plea.

"Jerry seemed friendly enough," McParlan said, "and I asked him why everybody was cuttin' me dead.

" 'Oh,' he says, 'I was over at the Hibernian House this mornin' " hoistin' a few with Pat Butler when in walks Mrs. Kehoe to the bar. Now that's somethin' I never seen her do before. I ask her where Jack is.

" ' "He had to go out some place," she says, "but I'm to tell you not to be doin' any talkin' to McKenna until Jack finds out if he's a detective like he heard." With that she walks out again. Pat looks at me and says, "I think maybe Jack's learned the truth. I been hearin' things about McKenna for the last couple weeks meself." ' "

Then Hughes, a six footer, looked down at McParlan.

"I believe it's a big mistake," he said, "but there's a lot of boyos don't think like me and Frankie. They'll need a deal of convincin'."

"Let's convince 'em, then, Frankie," McParlan said to his friend, and with this the little Irishman and McAndrew left the courthouse and went directly to Shenandoah.

"It was about eight o'clock when we got there," the detective recalled, "and I got to thinkin' again that Frankie would be in trouble keepin' me company so I told him he'd be better off not bein' seen too much with me. But he says to hell with them and what they think and that he's with me.

"So the pair of us head for Muff's. The place is packed with Mollies. Some of them got their pistols on the bar like they expect to be raided by the Mahanoy Modocs. They're all talkin' about what's gonna happen to poor Mickey Doyle and what about all the other arrests. They're goddamned sore about Kerrigan and are layin' plans how to take care of *him*. I don't doubt for one moment that they've been discussin' me, too.

"Everybody starts growlin' when they see me. They're handlin' their revolvers and givin' me looks like they could kill me. So I jumped right up on the bar and yelled, 'Quiet!' There's not a sound.

" 'Now look,' I tell 'em, 'I know what's bein' said about me. It's a dirty lie. I'll knock the hell out of any brother who calls me a spy.' Then I give the quarrelin' toast but I get no takers. They look around at each other and I can see they're not so sure any more *what* I am.

"Then I say to the bartender, 'A round for the house, and let's see who won't drink with Jim McKenna.' I'm still standin' on top of the bar lookin' to see who'll refuse but nobody does. I start smilin' and in a minute or two the boyos are laughin' and jokin' and forgettin' their troubles. Somebody yells out, 'Give us a song, Jimmy, lad,' and I do and I dance 'em a jig besides."

McParlan realized it wasn't enough to persuade members of the Shenandoah Division that he was not a detective: he had to convince Jack Kehoe as well. Actually, there were no substantial reasons for the undercover man to continue his masquerade. His usefulness was over and he could not hope to gather further evidence. This was the time he should have disappeared.

"I guess I was stubborn, and I wanted to see the job through. None of those miserable sons-of-bitches were goin' to tell *me* what I had to do. Besides, the Organization was still operatin'. Kehoe wasn't touched and he was a high constable. I didn't know what Mr. Franklin was goin' to do about him and when.

"Then, I had a grand idea. I figured I'd get all the boys together at one meeting. I'd send the word to Captain Linden in time and tell him to pull a raid with a hundred policemen and take the brothers all at once. It was a long shot but I figured it'd be worth the gamble."

The next morning McParlan rode to Girardville alone. There he confronted Kehoe in the back room of the Hibernian House.

"I looked him straight in the eye and I says, 'Jack, what's this all about me bein' a detective? I hear you warned the boyos not to talk to me any more.'

"He stared back at me. 'That's right, McKenna,' he says, 'and if I had any proof of this you'd be dead now. I'd be happy to do the killin' meself. Only I ain't sure. You've more guts than most of me boyos and if you ain't a spy I sure could use you. There's plenty of troubled days ahead for all the likes of us.'

"I says, 'Jack, where did you ever get the idea I was a detective?'

"He says, 'Now I'll be honest with you, McKenna. You'll remember it was in this same room me and you met for the first time a couple years ago and I had me doubts even then. But you convinced me you really was from Buffalo and was straight. So I backed you up and look how high you rose in the Organization.

" 'Then lately I had me eyes on you again. Too many things are goin' wrong. There's always somethin' happens when you go out on a job. The guy we're gonna take care of ain't around or when our lads get there he's bein' covered by the damned police. You're good at singin' and dancin' and keepin' the boyos happy. And when you collected all that money we need to pay the lawyers I was willin' to admit I was wrong. Then when Powder-keg starts squealin' I was sure of it.

" 'But when Linden picked up Tom Munley and Charlie Mc-Allister then I knew it had to be somebody else besides Kerrigan doin' the talkin'. Powderkeg didn't know a damned thing about who killed the bloody Englishmen no more than he knew where the Cat had his hideaway.' "

The Girardville bodymaster had one more point to make.

"Two days ago," he said, "I was on me way from Ashland to Girardville. The brakeman's a friend of mine and he whispers that he seen you put a letter in the mail drop over at East Mahanoy Junction. So now I don't know what the hell you are, McKenna."

"Let me prove what I am," McParlan replied. "Call a convention and give me a fair trial in front of all the brothers. I'll take my chances."

"I'll think about it, McKenna," Kehoe said, "and I'll give you me answer soon."

On the afternoon of Wednesday, February 9, McParlan received word that Kehoe wanted to talk to him. The detective went to the Hibernian House at once.

"I've thought it over, McKenna," the Girardville bodymaster told the detective. "You'll have a fair trial. Make up notices right away and I'll sign them and you can send them out."

"Who do you want?" McParlan asked.

"Every bodymaster and officer in every lodge in the county and all the witnesses they want to bring besides. It'll be on March first at Ferguson's Hall."

This could be the big "roundup" McParlan had hoped for. It took him several hours to prepare the brief notices and when he'd finished he called Kehoe in to the back room from the bar.

"I had 'em all lined up on a long wooden table, one on top

of the other with space showing at the bottom of each where Jack was to sign. As soon as he'd finish one I'd blot it, pull the letter out, fold it and put it in an envelope. Then he'd go on to the next.

"There was more than a hundred of 'em. I knew he wouldn't bother to be reading more than the first couple and maybe one or two in between, or that's what I hoped he'd do at any rate. Well, what Mr. Kehoe didn't know was that one of 'em was addressed to Captain Linden.

"Now I didn't have to get Kehoe's signature on that one. I could just as easy have slipped it in the mail with all the rest. But I thought it might be fun to watch him write 'Jack Kehoe, Bodymaster' on a personal invitation to the Captain."

The Girardville bodymaster had an additional assignment for McParlan. "Go out and raise two hundred dollars more, McKenna," he said. "I need it for Lawyer Ryon's fee."

While McParlan was making another round of Schuylkill County bars, where he expected to collect sufficient cash for the defense fund by his impromptu entertainment, Linden received his "invitation." His response was not what McParlan had hoped for.

On February 14, the Captain and a dozen Coal and Iron Police raided a saloon outside of Ashland. Among the twenty or more barroom habitués Linden arrested and took to Pottsville for "interrogation" was McParlan. When the pair were alone McParlan grinned at the big officer.

"Well, Captain, what do you think of my idea?" he asked.

"I think you're crazy, Jamie," was the answer. "It won't work. There'll be no county meeting, you damned little fool."

McParlan shook his head in disbelief.

"Why not?"

"With all that's goin' on do you think for one minute Jack Kehoe'll let you bring all his boyos together in one place at one time? This was just to set you off balance while he figures out plans to take care of you nice and easy.

"You're cooked, Jamie. You've done as much as anybody could. Quit now while you're still able to walk out on your own two feet. Don't go back to Shenandoah. Get so far away from the coal regions they'll never find you. If they do you're dead. Don't worry about what Mr. Gowen will say. I'll square everything with Mr. Franklin. I'll tell him I ordered you to leave."

But McParlan refused to listen to the policeman, and Linden, shaking his head sadly, said, "I'll be as close by you as I dare without spoiling your foolish plans." Then he took McParlan into the basement of the courthouse and around a narrow unlit passage, which led, labyrinth-like, through the huge cellar and came to an end at a door, dimly seen in the light cast by the Captain's lantern. Linden pushed the door open and the pair stepped through a closet into a large room.

"This was part of the runaway slave's underground railroad, Jamie," he explained. "But nobody's used it for twenty years but me and you'll be safe here if you get that far. And whenever I know you're in Pottsville, this is where you'll find me or somebody else you can trust."

McParlan returned to Shenandoah, still believing Kehoe intended to call a county meeting and sure that when it occurred, Linden, despite his skepticism, would be prepared to take appropriate measures.

At Fenton Cooney's he learned that the Brotherhood in the western end of the county was disturbed over a strong anti-Molly Maguire sermon preached by Father O'Connor at St. Joseph's in Girardville the preceding Sunday. What distressed McParlan was the fact that the priest warned his parishioners to get out of the Organization at once and save not only their souls but their bodies as well because "there is a detective in your midst."

McParlan realized he had to find out quickly just how much the pastor of St. Joseph's actually knew and, at the same time, try to allay fears of Molly Maguires inclined to believe the priest. McParlan passed the word at Muff Lawler's that he intended to call upon Father O'Connor the following day.

"Dave Kelly, Phil Nash, Tom Donohue, and Joe Dooley heard me say where I was goin'," McParlan recalled. "When I got to Mahanoy Plane the next mornin' and stopped into Callahan's Oasis Cafe for a shot, there's three of 'em. Joe isn't around and I could easy figure were *he* was.

"So I walked to the parish house. Father O'Connor's not in

231

the first time and I come back a half hour later. He asks me into his anteroom. Just as he shuts the door I hear steps outside and somebody pulls a chair alongside of the door. I'm sure it's Joe listenin'.

"I ask the Father if it's true that he said there was a detective joined the order, and he says 'yes' but that he didn't mention my name. He says, 'I know you're a detective, McKenna, and a stool pigeon beside. If you had knowledge of crimes beforehand, why didn't you prevent them?'

"There's no use trying to explain to the priest just how I had to operate and why certain things couldn't be done. So instead, knowing Dooley is outside listenin', I start telling Father O'Connor that there's nothing wrong with the Brotherhood; that it's a noble organization out to help the working man and that's all."

At this point Father O'Connor interrupted the detective and looked at him sadly.

"This will get us nowhere, McKenna," he said. "There's little value your telling me lies about yourself and the Organization. I've told the men time and time again that such will be their fate, but they would not listen to my voice and would not leave the Organization. Now they must suffer and so must their poor families."

The priest dismissed McParlan who left and stopped at Callahan's on his way back to Shenandoah. While he was having a drink, Dooley walked in.

"How did you make out with Father O'Connor?" he asked.

"All right," McParlan answered.

"I know you did, McKenna," Dooley said with a smile. "I heard every word. You gave us a good lift, all right. I'll tell the boyos not to believe all that's bein' said about you."

Chapter Thirty-Two

Because of his current fund-raising assignment, McParlan could learn at first hand how plans were progressing for the Ferguson Hall meeting and attempt to persuade dubious Schuylkill County bodymasters that it was their duty to attend the session.

"I was doing all right, too," McParlan said. "The boys were kind of edgy at first. They didn't know what to expect with all those arrests. They'd been ordered to lay low to see if Doyle would get a new trial and if he did they'd be told what action to take then.

"I was trying to keep 'em calm 'til March first. Then I wouldn't give a damn what happened. If Linden could round all of 'em up in one big move, he'd get a dozen squealers and my job really would be over. I didn't want to leave it half-finished.

"My main problem was the Doyle case. I was hopin' there was some way to reach Judge Dreher and ask him to hold off his decision. Or if I could be sure Mickey would get a new trial I'd be all right. If he did the boyos'd be cocky and think everything would blow over. But if he got turned down then I figured no bodymaster would gamble on me or anybody else they're suspicious of.

"I'd have to get away fast or they'd pull my tongue out as a lesson to all 'squealers' and 'spies.' "

On February 22, the birthday of both George Washington and Michael J. Doyle, Judge Dreher ordered the district attorney, the defense counsel, and the prisoner to appear before him.

"There was a large crowd at the Court House doors ready to enter . . . the moment the doors were opened," said the Mauch

Chunk *Coal Gazette,* "but they were doomed to disappointment, for orders were given to Crier Markley . . . that the proceedings were strictly private. Two newspaper representatives were present through the courtesy of the court.

"Doyle entered the courtroom with his guard. He looked in somewhat better spirits than when the jury returned the dread verdict three weeks ago."

Doyle only that morning told the Breneiser brothers he was sure he would be granted a new trial in view of the evidence, just revealed, that "somebody tampered with the jury." On February 20, Mr. Kalbfus, for the defense, had moved to amend the original motion for a new trial for that reason and His Honor announced he would render his decision the following day.

"Judge Dreher," continued the *Coal Gazette,* "went over the pleas made by the defense and announced his inability to see why a new trial should be granted. District Attorney Siewers rose and moved the sentence of the law be pronounced.

"Counsel for the defense made no opposing motion and the judge asked the prisoner if he had anything to say . . . Doyle answered, 'I don't care what you do. You will do what you like anyhow.'

"Judge Dreher said he would make no protracted remarks and advised the prisoner to 'put your trust in Him who is all powerful.' Then he said:

" 'And now the sentence of the Court is that you, Michael J. Doyle, be taken from this courthouse to the common jail in this county, and from thence to the place of execution and there be *hanged by the neck until you are dead,* and may God have mercy on your soul.'

"The prisoner's parents sat in the rear of him, and when he sat down, his mother put her arms about him and kissed him. She stood by him stroking his hair and trying to soothe him in a motherly way for some minutes. She resumed her seat only because she was so overcome with emotion that she nearly fainted."

On Thursday, February 25, Judge Pershing, sitting in Schuylkill County's Court of Oyer and Terminer, heard Thomas Munley's and Charles McAllister's petition for freedom in bail on a writ of *habeas corpus* which he denied. On Friday, February 26,

Judge Dreher rejected a similar petition filed by Mr. Ryon on behalf of Alex Campbell.

McParlan, who had been in the eastern end of the county, returned to Shenandoah after completing his assignment.

"I stopped that night at the Hibernian House with more than two hundred dollars for the defense fund I sung and danced for. Jack wasn't around so I turned over the money to Mrs. Kehoe and she gave me a receipt. Then I went over to Pottsville. I was feelin' a bit uneasy and I wondered where the Captain was holdin' out.

"I ran into Pat Butler again and he told me everybody was sayin' to him that I was a detective and that the boyos wanted action. I told Pat I'd take action upon myself and that I demanded a fair trial.

"Well, while I'm standin' talkin' to Pat, in comes Jack Kehoe with Manus O'Donnell from Wiggans. Jack hardly looked at me and when I asked where he was goin' he said over to see Lawyer Ryon. I said, 'What's the news?' and he said, 'I got a good deal of news; that there is about twenty-five hundred men banded together in this county for the purpose of prosecutin' the A.O.H. and I have proof there is a detective or two furnishin' 'em with whatever they been tryin' to find out.' "

McParlan pretended he was indignant and demanded that Kehoe tell him where he got this information.

"From Judge Ryon, himself," Kehoe replied, "and I've no intentions of discussing anything more with you now."

"Will there be a meetin' so I can clear my name?" McParlan asked.

"There'll be a meetin', McKenna," Kehoe answered and walked away.

The detective, still convinced he'd be able to assemble all leading Mollies under one roof two nights hence, told McAndrew and O'Donnell to wait ten minutes 'til he finished a job he had to do for Muff. Once outside the building, McParlan scurried down a flight of stairs into the basement and, unseen, followed the devious passageway into Linden's office. There he found the Captain waiting.

"I knew you'd be here, Jamie, and I was waiting," Linden

235

said. "They told me you were upstairs talking to the 'king.' Did you decide to call it quits?"

The detective grinned.

"Not yet. The meeting's still on. I'll be goin' back to Shenandoah this day to make sure nobody's backin' out and check up on a couple more things. Tomorrow I'll be travelin' to Girardville to see Jackie and find out if he's coming to preside at my 'trial.' From here I'll be off to Muff's and then back to Brother Cooney's.

"I'm gettin' slightly nervous and I'd enjoy the pleasure of your company, Captain, but at a safe distance. That's why I'm tellin' you my plans, just in case . . ."

McParlan left the big policeman and joined McAndrew and Manus O'Donnell. Kehoe was nowhere in sight nor was he in the smoker of the Shenandoah-bound Reading train the detective and his two companions boarded late that afternoon.

"Manus stuck with me most of the time," McParlan recalled. "I judged that's what Jack ordered him to. When we pulled into Mahanoy City to change engines I saw Mrs. Kehoe walk down the steps from the ladies' car. I got off, too, and went over to her. She was a very fine lady, loyal to her husband and thinkin' him innocent of everything, just tryin' to help out those who needed him.

"I said hello, asked her how she felt and where was Mr. Kehoe. She told me he was up in Frackville on some lodge business, and that she was in Mahanoy to visit her sick mother. Then she looked at me kind of funny.

"'I don't know who you are or where you're from,' she said sadly, 'but you're troublin' my poor Jackie and he's enough troubles of his own. Why don't you go 'way now while you still can?'

"This really made me suspicious but I only smiled at her and got back to my coach."

The train arrived in Shenandoah about eight and McParlan walked into Lawler's saloon alone. He was surprised to find the place deserted except for an aged bartender. No member of Muff's family or the bodymaster was around.

"I thought this was very strange," McParlan recalled. "I made sure my pistols were ready for action and I went about the streets.

I met some citizens but none of my old acquaintances that belonged to the Organization.

"I walked as far as James McHugh's saloon and spoke to Jimmy who was a member. He asked me if I wanted anything to drink and I said I didn't mind a bottle of porter. He got the bottle and could hardly take the stopper out he was so nervous.

"I noticed he was very pale. I asked him if he had the ague or was out on a spree or sick or somethin'. He said no, he had a cold. I asked him if he heard the report about me and he said yes, but he disbelieved it and he'd be around to the meeting on Sunday to see how things were goin'.

"Passing the Lehigh depot I met Mike McDermott. He was a member and he had been rather friendly with me always, but he hardly spoke to me this time. He passed me by very quickly, and just across the street I saw Ed Sweeney, another member, who was standing up against a lamp post."

The detective, pistols cocked, strolled over to the other side of the street.

"Is that you, Eddie?" he called out and when Sweeney answered "Yes" the detective said, "It's a damned good thing I asked you before shootin'. I've awfully itchy fingers these nights. Why don't you go home Eddie, before you get hurt?"

On nearly every one of Shenandoah's street corners McParlan found an armed member of the Brotherhood. A few nodded at him grimly but most of them did not return his salutation.

"I still didn't know whether the meetin' was on or off," McParlan said, "and I figured if I stay out in the open I'll have a better chance. There was plenty of people around, Mollies and lots of Coal and Iron Police and plain citizens. I was sure the Captain wouldn't be far away.

"I don't want to go to bed until I know which way the wind is blowin'. Around midnight I walk over to McAndrew's house. There's a party posted inside and out. A fellow named Grady is standin' in front of the door and a fellow named Doyle is lookin' out the front window.

"'What are you lads waitin' for?' I ask Grady, and he answers, 'We're waitin' for Frankie,' but *I* know they're waitin' for *me*. At that second Frankie comes along and Grady throws a piece of snow at him; I don't know why. Doyle comes out of the house; McAndrew sees him, and says, 'Go home now boys. Muff says to tell you we'll settle everything at the trial.'

" 'What does Jack Kehoe say?' Doyle asks and McAndrew don't answer; then Doyle walks off in one direction and Grady in the other. Frank don't say anything to me either, just shakes his head and goes into the house."

The detective moved off in Doyle's direction. A moment or two later he heard footsteps behind him and turned around. There he saw Grady, a dozen paces in the rear.

"I have my pistol cocked underneath my jacket and I wait until Grady catches up with me. Then I say, 'Walk in front, Grady, my eyes are bad and what with all the holes in the pavement, I might trip, fall down and hurt myself. Now you wouldn't want that to happen, would you, Brother?'

"Grady don't answer me and soon we part. I'm on my way to Cooney's for a night's sleep. Instead of walkin' down Jardin Street like I usually do I cut over a little swamp and come into Cooney's back yard. I'm real quiet. In the moonlight I can see a set of footprints in the snow leadin' to the kitchen door but no tracks returnin'. I think I know what *that* means.

"I sneak up to the window and sure enough, sleepin' next to the coal stove is Brother Jimmy Doyle, a big redhead from Mount Laffee. There's enough light from the hot coals for me to recognize him and see a pistol on his lap and an empty bottle by his side. I can hear him snorin' away like crazy.

"Well, I think to myself, 'This is no way to trap McParlan, Brother Doyle, you ugly bastard.' I felt like pluggin' him then and there but I know that would wake everybody including the party I'm sure is in front of the house waitin' for me."

"I can't let Brother Doyle think he's getting away with it, so I open the window and climb into the kitchen. I take his bottle away and I empty my bladder into it, and put it back by his side. I know that sometime later the big redhead's goin' to wake up thirsty and reach for the bottle."

McParlan then crept upstairs and went to bed. During the night he was awakened by sounds in the back yard.

"I wasn't sleepin' too well anyway. I look out my window and there's poor old Jimmy, sick as a dog, throwin' up, cursin' and shakin' his fist up at my window. I can hardly stop laughin'. I know damned well this is one story he's not goin' to tell anybody. As far as Mr. Doyle's concerned, I never came home to Cooney's that night."

The next morning, Sunday, February 27, McParlan left Cooney's after glancing carefully up and down the street. Among the many passers-by on their way to church he recognized no member of the Organization. He hadn't any plans except to stay alive long enough for his "trial" the following night and the roundup he hoped would ensue. He went to Mass first and afterward, coming out of St. Mary's, he met Frank McAndrew.

"You're supposed to be dead, Jimmy," McAndrew said. "Jack Kehoe ordered your execution yesterday when he was in Shenandoah. He said if you ain't killed you'll be hangin' half the people in Schuylkill County."

"Well, then, I think maybe I'll pay a social call on Brother Jack and surprise him," McParlan said.

"I'll go with you," McAndrew told McParlan. Despite the detective's protestation that this would accomplish nothing and endanger McAndrew, the latter insisted on accompanying his friend. "You might be glad I'm along," he said.

The pair rented a horse and cutter at Martin Delaney's livery stable and headed over the snow-packed roads for Girardville. They had traveled no more than a half mile when McAndrew turned around. Following a short distance behind was another sleigh and horse.

"It's Dennis Dowling and Ned Monaghan. They're gonna shoot you if they get close enough, Jimmy," McAndrew said.

"Well, what about you, Frankie?" the detective asked. "You're bein' seen in mighty queer company."

"Don't worry about me. I don't know what the hell you are except my friend and I'll stand up for you. I told the boyos you'll get a fair trial and then it'll be proved what you really are."

"You're a fool, Frankie," McParlan said, "but you won't be sorry. Take the reins. I'm a better shot than you and when they get close enough I'll plug 'em both."

"Then get Dowling first," McAndrew advised. "He was a sharp-shooter in the army."

But no shots were fired in either direction. When the pursuing cutter got within fifty feet of the horse McAndrew was driving, the detective turned, stood up and pointed both pistols at his would-be assassins. The cutter stopped; Monaghan who was driving turned the sleigh around, and the pair went off in the opposite direction. A half hour later McAndrew and the detective entered the Hibernian House to confront Kehoe.

"There was no more surprised man in the world than Jack Kehoe," McParlan recalled. "He stood there lookin' at me for a minute, then he says, 'I should have done the job meself instead of handin' it out to a bunch of stupid, yellow bastards, the whole lot of 'em.'

"I agreed with Kehoe. He wasn't stupid and he had guts, you had to admit. If he'd a done the job on me it would have been 'clane.' But it was too late for this. He knew it and so did I.

" 'Will there be a convention tomorrow night for McKenna to clear hisself?' McAndrew asks, but Jack only looks at him in disgust and says, 'You're bein' taken in worse than anybody, Frankie.'

"Then Kehoe looks at me and he says, 'There'll be no meetin' tomorrow. I don't know what the hell you are, McKenna. Maybe you are what you say—a Buffalo killer—and maybe not. I can't figure you out.

" 'Go 'way now and if you're a wrong one, a spy or a dirty informer, think how you betrayed your friends and all the poor people of the region and took the side of the bosses. See if you can face the priests with what you've got on your conscience, McKenna.'

"I'm thinkin' to myself, 'What I've got on *my* conscience, Mr. Kehoe? What about *yours?*' But I don't say anything. Frankie stayed and I turn and walk away.

"I knew there'd be no bullet in my back. Kehoe was a man even if he was a bad one. He really believed he was a kind of Robin Hood. Now I'm not tryin' to excuse what he did but maybe if things 'd been different, he could have been a leader of a decent group of miners fightin' for their rights instead of headin' a pack of night killers.

"I stepped out into the street. It was bitter cold, snow was fallin' again and the wind blowin' hard. I left the sled in the stable behind the Hibernian House for Frankie and took off by myself to the depot. I caught the next train for Frackville and sure enough when I boarded her there was Captain Linden, sitting in the smoker, waiting."

For a moment the two men looked at each other without speaking. Then Linden broke the silence.

"Well, do you believe me now, Jamie? You're finished; there'll be no county convention."

McParlan nodded his head.

"What are you going to do, Jamie?"

"I'm headin' for Philly to go over my last report with Mr. Franklin. Then I'm takin' off for Chicago and points west. You're a Protestant and maybe you won't understand what I'm gonna say. I want to 'rejoin' the Church. I've never missed Sunday Mass but I've not taken Communion nor went to Confession since I became a Molly. It would have been a sacrilege.

"I been on this job for over three years and a 'member' of the Organization for almost two. I'm tired and I want to get away."

"Aren't you afraid the boyos'll get you no matter where you are?" Linden asked.

"Maybe a little, Captain. But I'll have to take my chances." Then he grinned. "And so will they!"

When the train arrived in Pottsville, where McParlan had to change for the Philadelphia express, he and Linden shook hands and said good-bye. When McParlan walked into the Pinkerton headquarters on Chestnut Street, he found not only Superintendent Franklin and Major Pinkerton but also President Gowen. All three had been awaiting his arrival; two of the trio, Franklin and Gowen, hoped to persuade the detective to alter his plans.

Chapter Thirty-Three

Gowen, whose voice had certainly been heard, albeit off stage, was now nearly ready to direct the performance openly. He had no intention of mounting the podium, however, until he could command the appearance of Jack Kehoe, billed as the arch villain.

There was little doubt in Gowen's mind that the Molly Maguires, remaining symbol of coal region rebellion, were ready to run for cover. He fully believed that with their total destruction he would have removed the last major obstacle in his plan to gain complete control of the anthracite industry. To create the impression of infallibility and omniscience he had to emerge from the debacle as a towering figure, the mine owners' champion, adviser, confessor, and dictator.

He was only forty years old in 1876 and already had risen far higher than nearly all of his contemporaries among America's power elite. In Threadneedle and Wall streets, not to speak of Philadelphia's Bourse, Gowen was considered the man to watch. With less and less reluctance, conservative English and U. S. investors had been placing their pounds and dollars in the hands of this young, imaginative, and daring coal tycoon.

Older, wealthier, and more experienced anthracite barons were beginning to lean heavily on their brilliant colleague for advice and direction. The Reading, ruled by Gowen and backed by Philadelphia, New York and London funds, already controlled a $25,000,000 a year share of a potential $100,000,000 world market.

Unending coal region violence was the major obstacle to be removed before Gowen could interest enough additional money to expand his domain from kingdom to empire. The conservative Londoners from whom Gowen hoped to get the major portion of necessary capital may have been tolerant of bloodshed as long as it was not their own; they had no intention of placing more funds into an area that still managed to perpetuate the image of American savagery.

English and Welsh superintendents, lured by high salaries from the Old World to New, came home bearing scarcely believable tales of violence, told freely and printed daily by Fleet Street publishers. These stories added to a general feeling of revulsion toward America, still paying for its century-old mistake of breaking away from the only civilized nation in the world.

In the minds of many, particularly U. S. and English capitalists, the names "Molly Maguire" and "union agitator" were synonymous, an error that Gowen deliberately compounded. With Doyle waiting to be hanged in Mauch Chunk and the arrest of other Organization felons, Gowen had taken an important step towards reassuring lagging investors that labor tranquility was fast approaching in the hard coal regions of Pennsylvania.

The fact that 117 citizens were willing to testify against Doyle and 12 more were unafraid to convict him was evidence that the climate of public opinion had changed drastically in the anthracite fields. No longer could the Organization terrorize this area without fear of retribution. The chances were that at this point the Molly Maguires would have faded away, even without additional court scenes. Some leaders would probably have been hanged, vigilante style, while others, blacklisted in every colliery, would have tried their luck elsewhere or starved to death where they were.

Such a helter-skelter, undirected performance, however, would hardly have furthered Gowen's aims fast enough. It was not that the President of the Road was anti-Catholic, anti-Irish, or even anti-Molly. He had no personal animosity toward any member of the Organization, even toward those he hanged. It was merely that they stood in his way. He once told a friend he had a secret admiration for Jack Kehoe, who, he felt, with proper tutelage might have risen high in politics.

Gowen was reasonably certain that Kelly would receive the

same verdict as his colleague, Doyle. The cases against both the Mollies were based on evidence supplied by large numbers of respected citizens able to corroborate one another. This would not be so in the trials of the Commonwealth *vs.* other members of the Organization now lodged in jail. In these, the prosecution would be forced to rely basically on the evidence of a detective whose identity was not to be revealed and the testimony of an informer with personal reasons for turning State's evidence.

There also was a fair chance that Governor Hartranft could be persuaded that it would be politically expedient for him to grant executive clemency as soon as the tumult had died down.

Gowen tackled the second problem first. Even before Doyle had been sentenced, the President of the Road began to needle the Governor by spreading the word in Carbon County that the Chief Executive had promised Kehoe that Doyle's sentence would be commuted before the next election. When the Tamaqua *Courier* printed this rumor, Hartranft was placed in the unpleasant position of denying something he had never said in the first place.

Before the "feud" deliberately created by Gowen had ended, the Governor called the President of the Road a "liar" and Gowen returned the compliment. Should His Excellency now pardon Doyle or any convicted Molly, he would have proved the truth of Gowen's charge and ruined his own reputation as a "man of honor."

Gowen's next target was McParlan. When the detective arrived in Philadelphia for his "final" conference, the President of the Road treated him as a hero. He was a guest in Gowen's Mount Airy mansion, he was introduced to the Quaker City's business and political aristocracy at the Union League as "my good friend, Jim McKenna," and he shared a table for three with Gowen and Superintendent Franklin in the Rose Room of the La Pierre Hotel.

"Mr. Gowen really laid the cream on thick," McParlan recalled, "and I lapped it up, although I was old enough to know better. Like we were partners, he told me all about the problems every coal operator faced and how, more than anything else, he wanted to convince the miner he was his friend and that the team of Gowen and the worker couldn't be beat. Everybody would make a decent living and have peace if only the Mollies were destroyed forever.

"He told me how he liked the Irish and respected us for our virtues more above all other races. Then he tossed me a clincher.

" 'Jim,' he says, after we'd had a couple drinks together up in his house out in Mount Airy. 'When we first met, I promised you that nobody but me, Mr. Franklin, and the Captain would ever know who you really were, didn't I?'

"I nodded my head.

" 'Well,' he goes on, 'I hope you won't be angry with me for betraying your confidence but I must make a confession, Jimmy, I've told one other person.'

"I looked at him. 'Who?' I asked.

" 'The Archbishop of Philadelphia, himself,' Mr. Gowen says, 'and I know *he'll* never tell. Besides, he's all for you and he's entirely in sympathy with what you and I have been doin'. He hopes we succeed.' "

It was true that the Roman Catholic prelate had denounced the Molly Maguires in no uncertain terms and had excommunicated its members. It is probable, too, that at the start of McParlan's operation, Gowen had told the churchman that an Irish Catholic detective would be infiltrating the Organization. But it is hardly likely that the Archbishop would have approved of using his name to influence McParlan; he surely would have disapproved of Gowen's motivation.

"Far from bein' upset, I was quite happy that the Archbishop 'knew' who I was and blessed my work. Sure, if Mr. Gowen said it was so, who was I to doubt it? So when Mr. Gowen kept pointing out how hard it would be to convict the boyos on Kerrigan's testimony alone, before I knew it I was volunteering to do something I swore I'd never do and take the witness stand.

"At first Mr. Gowen wouldn't dream of it. He said that it would be too dangerous, that I'd taken enough chances already and he'd ask no man, no matter how brave he was, to do more.

" 'Think it over, Jimmy,' he says. 'It's a terrible risk you'd be takin'. You're bolder and braver than all the rest of us put together but this would be too much. I'll have to say no.'

"The more he says 'no' the more I say 'yes.' Finally, Mr. Gowen 'gave in' and agreed to let me take the stand and mighty proud I was that James McParlan, a simple Irish farm lad, had convinced the President of the Road to do my biddin'. How simple can a man get!"

Assured that his star witness would testify and aware of the sensation this would cause on both sides of the Atlantic, Gowen set the stage for his own entrance. He took a leave of absence from the Road and volunteered his services without pay as assistant to the Schuylkill County district attorney. Mr. Kaercher was delighted to accept this addition to his staff.

Meanwhile, the trial of Edward Kelly, Doyle's and Kerrigan's partner in the murder of John P. Jones, began March 27 and ended eight days later. It was without sensation except perhaps for the introduction of Powderkeg's confession. Even this was an anti-climax, for its contents were an open secret. Kerrigan, no longer a defendant since he had been granted immunity to become a prosecution partner, did not enter the courtroom. Presumably he remained under guard in the sheriff's quarters and waxed fatter and fatter on Mrs. Breneiser's cooking.

To the casual observer, the trial of the Commonwealth *vs.* Edward Kelly must have appeared much like that of Michael J. Doyle. The judge, courtroom, witnesses, counsel for the defense and prosecutors were as before. Only the defendants (and there were many who noted strong ethnic resemblances between Kelly and Doyle) were not the same.

The verdict, too, was the same.

Franklin Benjamin Gowen was now ready to make his reappearance in Schuylkill County's Court of Oyer and Terminer and General Jail Delivery, where fourteen years before he had been frustrated in every attempt to convict a member of the Molly Maguires. This time Gowen anticipated no such failures.

On May 4, 1876, the Commonwealth of Pennsylvania began the trial of James Carroll, James Roarity, James Boyle, and Hugh McGehan, charged with murdering Patrolman Benjamin Yost on July 6, 1875. A fifth defendant, Thomas Duffy, who may be recalled as the "cause" for the policeman's death in a complicated "return of the favor" deal, asked for and was granted severance.

It took less than forty-eight hours to select a jury to try the quartet of prisoners.

As usual, no Roman Catholic was accepted for duty. The prosecution was not even called upon to challenge anyone of that faith. This omission was explained by a contemporary historian, William Linn, who declared: "That the jury might not be influenced by sympathy . . . care was taken to exclude from it, as far as possible, Catholics. . . ."

As an additional safeguard for the protection of citizens' Constitutional rights, that historian added: "Vigilance committees had been formed and summary vengeance would be taken in case of lawlessness on the part of the Mollies . . . and this knowledge tended to strengthen the backbone of the jury."

But even before the second day of the trial ended, with a full panel still to be selected, Gowen made a move that threw the Molly Maguires completely off balance. On May 5 he ordered his Coal and Iron Police to arrest High Constable Jack Kehoe, three other Schuylkill bodymasters, three Organization officials, and two run-of-the-mill Mollies.

As a matter of fact, it was upon evidence furnished by McParlan that these nine were arrested, charged with atrocious assault and battery and intent to kill William "Bully Boy" Thomas, June 28, 1875. Notably absent from the open sled which carted the shackled prisoners through the streets of Pottsville on their way to jail was Muff Lawler, retired Shenandoah Division bodymaster, and Roarity, already in court charged with a more serious offense.

As Kehoe and his associates were being indicted by a sitting Grand Jury which held them without bail, the case of the Commonwealth *vs.* James Carroll, *et al,* continued. Five judges, including two associates, made up a full bench. Cyrus L. Pershing, P. J., presided. District Attorney Kaercher opened for the prosecution. His address was brief, to the point, and without oratory. Whatever drama was in store for the packed courtroom would have to come later.

The defense was again headed by Mr. Barthelemew and consisted of the same staff that had fared so badly in Mauch Chunk. This time, however, despite his chief's strong protestations, Mr.

Ryon insisted on bringing along defense witnesses in numbers sufficient to supply alibis to all four defendants.

The first courtroom surprise, although only a mild one, was the appearance of Mr. Kerrigan on the witness stand. The dapper Powderkeg arose with alacrity when his name was called and smiled affably at Their Honors, at the district attorney and Mr. Gowen, at Messrs. Ryon and Barthelemew, and even at the prisoners, who glowered at him in return. He answered all questions cheerfully, refused to become distressed by Mr. Ryon's sharp, sarcastic barbs, and after seven hours on the stand, retired to his seat with the modest air of a good man who has just performed a citizen's duty for which he expects no reward.

The real shocker came when Kaercher, who had hinted at a surprise witness in his opening address, called out, "James McParlan take the stand!" What an amalgam of consternation, anger, and hatred must have swept through the minds of the four defendants as they turned their heads to the rear of the courtroom and saw "Brother James McKenna," flanked by Captain Linden and Superintendent Franklin, walk down the aisle and mount the witness stand.

"This," said Linn, "was a complete surprise, not only to the Mollies, but to the public which had not hitherto known of his existence. This feeling of surprise deepened into one of wonder and amazement when . . . with perfect coolness and deliberation he told in detail the story of his career among the Mollies.

"When he told of being suspected as a detective and related his interviews with his intended assassins, his escapes, etc., judges, jury, counsel, and audience listened with breathless attention; and so completely spellbound were all these by his recital of things the existence of which had not been thought possible, that at any time the falling of a pin might be heard in the densely crowded room.

"Much of this narrative which was not relevant was not objected to by counsel for the defendants because of the intense interest they evidently felt."

From the start of his hazardous journey from Philadelphia in October of 1873 until the hour of his return to the Quaker City on March 1, 1876, the detective, under the skilled, methodical questioning of the district attorney, revealed in every detail the inner workings of the dreaded Organization.

He named killers; he pointed his finger at those who planned executions; he recalled the dates and places of murder assignations; he described payments of "blood moneys"; he told of the cruelly casual "returns of the favor." Then he relaxed his grim audience and sent it into gales of near-hysterical laughter when he twisted his arms, head and body to demonstrate a particularly difficult section of the "goods."

He was a superb witness. He talked clearly and calmly, and his musical voice had enough of the brogue to give it a pleasant lilt. He never spoke above a conversational tone and he never appeared to show personal animosity toward anyone. His reply to the district attorney's question, "What is your religion, Mr. McParlan?" was given with a quiet pride which gained visible nods of condescending approval from the all-Protestant jury. "I am a Roman Catholic, Mr. Kaercher," he said, "baptized in the Parish of Mullabrack, the County of Armagh."

Kaercher then moved from generalities to the specific task on hand, the prosecution of Carroll, Roarity, Boyle, and Mc-Gehan, for the murder of Yost. Here, again, the little Irishman was faultless. His obvious sincerity, his lack of vindictiveness, and his unimpaired dignity produced a most favorable effect upon the panel. When he unequivocally identified all four prisoners as the killers of the policeman, and supported his testimony with details no man could have invented, the jury was convinced.

McParlan had been on the stand for three full days before Kaercher turned to the chief defense counsel and said, "Your witness, Mr. Barthelemew."

By this time, attorneys for the prisoner had fully recovered from their shock at the detective's first appearance in court and were ready to tear him and his testimony apart. They probed his background; they ripped into his morals; they accused him of entrapment; they called him a stool pigeon, an *agent provocateur*, a scoundrel, a villain, and a perjurer.

McParlan never flinched nor lost his temper. No matter how vilifying the defense counsel's queries were, he responded with decorum. Rarely did he have to refer to his notes. Upon one occasion, when Barthelemew asked about a Molly Maguire meeting occurring in May when he obviously meant the following month, McParlan corrected him politely. "Sir," he said, "I think you meant to say June." Then, with a slight smile, he added, "I was there, you know."

On the afternoon of his fifth day on the stand, McParlan was permitted to step down.

"Only once during the whole time did I feel bad," the detective recalled. "That was when I looked down and saw Mary Ann sitting there. She was a fine, decent girl, and maybe if I'd been the marryin' type, or if we'd met under different circumstances, something would have come of it. As it was I hate to think of what I did to her pride. She must have thought all I wanted out of her was to use her to trap Kerrigan.

"She looked at me, oh so sadly, and then I felt I really was a proper Molly."

While none of the prisoners took the stand, their counsel produced a long line of witnesses ready to furnish all four defendants with complete alibis. But McParlan's reports to Franklin had prepared the prosecution for this move and everytime a witness swore that Carroll, Roarity, Boyle, or McGehan was in one place, the district attorney was in a position to summon others to negate that testimony. For example, when Kathryn Boyle, wife of the defendant, James Boyle, said that her husband was at home dead drunk the night of Yost's murder, Kaercher produced five men and women who swore they had seen the defendant on the streets of Tamaqua that night.

The prompt arrest of five alibi witnesses on charges of perjury was to have a far-reaching effect on subsequent Molly Maguire trials. Almost as soon as they left the courthouse, the five, including Mrs. Boyle, were taken into custody and promptly tried, convicted and sentenced to the penitentiary on terms of from one to three years. The lesson was not lost on future witnesses, who might otherwise have contemplated furnishing alibis for defendants not yet tried.

The most virulent of all witnesses was Mrs. Kerrigan, who attempted to place responsibility for Yost's murder solely on her husband's shoulders. What small portion of Powderkeg's char-

acter had been left intact, his wife of twenty-seven years anni-
hilated on the stand. He was a "liar, cheat, drunkard, wife-beater,
coward, and killer." Much of what the lady said had a ring of
truth. A glance at Mr. Kerrigan's reddened cheeks, his clenched
fists, and his tightly-sealed lips from which an occasional hissing
sound emerged, revealed the fact that some of his wife's barbs
landed on sensitive spots.

To an amused, tolerant Gowen was left the task of nullifying
any damage Mrs. Kerrigan's testimony might have caused. He
performed the job gently but effectively. When he concluded his
cross-examination, he had punctured Mrs. Kerrigan's palpably
false story with large holes. His attitude was that of a teacher
softly chiding an understandably angry child.

"After each of Mr. Gowen's questions," said Schlegel in his
biography of the President of the Road, "Mrs. Kerrigan appeared
to hesitate before each answer. To Gowen's inquiry as to the
reason for the pause she replied that it was her heart trouble,
whereupon the Attorney aroused a gale of laughter by asking,
'How is it you never get heart trouble when Mr. Ryon questions
you?' "

On the afternoon of May 24, the defense rested. Mr. Barthelemew, his associates, and witnesses had undergone a rough time
of it. The presiding judge was cold and seemingly inimical, although he sustained some of Barthelemew's many objections;
the jury looked stern and unfriendly; and throughout the courtroom there was what Ryon called "an atmosphere of guilt," a
feeling most experienced trial lawyers are able to sense. Gowen
was scheduled to make the opening address for the prosecution
when Court convened the following morning. It was a speech he
had been hoping to make for fourteen years.

But that evening, Juror Number Five, Levi Stein, who had
been nursing a cold which seemed to be getting worse throughout
the trial, collapsed. He died of a heart attack before a physician
could be summoned. When the eleven remaining panelists reported for duty on May 25, they were discharged, a mistrial
granted, and the case of the Commonwealth *vs.* James Carroll,
et al. held over until the next term of court.

Chapter Thirty-Four

Postponement of the Pottsville trial on May 25 by no means halted court action against the Molly Maguires. On June 21, Alex Campbell, the Tamaqua and Storm Hill saloonkeeper and body-master, was arraigned at Mauch Chunk, charged with being an accessory to the murder of John P. Jones. For this murder, Doyle and Kelly were already awaiting execution.

While the Commonwealth was proceeding with the Campbell case, Thomas Munley, the Molly Maguire who had been captured in the Cat's Gilberton hideout, was brought to trial before Judge Horace Green, in Pottsville, charged with killing Sanger. Here Gowen would be able to make the oration that the death of Juror Number Five had delayed.

The Mauch Chunk trial, except for the prisoner, could be called "routine," and the result anticipated. Prosecution evidence, presented by McParlan (who again covered himself with distinction), corroborated by Kerrigan, and reinforced by most of the same witnesses who had appeared against Doyle and Kelly, was overwhelming. On July 1, a jury of eleven Dutchmen and one Welshman found Campbell guilty. Although he had not fired a shot he was judged just as culpable as though he had pulled the trigger and was sent to join his colleagues in the death cells on the lower tier of Carbon County's jail.

Campbell's conviction for premeditated murder terrified many members of the Organization who had previously thought themselves out of the law's reaches because they, like the Tamaqua bodymaster, had confined their murderous activities to blue-printing.

With two trials occurring simultaneously in different county seats, forty miles apart, the defense staff was spread thin. Since Kehoe and other leaders were in jail and unable to exert pressure anywhere, and with McParlan hardly in a position to entertain barroom habitués or their voluntary contributions, funds had dwindled to a vanishing point.

Another serious fiscal blow was Judge Pershing's ruling that only prosecution witnesses would be paid customary fees; defense witnesses would have to shift for themselves. This meant that those who could afford it least were penalized for being on the "wrong" side of the law. Yet Mr. Barthelemew and his associates not only continued to function without withdrawals (and probably without pay) but were augmented by the addition of another pair of coal region attorneys, both of whom normally commanded high fees. These were Martin L'Velle and S. A. Garrett.

The prosecution had no personnel problems. Siewers and his staff proved themselves competent and needed little help from Kaercher. The latter had a plethora of eager, politically-conscious volunteer assistants, more than enough to operate in several courtrooms simultaneously. McParlan and Kerrigan, however, had to be shuttled between counties and courthouses. But as the former was still on the Pinkerton payroll and the latter under obligation to the Commonwealth, neither was in a position to complain.

On July 8, while the Munley trial was entering its sixth day, Carroll and the other three defendants in the Yost murder were rearraigned before Judge Pershing and his colleagues.

In the Munley trial, Gowen did most of the cross-examination. He was particularly adept at discovering scarcely discernible flaws in the warp and woof of testimony, using them to prove the shoddiness of the whole cloth. An excellent example of Gowen's shrewdness in this area came when the defendant's young brother, Michael, was on the stand, attempting to furnish an alibi for Thomas.

Michael, clean-cut and boyish looking despite his twenty-seven years, made an excellent appearance and obviously impressed the jury with his air of innocence and sincerity. He stood up well under a barrage of questions and could not be shaken in his claim that at the time Sanger was being murdered, he, the defendant, their sister Mary, and their father were having breakfast at home. Gowen baited the trap.

"You've a good memory, Michael, haven't you?" Gowen asked.

"Yes, sir, I do," Munley answered not without pride.

"Do you recall anything unusual about that breakfast?"

"No, sir," was the response. "My father said Grace, and we all ate together like we always did."

Gowen nodded his head as if to give personal approbation to such a display of sanctity and togetherness. He continued.

"Do you remember what you had for breakfast that morning, Michael?"

Young Munley paused for a moment as if to think and smiled.

"I do indeed, sir," he answered with an air of satisfaction.

"Would you mind telling us?"

"We had eggs, some of me sister's bread she'd baked ony that mornin' before Mass, and some ham."

"Did you all eat the same things?"

The witness pondered this one for a few seconds before replying.

"Yes, sir, we did, all except me sister. She ate no eggs."

"You seem to remember everything else so well, Michael, I wonder if you remember what day of the week that was?"

"No, sir, that one I don't really recall," the witness answered in a show of sincerity.

"Well," said Gowen, "I'll tell you. It was Friday, Michael."

The assistant prosecutor then turned to the jury.

"Now where," he asked rhetorically, "is there another good Catholic family in Schuylkill County that had meat for breakfast on a Friday?"

On the fourth day of the trial, a Mrs. Williams accompanied her husband to Pottsville. She was permitted to enter the courtroom, where an attendant escorted her to a front seat. She was there for only a moment when she glanced at counsel's table, and saw the prisoner. She jumped up and rushed from the courtroom to talk to her husband who was in an antechamber.

"What shall I do?" she asked him after declaring she recognized Munley. "Tell it to Mr. Kaercher," he answered.

Mrs. Williams spoke to the district attorney and shortly thereafter was called to the stand. In a particularly moving fashion she described the moment when, upon hearing shots and opening the front door of her home, she saw Sanger lying on the ground and a man, pistol in hand, rush by.

"The man looked right at me," she said, "and I slammed the door shut and stopped my boy from going out. And I saw him this morning for the first time since."

"Is that man in court?" Gowen asked.

"He is. That's him," she answered, pointing her finger at Munley.

Ryon attacked her on cross-examination.

"You said, Mrs. Williams, that the man you saw was running fast and you only saw him for a moment, didn't you?"

"Only for a moment," the witness answered, "but it seems to me I will always see that face, at night when I try to sleep or in the morning when I open my front door to look outside."

Sanger's employer and friend, Robert Heaton, the fat man who chased the fugitives, was called upon to identify not only the prisoner but Munley's colleagues in crime.

"I had a full view of them," he declared. "Every time I fired my pistol, they turned and faced me full. When I rested my pistol on the stump and fired, they turned around once more and I saw them. I'd know their faces anywhere."

L'Velle could not shake Heaton. The stout gentleman walked down the aisle and out of the courtroom followed by admiring glances from both male and female spectators.

Kerrigan, by now a courtroom fixture, professed little knowledge of the Sanger-Uren murders and was called upon to testify only about generalities which provided a background to Molly Maguire activities. But McParlan remained on the stand for three days and was subjected to relentless cross-examination.

He described in minute detail the night in his room at Cooney's boarding house when he was awakened from a restless sleep by Jimmy Doyle, to whom he loaned his coat. He described how a few moments later, he was disturbed once more, this time by Tom Hurley, who remained with the detective, upon Kehoe's direct orders, all the day of the Summit Hill murders so that word could not be "leaked" to Coal and Iron Police by McParlan, then under suspicion.

To the horror of the jury, McParlan described the calmness with which the murderers, "blood on their hands and clothes," strode into Muff Lawler's saloon and boasted of killing not one but "two English bastards."

L'Velle, unable to trap McParlan into contradictions, made considerable headway with the jury by forcing the detective to admit that several premeditated murders of which he had more than casual knowledge were carried out according to plan.

"If you are as clever as you want us to believe you are, McParlan," said L'Velle, "why didn't you stop them?"

Actually there was no easy answer to that question. The panel was obviously troubled by this thought, which seemed not to have occurred to it before, so carried away was it by McParlan's daring, poise, and ingenuity.

In his plea, begun after the defense had rested on the tenth day of the trial, L'Velle made much of the fact that until McParlan came to the hard coal regions, there had been considerable lessening of violence in that area. Recent murders—Yost, Sanger, Uren, Jones, Major, and James—occurred, L'Velle pointed out truthfully, only after the detective's arrival in Schuylkill and Carbon Counties.

In his final dramatic appeal to the jury, L'Velle attempted to negate Commonwealth testimony by denying the very existence of the Molly Maguires and terming the murder trials "battles between capital and labor."

"No such Society as the Molly Maguires ever existed," he declared, "except in the minds of the coal barons, the railroad moguls, the mine bosses, and the bitterly bigoted anti-Catholics. For God's sake, gentlemen, give labor an equal chance. Let it not perish under the imperial mandates of capital in a free country!"

Chapter Thirty-Five

Gowen made the final address. He anticipated correctly that his words would extend far beyond the backwoods courtroom. His primary interest in the case of the Commonwealth *vs.* Thomas Munley was not to hang one wretched Molly Maguire. What Gowen expected to emerge from this trial and others was a cheering message to investors in Philadelphia, New York, and London.

"Observe, gentlemen!" he would be saying. "In demolishing the only organized group of rebels in the anthracite counties of Pennsylvania and making their revival an impossibility, I have given to the hard coal area of the state the healthiest investment climate in America. Price ceilings can be as high as you wish and wages, in a glutted labor pool, as low as you care to pay. Furthermore, should anyone else attempt to interfere with capital's rights, all I have to do is label them 'Molly Maguires' and the public will do the rest."

Of course, to achieve these ends, Gowen had to take care of a task at hand, the conviction of Thomas Munley. This he proceeded to do in a superb address lasting seven hours. Gowen combined a lecture on the anatomy of the crime itself, destruction of alibi witnesses, a defense of McParlan's integrity, an attack on Jack Kehoe, an assault on the Organization, an appeal to racial prejudice, and a corollary proposition that the words "Molly Maguire" and "labor agitator" were synonymous and interchangeable.

"If there is anything which should be accorded to a member of a Free Government; if there is any right which the humblest

257

man in our country should possess, it is the right to labor for the support of his family without hindrance or molestation from anyone," declared Gowen.

"On September 1, 1875, a young English boss miner . . . who, as far as we know, did not have an enemy in the world, left his house in the morning to go to his daily job . . . This man was confronted by one of an armed band of assassins. He was shot in the arm . . . he turned to run . . . and was confronted by another of these miscreants and stumbled to the ground.

"When the foremost of this band of assassins came upon him, as he lay upon the ground, he discharged his revolver into Sanger and turned him over upon his back so that he could expose a deadly part for his aim, and then, with calm deliberation select a vital spot and shoot him. That man was Thomas Munley."

The courtroom was stilled as Gowen paused, walked over to the victim's widow who was sobbing softly in a conspicuous seat only a few yards from the panel, stood beside her for a moment, then continued.

"This woman, from whom he had just parted, hearing his cries, rushed out and reached her husband only to hear his last faltering words: 'Kiss me, Sarah, for I am dying.' "

With the stage thus set, Gowen, using vital portions of prosecution testimony, re-enacted the murder so graphically that women spectators, comprising the larger portion of the audience, were sent into paroxysms of emotion even greater than they had hoped for. As a matter of fact, according to the Mahanoy City *Tri-Weekly Record,* "Three ladies fainted with excitement before Mr. Gowen had half finished his masterful address."

Two of the State's important eyewitnesses, who unequivocally identified the prisoner, were Mrs. Williams and Mr. Heaton. Both made strong impressions on the jury. To counteract L'Velle's assertion that neither had the moral right to send an "innocent man to the gallows upon such fleeting visions," Gowen had this to say:

"If Robert Heaton, that morning, instead of taking with him a five barrelled pistol, had a rifle carrying sixteen cartridges and shot every one of these men down in their tracks and their bodies had been laid side by side for identification before the coroner's inquest, I submit with great confidence that there would have been, of the dead body itself, *no better identification of Thomas Munley than has been given of his living body now sitting before you.*

"Robert Heaton is not alone. We have Mrs. Williams, wife of a man working at that colliery, mother of a young son, an active and impetuous lad, who, when he hears sounds of fighting, is anxious to rush out as other men *ought* to have rushed out, and arrested these men.

"This mother, hearing the shots and knowing there was murder in the air, anxious that her son should not be exposed to danger and throwing her arms around his neck . . . strove with all her strength to force him from the path of the murderers. When so engaged with the dread of danger before her, she sees one of the murderers pass the door, head raised defiantly in the air, and with his pistol in his hands.

"It needed but one instant for that countenance to become indelibly impressed upon her mind. In the dark visions of the night, that face is ever before her. The face of the murderer haunts her forever.

Gowen turned to the smashing of the Molly Maguires and the benefits their destruction would bring to law-abiding citizens.

"Now that the light of day is thrown upon the secret workings of this association," he said, "human life is as safe in Schuylkill County as it is in any other part of the Commonwealth; that as this association is broken down and trampled into the dust, its leaders either in jail or fugitives from the just vengeance of the law, the administration of justice in this court will be as certain as human life is safe throughout the length and breadth of the county.

"The time has gone by when the murderer, the incendiary, and the assassin can appear before a jury and have an alibi proved for him to allow him to escape punishment. There will be no more false alibis in this county, the time for this has gone. No more confident reliance upon the perjury of relatives and friends to prove an alibi for him who was seen in the commission of the act. No more dust thrown in the eyes of juries.

Gowen spoke briefly of his own past and his previous failures to convict members of the Organization.

"A man who for two years acts as district attorney in this county . . . must be either very obtuse or willfully blind, if he could close his eyes to the existence of a fact as perceptible as this is to me . . . Murder, violence, arson, committed without detection and apparently without motive, attested the correctness of that belief.

"I made up my mind that if human ingenuity, if long suffering and patient care and toil could succeed in exposing this secret Organization and bring well earned justice to the perpetrators of the awful crimes, I should undertake the task.

"I knew that it could only be done by secret detectives."

To cover defense allegations that McParlan "invented much of his evidence only in order to benefit financially by the revelations of crime," Gowen quoted the little Irishman's employer, Major Pinkerton.

"'Whoever I choose for this job,' the head of the National Detective Agency told me when we first discussed hiring one of his operatives, 'is to be paid so much a week, no matter if he finds nothing. He is bound to me, never, under any circumstances, to take a reward for his services from anybody, and if he spends five years and obtains nothing in the way of information, he must be paid every week or every month exactly the same compensation as if every week he had traced a new murder and every month had discovered a new conspiracy.'

"Furthermore, Major Pinkerton said, 'The man who takes the job, takes his life in his own hands, and I will send no man on this mission of years unless it be agreed upon beforehand, and I can tell him so, that *he is never to be known in connection with the enterprise.*'"

Gowen had words of praise for McParlan.

"He came here pledged that he would not be used as a witness . . . the only object of his coming was to put us on the track so that we could discover the crime when it was being perpetrated. This is the best answer I can make to the charge that he willfully withheld his knowledge when he might have saved human life."

Gowen next attacked defense counsel's argument that crime in the hard coal regions was on the wane until McParlan arrived on the job.

"Mr. L'Velle tells you," declared Gowen, "that from the advent of Mr. McParlan into this county have all these crimes been committed. I fear that Mr. L'Velle has not been among you, or, if he has, his memory is sadly deficient when he says that all these crimes have been committed since the advent of Mr. McParlan in Schuylkill County."

Here L'Velle rose in protest.

"Sir," he said, "I antedated you in coming to Schuylkill County."

"Then, Mr. L'Velle," Gowen replied scornfully, "your memory is very defective. Does the gentleman forget Dunne, who was murdered within two miles of this town? Does he forget Alex Rae, who was stricken down near Mount Carmel? Does he remember the assassination of William Littlehales? If he does I am very sure that his colleague Mr. Barthelemew will not forget.

"For I remember that I stood here, just where I now stand, some years ago, defending a couple of men for murder, who, with other good citizens, when the house of a boss had been attacked at Tuscarora by a mob intent upon murder, had taken their old muskets, their rusty rifles, their pistols and their swords, some of them with no time to load their muskets save with marbles with which their children had been playing, and had sprung to arms to defend the house that was being attacked, and had shot down one of the assailants in his tracks, and were arrested and brought here charged with the crime of murder.

"Mr. Barthelemew, who was my colleague, joined with me in contending that our clients had done that which they ought to have done to protect themselves, and as I was standing here, arguing that case, there came over from Coal Castle the news that William Littlehales had been murdered.

"Does the gentleman forget all about this? Does he forget George K. Smith and Morgan Powell and Frank S. Langdon?"

Gowen then dwelt upon the Society itself and described its effect upon the area.

"This Organization we are now for the first time exposing to the light of day has hung like a pall over the people of this county. Before it, fear and vengeance of their pursuers. Behind it stalked darkness and despair, brooding like grim shadows over all of us.

"Nor is it for those whose names I have mentioned—not alone the prominent, the upright . . . but it is in the hundreds of unknown victims whose bones now lie mouldering over the face of this county.

"In hidden places and by silent paths, in the dark ravines of the mountains, in secret ledges of the rocks, they are. Who shall say how many bodies of the victims of this Order now await the final trumpet of God . . . to take their place among the innumerable throng of witnesses at the last day, and to confront with their presence the members of this ghastly tribunal, when their solemn accusation is read the plain command of the Decalogue, 'Thou shalt not kill!' "

From the Molly Maguires, Gowen turned to the ethnic group which comprised its membership.

"I shall say but little about the Irish except that I am one myself," the prosecutor declared, "the son of an Irishman, proud of my ancestry and proud of my race, and never ashamed of it except when I see that Ireland has given birth to wretches such as these.

"These men call themselves Irishmen! They parade on St. Patrick's Day and claim to be good Catholics! Where are the honest Irishmen of this country? Why do they not rise up and strike down these wretches that usurp the name of Irishmen? If a German commits an offense and engages in murder, do all the other Germans take his part and establish a false alibi to defeat the ends of justice?

"If an American becomes a criminal, do the Americans protect him? . . . If an Englishman becomes an offender, does the English nation take him to its arms and make him a hero?

"Why then do not the honest Irishmen of this country come together and . . . denounce this Organization? Upon what principle do these men, outcasts from society, the dregs of the earth, murderers, assassins, claim to be Irishmen and abrogate to themselves the national characteristics of the Irish?

"It is a disgrace to Ireland that the honest Irish of this county, probably five or ten thousand in number, should permit a few hundred villains like these to say that they are the true representatives of Schuylkill County.

"Does an Irishman wonder why it sometimes is difficult to get a job in this county? Does he wonder why the bosses hesitate to employ him? . . . The time has come when every honest Irishman in this county must separate himself from any suspicion of sympathy with this association. He must say they are *not* true Irishmen and that they are *not* representatives of Ireland."

Gowen passed on to the official attitude of the Church.

"Excommunicated by the Archbishop of Philadelphia and by the Pope himself, outcasts from society and from the communion of their own religion, the door of the Church shut in their faces and the gate of Heaven closed against them . . . these men, infidels and atheists, caring for no church and worshiping no God, set themselves up in this community as representatives of the Catholic faith.

"For many months before any other man in this world except those connected with the detective agency knew what was being done, Archbishop Wood of Philadelphia was the only confidant I had. He fully knew of the mission of McParlan.

"So much then for the assumption of Mr. L'Velle that these men claim sympathy on account of their being Catholics. I can hardly reply calmly to this argument . . . I am one of those who believe that there must be different sects in this country as there are in all countries and that a good Catholic is better than a bad Protestant."

Gowen attributed the detective's change of heart to a higher Authority and modestly ignored his own part in the conversion.

"It seems to me," the prosecutor said, "as if there had been a Divine interposition for the investigation and punishment of crime in this county. Remember that McParlan came here pledged that he should not be used as a witness. We placed no reliance upon him as a witness. We could not arrest a man because he told us anything about him, because he was protected by the pledge we had given him . . .

"I would have been the last man in the world to ask him to relieve me of this pledge, no matter the consequence . . . Some miraculous interposition of Providence had been vouchsafed to permit us to use the testimony and knowledge of McParlan. Then I breathed freer, and trod with elate step. Then I knew I had within my hands the power to crush these scoundrels.

"When, in all the history of criminal jurisprudence, did ever such a change in society come over a county as that which came here on the morning when McParlan first became a witness, that morning when Jack Kehoe, the county delegate, and twelve or fifteen other men, handcuffed to a chain, were pulled from the high places they occupied to take their solitary cells as felons within the walls of your prison.

"When I came to this courthouse on that memorable day, the courtroom was crowded with sympathizing friends of these criminals. Where are they today? They may be here, but they give no sign and we know nothing of them. The whole county sprang up like a giant unbound, and, ever excepting dramatic literature, there has never before been revealed such an awakening and such a change."

Gowen's final remarks were devoted to his championship of the working man.

"Counsel acting for the prisoner," declared the prosecutor, "say it is the old story of capital against labor. I now stand here on behalf of the laboring people of this county, people who have suffered more throughout the actions of these men than any other. I protest against the monstrous assumption that these villains are the representatives of the laboring people of Schuylkill County."

In the words of the Mahanoy City *Tri-Weekly Record*, "As Mr. Gowen concluded his magnificent address, not a sound echoed through the packed courtroom; spectators and jury sat enthralled.

" 'I have done my duty,' Mr. Gowen concluded. 'For God's sake let me beg of you not to shrink from doing yours. Solemn judges of the law and of the facts—you august ministers in the temple of justice, robed for sacrifice, I bring before you this prisoner and lay him upon your altar.

" 'The world awaits and trembles at the momentous issues involved in your answer. I ask you, will you let this villain go?' "

The answer for which Franklin Benjamin Gowen and the world waited came three hours later. "Guilty of murder in the first degree."

Chapter Thirty-Six

Less than twenty-four hours after Munley's conviction, the trial of the Commonwealth *vs.* Carroll, Roarity, McGehan and Boyle, interrupted by the death of Juror Levi Stein, was resumed. Its conclusion was foregone, and with the exception of the prisoners and jury, the cast of characters was the same. On July 22, all four were found guilty of murder in the first degree.

By August 8, Gowen was ready for Jack Kehoe, and the trial of the Girardville bodymaster and the eight Molly Maguires arrested with him two months earlier was begun. The charge was "atrocious assault and battery on the person of one William Thomas with intent to kill." The victim, Bully Boy, was very much alive and ready to enjoy every moment of the trial. Gowen was not yet prepared to charge Kehoe with murder.

By now, many metropolitan newspapers throughout the United States and England had been alerted to Gowen's systematic demolition of the Molly Maguires, whom many members of the working press reported as "Irish labor agitators and anarchists."

During the five days of his ordeal, Kehoe maintained his dignity and was an example of stoicism to those who faced with him a hostile judge, courtroom audience, and jury. Neither he nor any of his fellow defendants took the stand. When McParlan testified, as he did again at great length, the Girardville bodymaster regarded the detective with complete indifference.

The Bully Boy extracted only mild interest from the impassive Girardville bodymaster. No one could have guessed what response Kerrigan would have drawn, but Powderkeg was not called to the stand. Even the testimony of the youngest defendant, eighteen-year-old Frank McHugh, who turned State's evidence, drew no visible emotion—except perhaps scorn—from Kehoe.

Only once did he exhibit anger. This came when Schuylkill County Warden George Beyerle testified that "Kehoe told me, 'If I don't get justice, I don't think the Old Man up in Harrisburg will go back on us.' "

Kehoe's face grew crimson with fury at this and he muttered something to Martin L'Velle, who, because of the illness of Congressman Ryon and the unexplained withdrawal of Linn Barthelemew, now headed defense counsel. It is more than likely that Kehoe, who had been partly responsible for Hartranft's election, might have felt the "Old Man up in Harrisburg" owed him a favor. But it is not likely that he would have blurted out such a statement to his jailer.

The inner workings of Kehoe's Organization were once more revealed. Gowen could add little to what he, Kaercher, and the rest of the prosecution staff had already shown. In his address, Gowen dragged the Girardville bodymaster and his co-defendants through years of coal region violence. He concluded his eight-hour speech with another plea to "allow the laboring man to work unmolested, without the danger from armed bodies of Molly Maguires, who in the guise of labor reformers prevent honest men from earning their daily bread."

It took the jury less than a half hour to find all defendants guilty as charged. The panel rewarded McHugh with a recommendation of mercy and Judge Walker placed the youth on probation. From the day he left the courtroom that August 13, he was never again seen in Schuylkill County. The rest of the prisoners received penitentiary sentences of five to twenty years.

Gowen never let the Mollies recover their balance. Before the defendants in the Thomas trial had a chance to catch their breaths, all of them, with the exception of McHugh, were rearraigned in the same court, this time charged with conspiracy to kill William and Jesse Major, brothers of the murdered Mahanoy City Chief Burgess, George C. Major.

All were found guilty in a trial lasting only two days. McParlan's testimony furnished the bulk of the prosecution evidence. Kehoe and Canning, already under five-year sentences, received new seven-year terms, not to be served concurrently as L'Velle asked but consecutively as Gowen demanded. The other defendants were sent to jail for consecutive periods of from one to five years.

Still shaking from the Thomas verdict, the same defendants, this time without Kehoe but with the addition of Pat Butler, the Locust Gap bodymaster, were tried for aiding in the escape of Thomas Hurley, murderer of the Shenandoah Welshman, Gomer James. The verdict was "guilty as charged."

Those who wondered why Muff Lawler had not been brought into court had their answer on August 20, when Gowen announced to the press that the recently retired Shenandoah bodymaster had made a full confession of his crimes, "singing" as loud if not louder than Kerrigan. What Gowen did not reveal was that Muff had implicated Kehoe in a capital offense.

But Gowen wanted to be dead certain he had enough evidence to hang the Girardville bodymaster. This would take more time and patience, but for this one the special prosecutor had plenty of both.

Meanwhile, the other Molly Maguire trials continued. Thomas Duffy, who had elected to be heard separately for the murder of Patrolman Yost, was next on the schedule. The cell adjacent to Duffy's in the Pottsville jail was occupied by a perennial prisoner, an alcoholic minstrel christened (as far as anybody could learn) Manus Coll, but known throughout the hard coal regions as "Kelly the Bum," a one-time member of Pat Hester's Bloomsburg Division.

Even in an area abounding in "characters," Kelly the Bum was outstanding. The fact that he dressed in rags and rarely washed would not have set him apart from many men, but Manus Coll possessed additional distinctions. He could read and write; he was an authority on Gaelic literature and music; when he wished to, he could speak English flawlessly; and he appeared to be familiar with every remote seaport in the world. His ability to recite a complete Latin Mass led Tom O'Connor, the Mahanoy City editor, to believe Kelly the Bum had been a seminarian.

These by no means exhausted Manus Coll's abilities. He was an expert cutthroat, a skilled burglar, and a highly efficient arsonist. Unfortunately, alcohol was his curse, and he failed to achieve fame in any of his disciplines. Besides these accomplishments, Coll was a chronicler of coal region folk tales, and a balladeer and rhymster.

A day or so after Manus was released from prison he wrote seven stanzas of verse, obviously inspired by his quondam neighbor, Tom Duffy. For the price of a few drinks to assuage Kelly the Bum's everlasting thirst, the editor of the Shenandoah *Herald* became the owner of the coal region bard's only extant verse. It appeared in the *Herald* on September 9, 1876.

"*My name is Tommy Duffy, I am scarcely twenty-four;*
I was born in County Donegal, on Ireland's Emerald Shore.
I left my aging parents, like many of my race, ———
And now I'm held in durance vile, besmirched in black disgrace.

I was just about eighteen years old when to this land I came,
No sin lay on my conscience, and on my head no shame;
The first place that I earned me pay was in the Jeddo Mine,
And there, the men can testify how well I served me time!

The day I left my native land, I swore a solemn oath,
No liquor, grog of any kind would e'er go down my throat.
And now I'm still a-keeping it, and will until I die,
Be it on a bed of roses, or on a gallows high.

I stand accused of murder foul, the same I do deny.
And now my trial will soon come off—the traitors I defy!
But perjury has got its way throughout our happy land,
And like O'Connell, I'll have them swear on every upraised hand.

May God have mercy on these men, their deeds they can't
    secrete,
When called to face an angry God, before the Judgment Seat.
But such is life for Irishmen, and ever more 'twil be,
For it always was since that bad day, when Paddy's land was free.

By all that's holy Up Above, now what I say is true!
I never knew "Powder" Kerrigan, nor any of his crew.
I never kept his company, which he must know right well,
But to save his guilty neck, Alas; he'd swear a Saint to Hell.

So here's to all my kindly friends; my enemies also,
And to my foster parents, whom I have brought so low,
As for my loved and pretty wife, to me she is most dear,
I know that she will grieve for me, whilst I am lying here.

But wait, me lads, a little while, and soon you'll see me free,
To face the Bosses, one and all, that tried to bury me,
I'll walk among my fellow men, with head erect and strong,
To show my vile accusers that they are in the wrong!"

Duffy's fate was not as happy as the one projected for him. This fifth defendant to be tried for the shooting of Patrolman Yost fared no better than his four colleagues: on September 21, he was found guilty of murder in the first degree.

Not included in Kerrigan's original 210-page confession were details of the murder of mine boss Morgan Powell, which occurred in Summit Hill on December 2, 1871. Almost as an afterthought, Powderkeg, who'd been fading from the limelight, put the finger on three men who he claimed fired the fatal shots and three others who were, he said, accessories. Five of the six were arrested, promptly indicted and brought to trial October 19, in Mauch Chunk. There was no need to search for the sixth man. Alex Campbell was in jail awaiting execution.

In addition to Campbell those whom Kerrigan accused were John "Yellow Jack" Donohue, Thomas Fisher, Patrick McKenna, John Malloy, and Patrick O'Donnell, members of the Tamaqua and Mount Laffee Divisions of the Organization. The trial lasted only four days. With the exception of Malloy, who was able to substantiate his alibi, all were found guilty as charged. McKenna and O'Donnell were sent to prison for ten years while Donohue, Fisher, and Campbell were sentenced to be hanged.

There were no reasonable doubts about the guilt of two of the three sentenced to death, but there was a serious question about the nineteen-year-old Fisher's participation in or even knowledge of the crime. Except for brief membership in the Molly Maguires, from which he withdrew after only a two month "apprenticeship," Fisher's reputation was good. He vehemently denied the charge and admitted to only a tenuous acquaintance with any of the other prisoners. In this last he was supported by all the defendants. Fisher, like the rest of those charged with participating in Powell's murder, did not take the stand.

"If he had," said W. P. Ramsey, a member of the Schuylkill County Bar and distant relative of Fisher, "I doubt if he would have been found guilty. His conviction was a grave miscarriage of justice.

"As it was, the jury tarred Fisher by associating him with well-known criminals, including Alex Campbell, already found guilty in a previous homicide. It was easy to see how a jury would reason. 'What the hell,' they'd say, 'another jury found this fellow guilty before. Here he is again. You can't hang a man more than once so it's nothing on our consciences if we decide against him and the rest.'

"I checked with three witnesses who 'identified' Fisher. Two of them told me they never were sure it was Fisher they'd actually seen but they hated 'to disappoint Mr. Siewers.' The third witness, a woman, admitted that two years after the Mauch Chunk trial she saw a man on the streets of Tamaqua who looked exactly like the defendant. 'More so, I guess,' she told me. 'I think I must have made a mistake but it's too late now. Anyway, Fisher was a Molly and none of them are any good. What's the difference if we hung one more of 'em?' "

On November 1, Kelly the Bum was back in the Schuylkill County jail, charged with vagrancy and petty larceny—the theft of a bottle of whiskey. After three days of incarceration he was in desperate need of a drink. "Tell Mr. Gowen I'd like to see him," he told his jailer, and the latter complied.

"I know who killed Alexander Rea," declared the Bum to Gowen. "It was Pat Hester and some of his boyos."

While Gowen listened and a stenographer took notes, Manus Coll revealed details of Rea's assassination on August 17, 1868. He implicated Hester and several members of the Bloomsburg Division of which the Bum had been a member. His own part in the robbery-murder, he said, was merely that of bystander. Gowen took action at once.

"Hester and a man named Michael Graham were arrested and lodged in the Schuylkill County jail, charged with the murder of Rea," said the Bloomsburg *Columbian*, November 17, 1876, "Hester as an accessory before the fact and Graham as accessory after the fact. The chief evidence against them is that of a man in jail at Pottsville, charged with larceny, who has confessed the crime and given the names of the parties engaged in it and the division of the money taken from the body after the murder.

"Since writing the above, Patrick Tully, alias Pat Brown, has been arrested near Wilkes-Barre and taken to the Pottsville jail, charged with the murder."

The treasury of the Molly Maguires, Bloomsburg Division, was empty; consequently no funds were available for the defense of Hester (charged with the same crime once before) and his colleagues. Loyal members of the Organization, not in jail, determined to rectify the situation as soon as the opportunity was offered.

The opportunity presented itself on November 19. A few days before, Dillard Wright, a handyman, had learned that his employer, Nathan Henninger, had just received three thousand dollars in gold as settlement in a relative's estate. Wright, no Molly himself but hopeful he'd get a cut if money were stolen, passed this information to his friend, Philip Hughes, secretary of the Bloomsburg Division. Hughes and an unknown number of confederates decided to rob the farmer before his cash was placed in a bank.

"My grandfather was Nathan Henninger," said Mrs. Goldie Kerstetter, a retired school teacher and postmistress of Gowen City, named in honor of the President of the Road. "Grandpa's farm was in a very remote part of Mahoning Valley, about ten miles east of Bloomsburg, and his nearest neighbor was at least a mile away. My mother was only eleven years old the night the Mollies robbed Grandpa but the memory stayed with her until the end of her days.

"About seven o'clock, the family was finishing supper in the summerhouse, a stone building, about fifty yards from the main house. They were getting ready to butcher, so the big kitchen in the main house wouldn't be used for a week; that's why they were eating in the summerhouse.

"Grandma had to go out to milk her pet cow, but when she tried to open the door it wouldn't budge. She thought maybe it was Dillard playing a joke so she called out to him to quit it. When nothing happened, Grandpa, who was a big man, about six foot six, and weighed more than two hundred and fifty pounds, put his shoulder and pushed. The door sprang open and he could see a man in a white shirt standing there, holding a pistol in his hand.

" 'Don't come out!' this man yelled, 'or you'll get your head shot off.' "

At this, Henninger slammed the door and threw an iron bolt in place. He realized that someone (he suspected Wright immediately) was in the process of stealing the gold hidden in an attic chest. He told his family to lie flat on the floor.

"Grandpa and the hired man ran up to the second story," Mrs. Kerstetter continued, "and grabbed a couple of guns. They had plenty of bullets around, because of butchering. In those days they made their own bullets.

"There was some light from the moon and a little coming out of the kitchen window, so they could see. Grandpa got a glimpse of a white shirt and he fired. Then the hired man saw something moving near the big house and *he* fired.

"There were sounds of somebody running so my grandfather and the hired man rushed outside with their guns loaded. They found a dead man in front of the kitchen. There'd been a light snow and they could follow a trail of blood leading from the main house across the field into a woods where another man had run. They were too late to save the money; it was gone.

"Grandpa called the sheriff and he recognized the dead man, Philip Hughes, a Bloomsburg Molly. Nobody ever knew for sure whether a second Molly was killed, but Grandpa thinks so. There was so much blood, he figured the man died and his friends carried the body off where it wouldn't be found. They even thought it might be Dillard."

But Wright, who disappeared that night, returned to Bloomsburg six years later and surrendered to police. He admitted his participation in the crime and said the gold was stolen to provide money for Hester's defense. As far as he knew it was used for that purpose. The handyman was to have received ten dollars for his share. As it turned out, he fared better than Hester.

Chapter Thirty-Seven

For Franklin Benjamin Gowen, the most important section of Lawler's lengthy confession was Muff's claim that Kehoe was directly involved in the murder of Frank S. Langdon, the Audenried ticket boss slain July 4, 1862. The special prosecutor would have preferred to charge Black Jack with a more recent homicide but Coal and Iron Police, who began a complete investigation of Langdon's murder the moment Lawler turned informer convinced Gowen that here he had a foolproof case against the Girardville bodymaster.

Lawler himself was in no way involved with Langdon's slaying, but he knew enough about the case to furnish Gowen's investigators with background information so detailed that they could supply many witnesses to a fourteen-year-old homicide.

It may well be that the case of the Commonwealth vs. John Kehoe was an anticlimax. The Mollies were finished as organized pockets of resistance and rebellion. They knew it and so did the people. Nevertheless, residents of hard coal counties and newspaper readers in far-off New York and London, who had been following the Molly Maguire court scenes with avid interest, were far more excited over the prosecution of the "Molly King" than over the trials that preceded it.

"John Kehoe was brought to court this morning," wrote Tom Fielders in the Shenandoah *Herald,* on January 9. "His appearance has not been improved by confinement and he looks much thinner and careworn . . . John W. Ryon, Esq., on behalf of the prisoner, said a continuance was desired . . . Court did not sustain the motion and the work of drawing the panel got underway."

Again Judge Pershing presided and again no Irishman was among the twelve men of the jury.

"Mr. Farquhar opened the case in which John Kehoe is charged with the murder of F. S. Langdon," said Fielders the following day. "He promised the jury to lay before them such testimony as would warrant them in returning a verdict of murder in the first degree.

"The first witness was H. S. Reitz, a mining engineer, who produced a map of the scene of the murder and explained it. Mr. Ryon, for the defense, asked the witness who employed him to make the map and who paid for it. The witness said he had been commissioned by General Albright and that the county commissioners had paid for the work."

And so, down the line and up the stand went a long parade of prosecution witnesses. There was Pat Brady, a night watchman, who swore he heard Jack Kehoe say to Langdon, "You son-of-a-bitch, I'll kill you before long." There was William Canvin who testified that he saw Kehoe spit on the American flag and heard Kehoe or one of the bodymaster's cronies shout "If we get the son-of-a-bitch we'll kill him." There was John Tyrell, Jr., a carpenter's helper, who swore he saw Kehoe and Neil Dougherty follow Langdon and knock him down. There was John Brian, a miner, who claimed he saw Langdon run past Boch's saloon closely pursued by Kehoe and three or four others whom he did not recognize. Still others described the merciless manner in which Langdon was beaten that Saturday evening, his desperate flight, the cowardice of those who turned their heads and ran away, and the ticket boss's last moments.

"When Frank came home Sunday morning," said Langdon's widow, "death was staring out of his eyes."

Several witnesses to some part of Langdon's murder admitted they had been afraid to testify at a coroner's inquest held shortly after the ticket boss's death. One of these was George Arn, a store clerk, who probably expressed the attitude of many residents of the hard coal regions.

"Back in '62 and for a long time after," he said, "it took more courage than I had to appear against the Mollies. I ain't afraid no more."

The defense made its strongest stand on the fifth day of the trial by producing a number of witnesses, including several "respectable" citizens, who testified that Kehoe had not left Boch's saloon during the attack on Langdon. Because witnesses who could have negated this evidence had died during the years that had elapsed between the murder and trial, much of this testimony went uncontradicted.

"At the adjournment of court yesterday," wrote Fielders, "the case against Kehoe looked anything but cheerful; still, men have escaped from positions just as dangerous."

But as the sixth day closed, "prospects of the County Delegate, Kehoe, took a turn for the worse," the *Herald* reporter continued, adding an unsolicited suggestion to the prisoner. "If he hasn't already done so, Kehoe might as well throw up the sponge."

The defense rested on January 15, two days after the Commonwealth had concluded its case. To the surprise of an expectant audience and the working press, Gowen, who had sat at counsel's table during the trial, yielded the honor of addressing the jury to his colleague Kaercher. There was little the special prosecutor could gain by presenting the State's final plea; he might even be criticized for usurping the spotlight.

Gowen had won all he needed. No one in Schuylkill County or elsewhere questioned the special prosecutor's position in the demolition of the Molly Maguires and the toppling of "King Kehoe" from his throne. Perhaps Gowen felt that in view of his much-publicized avowal to destroy the Girardville bodymaster, he might be accused of persecution rather than prosecution had he not relinquished the trial's top spot to the district attorney.

Nearly all records of this and other Molly Maguire trials have disappeared from Pottsville's courthouse, stolen, officials say, by descendants of Kehoe and his colleagues. Likewise, books and articles, written by contemporary authors, have vanished from the shelves of libraries throughout the anthracite area. So there is no record of what Kaercher told the panel.

"At nine o'clock this morning, Mr. Kaercher commenced his address to the jury in the Kehoe case," wrote Fielders. "For two hours he occupied their attention . . . The Court, in its charge, reviewed the testimony at length and closed at ten minutes past twelve. The jury retired immediately afterward.

"Concluding that the deliberations would take some time, Judge Pershing ordered court adjourned until the ringing of a bell, announcing that the jury had made an agreement.

". . . At half-past two, the bell rang, warning those who wanted to see the last act of the drama to make their way to the courthouse. Within five minutes, an immense crowd was on hand and the jury entered the box at twenty-five minutes to three, having deliberated two hours and twenty-five minutes."

Betting was that Kehoe would be convicted of murder in the second degree, the sentence handed down to two other defendants. Neil Dougherty and John Campbell (Alex's first cousin) had been tried at Mauch Chunk the previous year, and, even after admitting participation in Langdon's murder, had escaped the maximum penalty. Neither was a witness at the trial of the Girardville bodymaster.

"Kehoe," continued Fielders, "sat at counsel table, looking pale as death. His wife occupied a chair next to him and appeared composed. Dead silence reigned when the clerk of courts asked the ominous question: 'Gentlemen of the jury, have you agreed upon a verdict?'

"There was a pause for a few seconds when Foreman Schenk, handing papers to the clerk, said: 'We find the defendant guilty of murder in the first degree.'

"It must have been a horrible surprise for Kehoe, as he really entertained hopes of a lesser degree, if not acquittal. He gazed upon the jury as if to stamp the face of each member indelibly into his mind. As each juror was polled, the eyes of the convicted felon never left his face.

"Mrs. Kehoe did not flinch while the verdict was rendered but when Kehoe left the room, she broke down . . .

"It was learned that the jury agreed upon the first formal ballot. . . ."

On April 16, 1877, Kehoe was brought from his cell to receive the Court's sentence. Thin and drawn-looking, he sat next to his wife and held her hand. He got up only to shake his head when asked by the Court if he had anything to say before sentence was imposed.

"The three judges and Court Crier then arose," said the *Herald,* "and remained standing while President Judge Pershing spoke as follows:

" 'The sentence of the Court is that you be taken hence to the county jail and thence to a place appointed for the execution, and there you be hanged by the neck until you are dead, and may God have mercy on your soul.'

"During the entire charge, Kehoe was composed, but his face was ashy pale . . . His wife, who sat with him, exhibited no emotion until her husband had entered the prison, when she burst out crying and walked down the pavement, a melancholy picture of sorrow."

All Kehoe had left was the hope that the "Old Man" would not forget to "return the favor."

Meanwhile, Hester and two confederates, Peter McHugh and Patrick Tully, arrested with him the past November, went on trial at Bloomsburg, February 8, 1877, charged with the murder of Alexander Rea. The prosecution's chief witness was Kelly the Bum.

Modestly but immaculately attired and probably the victim of a recent bath, Manus Coll entered the courtroom in triumph, escorted by his permanent bodyguard, none other than Captain Linden.

The moment Kelly was sworn, John W. Ryon, chief defense counsel, who presumably never gave up, questioned the Bum's competency. He based his objections on the fact that Coll, in 1867, had been sentenced to a term in the Schuylkill County jail for highway robbery and that the sentence had not been fully served.

"But," said the *Columbian,* "the Commonwealth answered the objection by producing a pardon from the Governor."

Whether Hartranft pardoned Coll because the latter was a Molly Maguire or an enemy of the Organization was not established. The distinguished Governor of the Keystone State, according to contemporary authorities of Pennsylvania's politics, could have adjusted his malleable conscience to fit either situation.

That Coll's conscience was as pliable as that of the "Old Man" up in Harrisburg was evidenced by an example of the Bum's ethics.

Cross-examined by Ryon, who asked what he was doing in 1867, Coll replied that he was "electioneering."

"For whom?"

"For Kase, who was running for district attorney on the Democratic ticket."

"But weren't you getting expense money and traveling on a railroad pass furnished by Mr. Fiske, the Republican candidate?" questioned Ryon.

"Of course," returned the witness. "You see I was working a little for both sides."

Coll maintained certain standards in his principal vocation, however.

"Wasn't it your custom," asked Mr. Ryon, "to knock a man down then pick his pockets?"

"Certainly not, sir," came the answer. "I used to get my man drunk first, then when he had lain down, go through his pockets. I *never* hit him."

The Bum placed most of the blame on Hester, although he admitted that the Bloomsburg bodymaster was not present when Rea was waylaid, robbed, and murdered. Coll definitely put himself, Tully, and McHugh at the murder site and described in detail how they shot and killed the mine superintendent.

"With apparent unconcern," reported the *Columbian,* "Kelly sat upon the witness stand for two days and told the story of the bloody deed. According to his own testimony . . . he it was who fired one of the first balls that went crashing through the skull of the unfortunate victim; he it was who rifled the pockets of the dead man and took the lion's share of the plunder; he it was who took the watch and money of Mr. Rea, and afterwards generously gave to each of his companions a few paltry dollars as the price of blood."

Some portions of Coll's testimony were corroborated by other witnesses, but the bulk of the prosecution's case rested on the Bum's testimony.

To his surprise, Tom Fielders of the Shenandoah *Herald* was called as a witness for the defense. He was asked to read the notes he had taken when Coll first discussed the Rea murder in front of Magistrate Reed in Pottsville. Ryon's efforts were directed at proving that Coll had changed his story between the time he testified in Schuylkill County and the current trial, but except for showing minor discrepancies in the Bum's story, the defense gained nothing by putting Fielders on the stand.

On Saturday, February 14, court recessed until Monday morning. On Sunday, the jury, no doubt pleased to have one day devoted to subjects other than murder, attended services in Bloomsburg's St. Matthew's Lutheran Church. Here they were treated to a fire and brimstone sermon preached by the Rev. Dr. James McCron. Dr. McCron's topic, chosen from the sixth chapter of Saint Mark, was hardly coincidental, a fact noted by defense counsel the following morning when the trial was resumed.

"I move," declared Mr. Ryon, "that in the case of the Commonwealth *vs.* Hester, Tully and McHugh, the court discharge the jury from further consideration of this case because at one of the churches at which the jury attended services . . . the subject of murder in all its various bearings was discussed by the minister in their hearing, the special subject being the murder of John the Baptist by Herod; and the tenor of the discourse seemed to give credit to the testimony of Kelly, or Coll, the witness."

The petition was denied.

On February 24, the jury returned a verdict of guilty of murder in the first degree against all three defendants. As far as the record shows, Manus Coll never was indicted for this or any murder. In return for the favor, the Bum cleared up an additional homicide by recalling details in the slaying of George K. Smith of Audenried in 1868.

Smith's murderers, declared Coll, were James McDonnell, the Hairy Man of Tuscarora, and his friend Charles Sharpe, both of whom had been suspected of the crime for many years. The two were later arrested, brought to trial in Mauch Chunk, found guilty of murder in the first degree, and sentenced to be hanged. In the case of the Commonwealth *vs.* McDonnell and Sharp, the Bum's testimony was corroborated by another prosecution stalwart, Powderkeg Kerrigan.

Unlike his colleague, Kerrigan was given official recognition for services performed in a petition filed by the Carbon County district attorney.

"And now, April 10, 1877, upon motion of Messrs. Hughes, Albright and Craig, it appearing that James Kerrigan, the defendant, having been indicted for the murder of John P. Jones, January 17, 1876, and more than two full terms having elapsed since the indictment, the said defendant is therefore discharged from the further custody of this court, upon said charge the District Attorney not being prepared to prosecute said defendant.

"I have no objections to the above motion for discharge.

"E. R. Siewers, District Attorney."

Judge Dreher concurred, and gave Powderkeg his immediate freedom.

"Within ten minutes after Jimmy's discharge, he visited the Coal Gazette office," declared the *Coal Gazette,* "and was interviewed with the following result:

"REPORTER. Well Jimmy, I suppose you are happy on account of your release.

"MR. KERRIGAN. Yes, sir, I am. I had no knowledge that I was to be released until just before dinner. The whole thing was a complete surprise to me. I have spent a little over nineteen months in jail, and while I have no fault to find with the way I was treated there, I am very glad to get out.

"REP. What do you propose to do?

"MR. K. Well, I am going to Tamaqua tonight.

"REP. Is there not some danger in your going back at this time?

"MR. K. I think it is a duty I owe to my family to go to them at the earliest moment. I will start on the six o'clock train.

"REP. Have you anything you wish to say through the columns of the Coal Gazette to the public?

"MR. K. I want to say that I am very thankful to the Commonwealth's attorneys for their treatment of me, and especially General Albright. He always told me to tell nothing but the truth in my evidence, and gave me good advice not to drink and to attend well to my church duties.

"REP. What do you intend to do?

"MR. K. My plans are not matured. However, I intend to let drink alone and keep out of bad company. . . ."

"And Jimmy left smiling like a boy with a new toy."

Chapter Thirty-Eight

Defense counsel's formal appeals to Pennsylvania's Supreme Court for reversals of lower court decisions and its request to grant new trials for all the Molly Maguire defendants under sentence of death were rejected one by one.

Death warrants were received by the sheriffs of Carbon and Schuylkill counties.

"These documents," said the *Coal Gazette*, "fix as the day of execution, June 21st. Sheriff Raudenbush, accompanied by District Attorney Siewers and some other gentlemen, entered the cell of 'Yellow Jack' Donohue and told him his business. The prisoner, a large hearty man, seemed full of spirits and made a joking reply which ill befitted the occasion. He exhibited the utmost indifference and after the party had left he indulged in some dances and songs.

"Edward Kelly was the next visited. Since his confession Kelly has evinced a full appreciation of his situation and met the Sheriff in a mournful and touching way. When the reading was finished he said if it was God's will that he should die he was ready for the solemn event. Kelly has paid close attention to his religious duties for the past month and is frequently found praying earnestly. He is a very young man and there has been a good deal of sympathy for him expressed of late.

"Michael J. Doyle was . . . depressed in spirits and in bad health. During the reading of the warrant he trembled and at the close sank down on his bed. He is thin and pale and it is not thought he would live long in prison. When he entered the jail he was a man of large physique and looked very healthy. He has a bad cough and looks as though his disease was rapid consumption."

This seemed like an appropriate occasion for mine and railroad operators (frequently the same corporation) to lower wages throughout the hard coal regions. The Lehigh Valley Railroad led off, and, said the *Coal Gazette*, May 13, 1877, "ordered a ten per cent reduction on the salaries and pay of officers, conductors, baggage-masters . . . and laborers . . ."

At about this time, the national office of the Ancient Order of Hibernians took long-anticipated action against nearly all of its divisions in Schuylkill, Carbon, Northumberland, and Columbia Counties by revoking their charters. This was accomplished almost without opposition at a convention held in New York City, May, 1877.

Less than a week before the first ten Molly Maguires were scheduled to be hanged, defense counsel made its next to last appeal (the last was a direct plea for executive clemency) for a stay of execution or a commutation of sentences.

On June 19, the Board of Pardons announced it had turned down all defense pleas. Now only the faintest glimmer of hope, the "Old Man" up in Harrisburg, remained for the condemned men. But on Wednesday morning, June 20, Governor Hartranft, who all along had indicated his unwillingness to intervene, said no, and the prisoners prepared themselves for death.

Pottsville and Mauch Chunk, forty miles apart, were like armed camps. In the Schuylkill County city, Captain Linden, in command of a greatly augmented Coal and Iron Police force, guarded the jail from both inside and out. The streets of this county seat and the roads leading into it were patrolled by two military units, the Gowen Guards and the Pottsville Light Infantry.

No one was permitted to enter the town unless he could furnish a satisfactory reason for being there. Heavily armed posses of deputized sheriffs roamed the lonely hills surrounding the town looking for the bands of Mollies reported to be gathering in isolated mountain hideouts, preparing to make a mass assault on the prison.

How difficult it would be to make any last minute attempts at rescue was pointed out by a correspondent for the *New York Times*:

"The Pottsville jail is absolutely impregnable except to the assault of an organized army aided by artillery," wrote their reporter. "It occupies the top of a high hill surrounded by other hills, and they, by mountains north of the town, and is square in extent.

"It is encircled by a thick stone wall over 25 feet in height, except at the entrance on the south, where there is an immense castellated and turreted pile of brown stone of sufficient strength to resist an earthquake. The front of the entrance is neatly laid out as a cultivated garden, shaded by beautiful trees. The doors are all of heavy iron slabs, pierced with diamond headed iron bolts. To assault the place even unguarded would be madness."

In Carbon County, strong rumors persisted throughout the week that five hundred armed "do or die" members of the Organization, aided by thousands of armed sympathizers, were planning to catapult blazing torches to the rooftops of Mauch Chunk. While firemen were busy putting out the spreading conflagrations and police and military were saving citizens from death, attackers would then dynamite the prison and rescue their four condemned brothers.

It was even claimed that the fearless Powderkeg Kerrigan himself, remorseful over his betrayal of the "Cause," would be in charge of the demolition squad. But this was wishful thinking. No remaining Mollies contemplated dramatic prison deliveries, and as for Kerrigan, it was more than likely that this gentleman had been further rewarded by being ensconced in some safe spot with a clear view of the gibbet where he could taste the fruits of his infamy.

Carbon County authorities, however, were taking no chances. They knew only too well that the terrain might easily have lent itself to such a desperate enterprise. As the *New York Times* described it, "Mauch Chunk rests in the very midst of the mountains, the towering hills, densely wooded to their summits, almost overhang the town."

A cavalry troop, the Easton Grays, eighty strong, rode up and down the streets of Mauch Chunk and patrolled the roads leading into the hamlet. For fifty yards on each side of the jail, Linden's Chief of Staff massed his Coal and Iron Policemen and barred passers-by from the vicinity of the huge, iron prison gate. Squads of Sheriff Raudenbush's deputies, bearing Civil War rifles, cleared the borough's roads and alleyways.

Inside both prisons, the artifices of execution were gotten into readiness.

"Gallows were taken into the Pottsville jail yard at three o'clock in the morning," said the *New York Times*, "and were put together at once . . . They were made in town, but with the greatest privacy, and a statement was given out that they were manufactured elsewhere. These precautions were taken to prevent their destruction by the Molly Maguires, for fear they would set fire to the carpenter's shop.

"There are three gallows of unpainted pine. Each consists of two stout braced uprights 16 feet, 4 inches high, and a cross beam with two ropes of half-inch Italian hemp. These latter were given free by a Philadelphia firm who hope thereby to secure an advertisement.

"Seven feet 9 inches from the ground is a double trap door, secured by hinges in the uprights and making a platform seven feet by seven and one-half feet. Under where they meet is placed a double post, hinged in the centre and furnished with cushions at top and bottom. A rope attached to this passes out through a hole in a wooden screen in the rear."

No details of the *modus operandi* were left to the imagination of *New York Times* readers.

"The executioner," continued this newspaper, "stands behind the screen holding the three ropes, the three gallows being placed side by side, and when he pulls them at the signal the supports double up, cushions preventing them from making any noise, the drop-doors fall forward and the murderers are left swinging in mid-air. A drop of four and a half feet is provided for each man. There is no screen in front to hide the bodies.

"The jail proper, with an extension, forms an L inside the high wall, leaving a large, sloping grass-covered plot . . . About 15 feet from the east wall . . . is the place selected for the gallows. They face due west. Two of the six condemned men are in cells facing the fatal green, and could distinctly hear the hammering all day. Their relatives, in taking leave, were compelled to pass where they could see the work going on."

At Mauch Chunk, a similar event took place. Here, however, there was no prison yard and the condemned men were to be executed inside the jail itself, a narrow building with a gloomy, high ceilinged open area in its core. Around this ran a tier of upper and lower cells with a balcony encircling the top tier and leading off into the warden's quarters, where Kerrigan had passed many a pleasant hour.

The gallows were placed in the rear center of the areaway in full view of all four prisoners, who could watch the carpenters hammering away for hours, not a dozen feet off. Space was so limited that only one hundred fortunate spectators would be permitted to view the proceedings.

Mauch Chunk, more provincial than Pottsville, lacked the go-getter type of businessman which provided this latter community with an undertaker with imagination. Displayed in the front windows of Kline's Funeral Parlor on Market Street a week prior to the execution were six coffins. On placards placed at the front end of each wooden box, clearly visible to potential customers who stood gaping all day, were shown the recipient's name and measurements. "Thomas Duffy, 5′ 6″; Thomas Munley, 5′ 8″; James Carroll, 5′ 10″; Hugh McGehan, 6′ 0″; James Roarity, 5′ 10″ and James Boyle, 6′ 1″."

The coffins, according to a large poster which hung above the windows, were donated to families of the condemned men "Through the generosity of Herman Raudenbush Kline, prop." A pious postscript "The wages of sin is death (Acts XX, 23)" was appended.

To quiet any alarm which Mr. Kline's creditors may have felt at this philanthropic gesture, came the *New York Times*. "These coffins," said an observant reporter for this newspaper, "are only stained poplar, studded with cheap silverplated stars . . . the sides are silverplated and in the center of each lid is a poor imitation of a crucifix, silvered and roughly tacked on . . . Around them is a band of tinsel."

All of this led Jake Haas to add his own Biblical quotation

selected from Philippians II, 12. "Touch not . . . handle not." Except for its public relations value, Mr. Kline's benevolence was wasted; the Commonwealth of Pennsylvania provided sturdier, if less ornate, coffins built of rough pine.

Inside both jails, a constant stream of relatives paying last minute calls on the condemned men made the prisons seem like macabre picnic grounds or ghastly wakes where corpses were able to talk to their mourners.

Not only were kinfolk of the condemned allowed free access to loved ones, but widows, orphans, mothers and fathers of victims drifted in and out, pausing before the murderers' cells to excoriate, forgive, or even pity those who were about to die.

"Yellow Jack" Donohue, smoking a short black pipe, sits in Cell Twelve with his wife and their eight children, who range in age from three to fourteen years. "They spread themselves on the bed and floor," reports the *New York Times*, "and the cries of the women and children resound throughout the prison."

In Cell Six, Alex Campbell, calm and reflective, is having a subdued conversation with his wife, soon to be a widow. According to the Mahanoy City *Tri-Weekly Record*, "The Tamaqua bodymaster does not resemble in any way the archvillain he's been painted."

In Cell Ten sits Edward Kelly, scarcely nineteen years old now; only eighteen when he killed John P. Jones. His handsome face is wan and drawn and there is a look of bewilderment in his bright blue eyes. He seems more like an acolyte who has forgotten his lines than a man with only hours to live. With Kelly is his oldest brother, Dan, a decent lad of twenty. His mother is too ill to visit her son; his father was killed in a mine accident the day after Edward was taken into custody; his four younger brothers and sisters have already said farewell.

Kelly, so far the only one who has confessed to his crime, has told the sheriff his one wish was to beg forgiveness from his victim's widow. Now Mrs. Jones stands before him, young, and, in the words of the *New York Times* reporter, "very handsome."

The prisoner, his words coming in a whisper between barely controlled sobs, falls to his knees at the door of his cell. Mrs. Jones, voice filled with emotion, stretches her black-gloved hand through the bars and pats the youth's head. "I forgive you," she says, "and I will pray to God to forgive you."

Then she and her late husband's mother and sister, who have been standing behind her, turn toward Cell Six. Michael J. Doyle is its temporary tenant. With Doyle are his parents, a brother, and two sisters. The murderer's mother, sitting beside her son, suddenly looks up and recognizes Mrs. Jones, draped in black, staring with fascination upon the face of the man who killed her husband.

Mrs. Doyle jumps up and stands in front of Michael, screaming with rage as she shields her son from view. "Go away! You can't look at him! You ought to be home."

The widow regards Mrs. Doyle contemptuously. "If you had brought your son up better this wouldn't have happened," she says with scorn. Mrs. Doyle collapses into the arms of her son, who switches roles from comforted to comforter.

In the Pottsville jail, where similar scenes are taking place, a rumor comes alive that Carroll has made a complete confession admitting not only his own participation in Patrolman Yost's murder but implicating Duffy, McGehan, and Boyle.

"Thank God!" says Warden George Beyerle. But the rumor is false and Carroll is ready to die with lips sealed.

When the courthouse clocks in Mauch Chunk and Pottsville struck nine, visitors were ordered to leave. The last straggler was Alice Doyle, Michael's fifteen-year-old sister, discovered almost at once by Sheriff Raudenbush who followed the prisoner's nod and found the weeping child hidden beneath her brother's cot.

"After all had left, the prisoners engaged in a light repast and retired," reported Tom Fielders, who covered the Pottsville hangings. He had nothing more to say about the condemned men's last night on earth.

"By eleven o'clock all was quiet in the prison and the hours passed slowly by without any signs of trouble," reported Tom Foster, who covered the Mauch Chunk executions.

"Two policemen slept upon the scaffold during the night and others walked in the jail corridors. John Donohue spent part of the night reading 'Preparation for Death' by the light of a candle. He was chained to the floor, as the law prescribes all men should be on the night previous to an execution. The candle burned low in its socket and was flickering just before its light failed when 'Yellow Jack' blew it out and stretched himself out on his bed.

"Michael J. Doyle . . . was thin and wasted away. His long fingers he ran through his hair and kissed his crucifix repeatedly. At twelve o'clock he laid himself down for a sleep, if nature could come to the relief of his troubled mind.

"Kelly's face is one that attracts rather than repels and there was something about it last night, even in all the mental torture it endured, that drew sympathy toward him. He kept awake until 11:50 and then placed himself upon his couch.

"Aleck Campbell showed no signs of mental exhaustion. He read his catechism and kissed his crucifix repeatedly. Shortly before twelve o'clock he laid on his couch.

"At 12:15, the guards passed the cells of the condemned men and the labored breathing and an occasional snore showed all of the wretches to be asleep."

Chapter Thirty-Nine

"The day dawned dark and gloomy over Mauch Chunk this morning, clouds were scattered about in the heavens and looked as though, at any moment, they would deluge the place with rain," wrote Tom Foster.

In Pottsville, even while overhead lamps were glowing in the misty haze which blanketed the town's dark streets, Tom Fielders, in his own words, "presented himself at the jail and was admitted." Then, with a touch of justifiable journalistic pride he added, "Until almost nine o'clock the Herald correspondent was the only newspaper representative within the jail."

Carroll, the ambitious Tamaqua saloonkeeper who had hoped one day to be a bodymaster, was the first prisoner to awake. Refreshed from five or six hours' sleep, he was stretching his arms and pacing up and down when Warden George Beyerle, Deputy Warden Moses Innis, and Albert Fessler, the prison barber, entered his cell.

"During the operation," reported Fielders, "Carroll appeared to be in very good spirits and chatted pleasantly. . . ."

Roarity, the Coaldale bodymaster who with no more than a year's schooling managed to own and operate a profitable tavern, had to be aroused from a sound sleep before Fessler could trim his hair and shave him.

"Make it good, Al," he jested, "or you're liable to lose a customer."

Munley, a victim of the ham he never ate that Friday morning, appeared subdued, and, said Fielders, "submitted to being shaved without indulging in any more conversation than was necessary."

McGehan, whose family had starved while he was blacklisted for "speaking up" too often to his bosses, now had nothing to say. He merely shook his head in response to Fessler's attempts at humor. Except for the sound of the barber's shears snipping McGehan's long blond hair, the cell was silent.

Boyle, the Lansford gunman, quipped grimly when the barber's razor nicked his face. "You better watch this fellow, George," he said to the Warden, "or he'll do the hangman out of a job."

Duffy, whose quarrel with Yost began the murder chain which finally linked all six prisoners, was concerned with the welfare of his colleagues.

"How are the boyos takin' it?" he asked the Warden, and when Beyerle answered, "Fine," Duffy said, "Good. We'll show 'em how men die!"

A coffee break came at six o'clock. "After this," reported Fielders, "the men dressed themselves and engaged in prayer while awaiting their confessors. Shortly after, a number of friends applied for admission and were allowed to visit the condemned men. Munley's wife, father, and two sisters walked from Gilberton, a distance of fourteen miles, and were in an exhausted condition and by no means strong enough to undergo the pain of a final separation.

"The father and brother of Duffy were also present, as were Mrs. Roarity and several others. The scenes that occurred in the cells of the condemned men were horribly suggestive of death. The women hung about the necks of the unfortunate culprits and fairly shrieked their agony.

"Strong men wept, and little children, not old enough to realize the situation of their fathers, followed the example of their elders, making the parting scene a never-to-be forgotten incident in the memories of all who witnessed it."

A bit later, the tall, slender ascetic Father Daniel I. McDermott, who had for so many years denounced the Molly Maguires and predicted the fate of those belonging to the Organization, entered the prison. Without a single "I told you so" he celebrated Mass in a spare cell and administered the Holy Sacrament to the condemned.

Foster, unlike his protégé, was forced to cool his heels outside prison walls and for the moment write about actions occurring only on Mauch Chunk streets.

"The guards came in from road patrol and reported all was quiet," said the editor of the Shenandoah *Herald.* "People went out of their homes and discussed the tragical event that was about to happen. As early as 9 o'clock the crowds started flocking to town and headed for the jail. There they learned the execution would take place inside and could not be seen from the street. . . ."

Substitute entertainment, however, was provided by the Easton Grays, eighty strong. This military unit, not as aristocratic as Philadelphia's First City Troop, nevertheless carried on its rolls a satisfactory number of gentlemen, including sons of John F. Hartranft, Governor of the Commonwealth, and Cyrus L. Pershing, presiding judge at several Molly Maguire trials.

"The Grays arrived and marched up the streets headed by a drum corps," wrote Editor Foster. "After several intricate drills, they cleaned the street in front of the jail for a square, files of men being placed above and below the jail and across a narrow street opening into Broadway, directly opposite the jail. Sentinels paced back and forth and all who dared to enter without a pass were quickly thrust out."

Foster was still concerned with the right of citizens to bear arms and seemed to hope they would be fired.

"Nearly everyone you met had a pistol concealed on his person and would not have hesitated to use it if the occasion arose," said the Shenandoah publisher.

Inside the prison, preparations for the executions went on according to schedule.

"New suits of clothing, purchased at the expense of the county, for Kelly and 'Yellow Jack' Donohue arrived at 8 o'clock and were taken to their cells and left with them," said Foster. "At 9 o'clock the priests arrived and the crowd that blocked the jail entrance gave way. They were received by the Sheriff and conducted to the cells of the condemned men, where they donned their surplices and at once administered the Holy Sacrament."

On the front stoop of a house directly opposite the prison gate sat a disconsolate figure, Alice Doyle, waiting to claim her brother's body; her parents had collapsed. Within the house, shielded from public view, were other relatives of the condemned men. With all hope gone, they sat in silence awaiting the inevitable.

At ten o'clock a mob of reporters, officials, sheriff's deputies, jury, and citizens with sufficient political pull to rate admission passes, entered one by one and took their places. The choicest locations were on the balcony. From that vantage spot there was a clear view of all the cells, the "last mile" to the gibbet, the hangman, and the drop.

At 10:10 a deputy warden made a hideous error and brought Campbell from his cell and led him to the gallows steps.

"Take him back!" the sheriff shouted. "We're not ready yet." Campbell, given a twenty-minute reprieve, might have been grateful for even this small extension of life; it is more likely that he was chilled with the thought of facing this same horror again.

But by 10:30 all preparations were completed and Raudenbush mounted the scaffold, stamping heavily on each of the ten steps to test their stability. On the platform itself he placed four pairs of handcuffs and four long white hoods. Then he tugged hard at each rope.

"Finding all in order," said Foster, "the Sheriff beckoned to a guard who rapped on the door of Cell #14. Almost immediately it opened and Aleck Campbell stepped nimbly out accompanied by Father Wynne, of Summit Hill. Campbell did not seem to wait for the priest but walked quickly to the steps of the scaffold and ran up to the platform.

"The priest followed and read a prayer while Campbell kissed the crucifix. When the priest finished, the Sheriff nodded to the same officer, who rapped on the door of Cell #12 and Doyle made his appearance, accompanied by Father Bunce, of Mauch Chunk.

"Doyle ascended the steps slowly and was placed on the platform facing Campbell. The Sheriff motioned to the officer again and he rapped on the door of Cell #13. Scarcely was the sound of the rap ended when 'Yellow Jack stepped into the corridor in his slippered feet, accompanied by Father Heinman of East Mauch Chunk. . . . He was placed on the platform by the side of Campbell.

"For the fourth time the Sheriff motioned to the officer, who went to Cell #11, and this time Kelly stepped out, accompanied by Father McElhone, of Laurytown. Kelly ascended the steps slowly and appeared to be exceedingly pale. There was a slight tremble in his hand as he held the crucifix to his lips. He was placed by the side of Doyle, his accomplice in the murder of John P. Jones."

There were thirteen men on the platform: four priests, four prisoners, two Coal and Iron Policemen, Coroner Stupp, a deputy, and Sheriff Raudenbush. All knelt as the aged Father Bunce softly recited the Miserere, which he followed with a prayer for the departed. Each of the condemned men responded so clearly that every word was heard by the hushed spectators.

Prayers ended, the four priests kissed the prisoners on their cheeks, gave the sign of the Cross, and walked down from the gibbet. Sheriff Raudenbush turned to Campbell.

"Alexander Campbell, have you anything to say?"

"I forgive everybody," the prisoner answered.

"Michael J. Doyle, have you anything to say?"

"I beg the forgiveness of God whom I have offended and the forgiveness of all those I have injured," Doyle responded.

Yellow Jack was asked for his last words.

He shook his head, shrugged his shoulders, and looked Raudenbush directly in the eyes. "I have nothing to say."

The last was Kelly who answered in a voice charged with emotion.

"May God forgive me and grant me mercy," he said. "If I had listened to my priest I wouldn't be here today."

The two Coal and Iron Policemen, Officers Brink and Taylor, then handcuffed the condemned men behind their backs and tied each man's legs together loosely. At this Kelly faltered and nearly fell down.

"Pray, Edward, pray," Father McElhone called from the bottom of the platform. Kelly heard and stood erect once more.

Each of the condemned men was silent and motionless except for the trembling of his lips as a rope was adjusted around his neck and a white hood placed over his head. This accomplished, Raudenbush motioned to the coroner, the deputy, and the policemen to leave. As they walked down the steps he placed his hand on a lever which held the trap in place. The sheriff then looked at Father Bunce.

"The priest, at a prearranged signal," continued Foster, "dropped his handkerchief. The Sheriff, with a tremendous effort, pulled on the rope, the trap doors parted with the rapidity of lightning and, in a second, the men were suspended between heaven and earth, spinning around rapidly.

"Campbell and Doyle gave no movement further than that caused by the twisting of the rope. Kelly drew his arms up near the center of his back and made no further movement. But Donohue must have died hard. He drew his legs up and kicked violently, the chains on his feet making a clamoring noise with each movement. The priests, as soon as they noticed how hard Donohue was dying, placed ointment upon his hands.

"At 10:57, Coroner Stupp recorded the last heart beat; it belonged to Campbell."

An awed and troubled crowd filed quietly out of the prison and cleared a path for relatives entering to claim the bodies of their prodigals. In half an hour, the streets of Mauch Chunk were stilled, and as Foster said, "The curtain fell upon the greatest tragedy that this State, or perhaps any other state of the Union, has ever known."

But the day's performance had not yet ended; there was still another act to follow. Even while Coroner Stupp was completing his gruesome chores, the six Molly Maguires awaiting death forty miles away were being led to the scaffold before an impatient audience, estimated at one thousand men, women, and children.

" 'Here they come!' was the cry and all was attention," wrote Tom Fielders. "Slowly and with solemn tread came the mournful procession down the brick pavement that leads to the scaffold in the outside courtyard. First in the procession walked

Sheriff Werner, followed by Father Beresford, of Port Carbon, upon whose arm leaned James Boyle, who carried a full-blown rose, red in color, in his right hand. Following came Hugh McGehan, leaning on the arm of Father Walsh. Warden Beyerle and Keepers Innis and Shoenman brought up the rear.

"McGehan, like Boyle, carried a rose, which he, every now and then, pressed to his face as if inhaling the perfume. Slowly the steps by which the traps were reached were ascended and when at last the procession halted on the scaffold, the condemned men faced the crowd and gazed curiously about them."

At this moment the sun broke through the clouds and from their vantage point the condemned men had a clear view of the fading pink and laurel blossoms which still covered the mountain sides surrounding Pottsville.

"Amid the hush that had fallen on the crowd," Fielders continued, "the beautiful service for the dying was repeated by the priests who held crucifixes upon which the men about to die fixed their attention.

"'He would have died for you,' said the priest attending McGehan, 'if you were alone in the world but He died for you with others and now He calls you home to His Kingdom. Remember and trust in Him and go to Him in the last moment of your agony. He will save you. Kiss his face.'

"McGehan at once kissed the crucifix and was followed by Boyle. Then came a prayer for the dead in which both men joined.

"As the muffled tones of four voices quivered in the sunlit air, the courthouse clock tolled eleven. Both men shook as the solemn tones of the bell floated through the air . . . As the last stroke pealed out, their attention was again attracted to their spiritual advisers, who, after finishing the prayer, kissed both men on the cheek, and took their stations on either side of the trap doors."

Before they were dropped to eternity McGehan and Boyle were asked for their last words. Their responses were much the same as those of their brothers who had preceded them at Mauch Chunk, and the hangman went ahead with his duties.

Carroll and Roarity followed in twenty minutes. The latter died protesting his innocence. "I never killed anybody," he shouted. Then his troubled eyes wandered over the crowd and caught sight of his lawyer standing near the front. "God bless you, Mr. L'Velle," he called. "God bless you, Jim," L'Velle replied.

Munley was the fifth and Duffy the last of the condemned men to mount the gibbet at Pottsville that day.

"The final pair made their appearance accompanied by Father McGivern, of Minersville, and Father Depman, of Pottsville," reported Fielders. "Both men walked to the scaffold and faced the crowd unblushingly.

"When good-byes had been said to the Sheriff, his assistant and the priests, Mr. Werner said to both: 'Have you anything to say?' Munley replied: 'It is too late,' and Duffy added: 'It's no use.' Without another word Duffy and Munley were launched into eternity.

"All was over."

Many of the newspaper editorials which appeared by the hundreds throughout the nation on Friday, June 22, 1877, were in agreement with the conservative Philadelphia *Public Ledger*:

"The doomed men behaved with decorum, and generally with a humility remarkable to men of their coarse natures and wicked lives," declared this leading Quaker City publication. ". . . None of them indulged in bravado; and none of them professed that loud and boisterous piety and ostentatious confidence of forgiveness and blissful immortality . . . Law and justice have been vindicated."

A minority opinion was filed by the *New York Times*.

"The 'Molly Maguires' were duly hanged in Pennsyvania yesterday," said this distinguished journal. "No one will question the justice of inflicting the extreme penalty of the law on their crimes, which were revolting. But we do not think the way in which the hanging was conducted will tend to make capital punishment regarded as the proper means of repressing murder.

"There were large crowds to witness the executions. The prisoners were paraded, as usual, on the scaffold. They were allowed to show such indifference to punishment as they could muster, which was considerable; to make prayers for the forgiveness of everyone; to protest their innocence in more or less braggadocio fashion, and generally to do everything to make their killing partake of the character of a cheap tragic show rather than a solemn scene of retributive justice.

"We venture to say that a very small part of the great numbers who saw the hanging have any deepened sense of the terrors of the law, while by many, the most hardened of the condemned murderers will be remembered as heroes not without a slight halo of religious sentiment about them."

Chapter Forty

Despite Tom Fielders' words it was not all over. March 25, 1878, must have been quite a day in Bloomsburg, seat of Columbia County. Not only did they hang Pat Hester, Pat Tully, and Pete McHugh there for the murder of Alexander Rea, but the large and unruly mob which viewed the triple execution was given an added fillip when a chicken shed on which a dozen spectators were standing collapsed and smothered thirteen-year-old Sunny Williams to death.

"Sheriff John W. Hoffman," declared a reporter from Mr. Dana's New York *Sun,* "was drunk when he pulled the rope." Joseph Engst, a Mahoning Valley farmer, "imbibed too freely and fell from the Exchange Hotel and crushed his skull on the pavement far below," said the *Columbian.* Early that same afternoon, added the Bloomsburg newspaper, "A boisterous bunch of young men marched arm and arm through the streets and swept aside everything that stood in their way. The buggy of William Yiengst was knocked down and Mrs. Yiengst was injured when she tried to run away."

A thief stole a gold wedding ring from the body of Pat Hester, which, said the *Columbian,* "Mrs. Hester placed on her husband's finger when bidding him good-bye. "The band was returned on April 5, however, with an accompanying letter addressed to Sheriff Hoffman. "Dear Sir," it read. "Please enclosed find Hester's ring that I removed from his finger when I was up to see the execution this week. Please return to his family and oblige, Abby Engle, P. & R. Employee."

Among the few who behaved with decorum that March 25 were the condemned men.

"As the ropes were placed around their necks," reported Tom Fielders, "in full view of the men facing death, their coffins were carried into the yard and deposited on the ground with a bang. But this did not seem to startle them and it became evident that they intended to die game."

On March 28, Tom Fisher was executed at Mauch Chunk for the murder of Morgan Powell. The previous evening Kelly the Bum informed Sheriff Hoffman at Bloomsburg that whatever he had said previously about Fisher was a lie and that the prisoner awaiting execution had nothing to do with the Summit Hill mine boss's death. Hoffman, who believed the Bum, telegraphed this information to Governor Hartranft, but the latter chose to ignore it.

Fisher was probably innocent of this or any felony. Legend has it that as the youth, weeping bitterly, was dragged to the gibbet he placed his right hand on the wall of Cell #8 and said, "My mark will stay here as long as this prison remains."

Fisher was only half-Irish. His father was a Pennsylvania Dutchman who believed in *hexerei,* so it did not surprise Sheriff Raudenbush, of German extraction, to find the dead man's mark when he returned to Cell #8. Even the Sheriff, however, could not have dreamt that Fisher's visible protestation of innocence would remain long after his executioner's death. Yet, on December 16, 1931, the Philadelphia *Evening Bulletin,* which has a stand-off policy on witchcraft, ran the following story under a Mauch Chunk dateline:

"The imprint of the hand of Tom Fisher, convicted of murder and hanged 54 years ago, is gone from the wall of the cell he occupied in the jail here.

"For more than a half-century the imprint has been there and reappearing under each fresh coat of whitewash and paint. Thousands of Pennsylvanians have traveled from all parts of the state to see it . . .

"Before being taken to the scaffold, Fisher raised his right hand and placed it on the wall, prophesying that the imprint would remain forever as evidence of his innocence. Sheriff R. L.

Bowman, tired of the tradition, and with a matter-of-fact knife, scraped away the surface of the plaster where the imprint showed, filled it up with cement, then painted it over."

To anyone with respect for the integrity of this usually reliable newspaper, it comes as something of a shock to catch a member of its reportorial staff in a glaring error. Yet, the truth is that the imprint is *not* gone. It remains to this day on the wall of Cell #8 and according to the present sheriff it is Mauch Chunk's (recently renamed Jim Thorpe) greatest attraction.

On June 11, Dennis "Buckey" Donnelly, Jack Kehoe's Girardville neighbor, was hanged at Pottsville for the killing of Thomas Sanger. Despite the fact that this was merely a single execution, it drew a large crowd. Unfortunately, the new sheriff, William Matz, was not as efficient as his predecessor. According to the Philadelphia *Times* of June 12, "This was the most violent death by hanging that has taken place since McParlan's first exposition of the Molly Maguires.

"The rope, which had not been properly adjusted back of the left ear, slipped forward, and bound as he was, arms, knees and feet, Donnelly twitched and moaned till the stoutest heart was melted."

Another flaw which marred the event was the horrifying scream of Donnelly's wife (not quite widow) who witnessed the bungled execution from a window in the warden's quarters and had to be restrained from rushing to the gibbet.

Sunbury made the headlines on August 15 when Peter McManus and John O'Neill were brought to trial there for the slaying of Frederick Hesser, the Hickory Swamp night watchman and Northumberland County coroner, on the night of December 18, 1874. Much of the evidence which convicted both men of murder in the first degree was supplied by Dennis Canning, bodymaster and county delegate. Canning, in jail, where he died before completing his fourteen-year sentence for attempting to kill Bully Boy Thomas, still could not recall why he had ordered Hasser's execution. "It slips my mind," he told the district attorney regretfully.

Another prosecution stalwart in this case was Muff Lawler, brought from Philadelphia where he was under "protective custody." There was not much question about McManus's guilt but if contemporary observers are to be given credence, the eighteen-year-old O'Neill was a harmless, affectionate, and handsome low-grade moron, labeled a "poor silly boy" by his grief-stricken mother.

Lawler and a half-dozen defense witnesses in a position to know, completely exonerated O'Neill, but the jury chose to ignore them and place its faith upon two prosecution witnesses bearing dubious reputations and upon Canning, who certainly expected something from the Commonwealth in return for this favor.

On January 17, 1878, a messenger from the Pardon Board at Harrisburg delivered two of that body's decisions to Schuylkill County Sheriff Hoffman. One was a month's reprieve for Martin Bergen, convicted of murdering Patrick Burns, a night watchman. The other was a rejection of Jack Kehoe's appeal for a stay of his execution scheduled to take place the following morning.

"Yesterday afternoon," said the *New York Times*, January 18, 1878, "Kehoe's wife carried to his cell the news that the Board of Pardons had rejected his last appeal and from that time he made his preparations to meet death with calmness and courage.

"He spent most of the evening in conversation with his guards, retired about 11 o'clock, and slept soundly. He arose this morning at six o'clock. While dressing he was asked how he felt, and replied: 'First rate. I never felt better in my life.'

"Mrs. Kehoe came in about 7 o'clock, and as she met her husband, the spirit which has sustained her through the long, hard struggle to safe his life, gave way, and she wept bitterly. For the first time Kehoe's stoicism deserted him, and he seemed as much affected as his wife, but regained his composure after a time. Soon afterwards, Fathers Brennan and Gallagher . . . arrived and celebrated Mass . . . At its conclusion Kehoe ate a light breakfast and again engaged in religious exercises."

Kehoe's six children, his mother and father, all of whom had spent the preceding day with the condemned man, did not attend the execution. They remained in seclusion at Girardville. "I am prepared to die," Kehoe told Martin L'Velle, and when counsel left the cell, the prisoner was told to get ready for the execution.

Standing erect, shoulders squared, the "King of the Mollies" strode from his cell and mounted the gibbet with firm steps. Only once did he glance at the audience, which he eyed disdainfully.

"Mrs. Kehoe," continued the *Times*, "had been dismissed by the priests a short time before this, but the Fathers went with Kehoe to the scaffold where they administered Extreme Unction and knelt in prayer. Kehoe's last words, uttered in response to the Sheriff's question, were: 'I am not guilty of murdering Langdon. I never saw the crime committed.'

"Having said this, he stepped back and nodded to the Sheriff, as a signal that he was ready. His ankles were then shackled, his arms and legs strapped and a white cap was drawn over his head. At 10:27, the drop fell and after a few moments of convulsive struggling all was over . . .

"About 150 people, including reporters, sheriff deputies, and prison officials witnessed the execution . . . A crowd of 200 people stood shivering in a driving snowstorm outside staring at the prison walls until the body was cut down."

What began as the routine hanging of two more Molly Maguires, the first of the new year, 1879, ended in near chaos. On Wednesday, January 15, James McDonnell, the Hairy Man of Tuscarora, and Charles Sharpe were scheduled to be hanged in Mauch Chunk for the murder of George K. Smith at Audenried, November 5, 1863. There was little doubt about their guilt, and while the Hairy Man denied complicity in Smith's murder, he admitted participation in another, that of Patrick Burns.

Chief defense counsel William Longstreet fought a delaying action ever since the conviction of his two clients. Longstreet was certain that an 1877 law requiring a writ of error to be taken within twenty days after sentence of death was unconstitutional. Should Longstreet be able to prove to the State Supreme Court that the act was unconstitutional, he would have a legitimate reason to demand a new trial.

Defense counsel, however, needed more time to prepare his argument for the Commonwealth's highest court. Longstreet's first problem was to convince Governor Hartranft to grant a further stay so that counsel could discuss the matter with Pennsylvania's attorney general. The Governor's executive secretary arranged an appointment for Longstreet to see Hartranft on Monday, January 13. But when defense counsel arrived in Harrisburg he found to his shock that the Chief Executive was in Washington.

At Longstreet's insistence, the secretary reached the Governor by telegraph and the latter replied that he would return to the state capital the following morning. When the Chief Executive stepped from his train he was met by Longstreet. The pair had breakfast together while defense counsel presented his argument.

"Just give me time to see the attorney general," he begged. "If you authorize it, he said he'd talk to me this Sunday. All we need is a four day reprieve."

The best Longstreet could extract from the governor was a promise to make his decision before eight o'clock the following morning. This would be the day of the execution; there was nothing further defense counsel could do except wait. No word came from Harrisburg and at 8:30 A.M., January 15, Longstreet entered the condemned men's cells and gave them the bad news. Both took it calmly and preparations for the hangings continued.

Sharpe's young wife, who had said farewell to her husband a few minutes earlier although she still had some hope left, was waiting for Longstreet in a house opposite the prison. It was 10:15 when defense counsel shook his head sadly at Mrs. Sharpe and informed her there would be no reprieve.

At this, Mrs. Sharpe, who had barely been able to keep herself under control, went berserk. Pushing Longstreet aside she forced her way through the crowd standing in front of the prison and beat her fists frantically against the door. Guards who heard the pounding and Mrs. Sharpe's piercing screams notified the sheriff, who sent his wife, Dr. DeYoung, and a deputy, to pacify the hysterical woman.

At 10:25, Raudenbush, standing alone on the gallows platform, nodded to a guard, who entered the condemned men's cells, and the procession—prisoners, priests, deputies, and Coal and Iron Police—slowly mounted the gibbet. At 10:32, the Mauch Chunk telegraph operator was given a signal to clear his wires for an important message coming from Harrisburg. At 10:37 the message arrived—a five-day stay of execution.

Philip Laudenslager, the operator, dashed from his office in the railroad station and sprinted along Mauch Chunk's icy streets as fast as his legs could carry him. He made it in under four minutes, and gasping for breath, banged his fists against the prison doors.

Inside, where all was hushed except for the priests' softly murmured prayers, Sheriff Raudenbush and the others heard sounds at the outside gate. Father Bunce, standing beside Sharpe who was oblivious to everything, looked questioningly at the sheriff. But Raudenbush shook his head and whispered, pointing at the condemned man, "It must be his wife again."

At 10:42, Father Bunce, now at the bottom of the gibbet, lowered his handkerchief; the sheriff pulled hard at the ropes and Sharpe and the Hairy Man of Tuscarora dropped through the opened trap. While Dr. DeYoung was checking heartbeats of the hanged men, Raudenbush hurried to the prison door where the noise was increasing. There, in a state of near collapse, was the messenger, Laudenslager; standing beside him was Mrs. Sharpe, shrieking wildly.

In moments, word of the last-minute reprieve had spread like fire throughout the town. Citizens who only a few minutes before could not wait until the pair of Molly Maguires were hanged, now turned against the sheriff. Raudenbush quickly slammed the door against Mrs. Sharpe, who tried to claw him with her nails, and the pressing mob which attempted to force its way in.

News of the telegram had already entered the prison, where restless reporters were impatient to flash this new development to their editors. Raudenbush motioned the guards to keep everyone inside until he was able to bring about order. But as he passed Michael McDonnell, kneeling over the body of his brother James, whose heart was still pumping, albeit slowly, the former leaped to his feet.

"You've murdered Jimmy!" he shouted, pointing his finger at the sheriff. Deputies quickly seized Michael before the latter could land any blows on Raudenbush.

It was Father Bunce who brought the situation under control. The priest first assured Michael McDonnell that what had happened was no fault of Raudenbush; then the priest quieted Mrs.

Sharpe. Arm in arm with the sheriff, he walked through the streets, where angry men were congregating, and into the office of the *Coal Gazette*. There, the cleric persuaded the publishers to print a notice exonerating Raudenbush completely. This was posted on a dozen corners and order was soon restored in Mauch Chunk.

Martin Bergen, the Hairy Man's associate in the 1870 murder of Patrick Burns, the "renegade" Irishman, was hanged at Pottsville, January 16. The twentieth and last Molly to mount the gibbet was Peter McManus, executed at Sunbury on October 9, for the murder of Frederick Hesser. A last-minute reprieve, delivered in ample time, saved the life of McManus' colleague, John O'Neill, the handsome moron, who was committed to prison for life.

"And now, gentle reader," as Messrs. Eveland and Harris said in the conclusion to their *"Molly Maguires: Or The Cut-Throats Of Modern Times,"* "our task is well nigh done, we have given you a plain, unvarnished tale; we have set down naught in malice and nothing extenuated; we know the tale we have unfolded is a horrible one, but it was due to the truth of history that it should be written. . . ."